RICHARD McKEON

RICHARD McKEON

A Study

George Kimball Plochmann

The University of Chicago Press   ·   *Chicago and London*

George Kimball Plochmann is professor emeritus of philosophy at
Southern Illinois University, Carbondale, and adjunct professor of
medical humanities in the School of Medicine at Southern Illinois
University, Springfield.

The University of Chicago Press, Chicago 60637
The University of Chicago Press, Ltd., London
© 1990 by The University of Chicago
All rights reserved. Published 1990
Printed in the United States of America

99   98   97   96   95   94   93   92   91   90   5 4 3 2 1

Library of Congress Cataloging-in-Publication Data
Plochmann, George Kimball, 1914–
   Richard McKeon : a study / George Kimball Plochmann
     p.   cm.
   Includes bibliographical references.
   ISBN 0-226-67109-7 (alk. paper)
   1. McKeon, Richard Peter, 1900–1985.   I. Title.
  B945.M48P56   1990
191—dc20   89-28254
                                                    CIP

Dedication

Franz Kneisel, who almost singlehandedly brought the great European tradition of fine chamber music-playing to America, was an unrelenting taskmaster. After putting one pupil through the scales and every other imaginable difficulty for many years, he said: "You are now ready to go out in the world. If you remember twenty-five percent of what I have taught you, you will be all right." I often think that Richard McKeon could have said something like that to us, his pupils. This book is about him. It is dedicated to my fellow students.

Contents

List of Figures   ix

Preface   xi

1   Reminiscences of the Years 1932–49   1

2   Conspectus   14

3   A Learned Apprentice   36

4   The Structural Dialectic of Philosophic Discourse   45

5   Metaphysical Bearings   71

6   Discourse, Controversy, and Resolution in Society   94

7   The Arts: Principles and Methods   125

8   Theses and Distortions   166

9   Concessions, Queries, Objections, Refutations   176

Notes   205

Bibliography   233

Index   243

Figures

3.1. McKeon's Conception of Spinoza's System 39

4.1. The Earliest Dichotomy 46

4.2. Concepts and Methods Divided 47

4.3. Threefold Divisions between Types 49

4.4. The Trivium with Applications 51

4.5. Three Approaches to Methods and Principles 53

4.6. Numerical Translation of the Matrix 58

4.7. Possible Diagonals of the Matrix 59

4.8. The X Matrix 61

5.1. Contrasting Theories of Space 76

5.2 Mixed Approaches in Physics 77

5.3. Involuted Threefold Approaches to Things, Thoughts, Words 80

5.4. Reconstructed Z Matrix 84

5.5. Simplified Square of Philosophic Semantics 89

5.6. Mixtures of Pure Approaches 89

6.1. Oppositions of Dialecticians and Nondialecticians 98

6.2. Four Types of Advance and Regression 105

7.1. The Four Types of History 134–35

7.2. Seventeenth-Century Combinations of Methods 145

7.3. The Expansion of Types of Rhetoric and Dialectic 161

7.4. Modality of Metaphysics in Kant and McKeon 163

Preface

During the later years of Richard McKeon's life and after his death on the last day of March in 1985, books and papers heavily influenced by his thought and teachings have already begun to appear, although unlike John Dewey and Bertrand Russell and a few others his opinions did not bring him constantly into public consciousness. He had a multitude of loyal followers, many of them well acquainted with each other and continually discussing his latest lecture or exegetic session; but because his teaching career spanned about five decades many of the students and associates were still unborn when their elders had undergone the various disciplines or had read the publications of this quite extraordinary man. In course of time more and more books and articles will appear, and I trust they will amplify or correct what I have to say.

My effort has been not to write a definitive study but to sketch some directions that such a study might undertake. The few biographical notes and asides here do not constitute a biography, the references do not form a complete bibliography, the expository sections would need much fleshing out to be more comprehensive. I have limited my treatment of the writings on politics far more, proportionately, as they are the most voluminous of all his publications. The writings on law have been left to one side, as is the one paper (coauthored) that McKeon wrote on mathematics. The critique at the end deals with but one aspect of the materials surveyed earlier, though I consider this perhaps the most individual aspect of his life work. But there is, even so, enough to introduce the thoughts and career of a man who had a compelling influence in his lifetime on those in contact with him and who bids fair to have even wider effect in the rest of this century and in the next.

Instead of the usual summary cast in terms restrainedly glowing of the contents of the book, I shall take a different tack. A recent commentary on the *Republic* advises the student wishing to get to the heart of Plato's theory to begin immediately with Book IV. The boldness of this suggestion (I do not remark on its possible grave wrongheadedness) prompts me to offer my readers some advice of the same sort. Those who feel that the personal characteristics and qualifications of anyone as teacher of philosophy are irrelevant should bypass chapter 1. Those who feel it unnecessary as well to glance at the writings taken as a group should omit chapter 2. Those who do not care to examine this thinker's earlier works, remarkable though they might be, ought to omit chapter 3. Those who, like Professor Irwin Edman at Columbia, would define logic as "the showy ornament of philosophy" should move rapidly past chapter 4. Persons familiar with the writings of McKeon on metaphysics, politics, and the arts, in that order, need never glance at chapters 5– 7. Readers who dislike ways that doctrines can be restated and then distorted should give chapter 8 no consideration whatever, and those who do not like to see objections brought against a philosopher should avoid most of chapter 9. However, in its final pages that chapter contains some general estimates of the value of McKeon's work, and I would urge, though mildly, that anyone happening to thumb through this book read at least those pages; for I am not so modest as to believe—really believe—that *nothing* in this book is worth reading.

Whether it required fifty years to write or merely a matter of a good many months it is hard to say. The reminiscences in chapter 1 are extracted from the half-century during which I knew McKeon. They are not especially intimate; McKeon and I had many conversations over the years, commencing early in 1934, but I now realize how few of them touched even briefly upon any of the details of health, family life, travel, academic politics, national economy, or indeed any of the topics most often thought to clear the way for and be the substance of closer personal contact. When I was a student our topics were chiefly readings and term papers—the common stuff of undergraduate and graduate concern. Afterward it was mainly at meetings of philosophical societies that we talked, and this was often in company with others, so that only the most unreserved of men—which McKeon was not—would have disencumbered himself of any revelations of his inner life and feelings. Perhaps this reflected my own nature as well; but the men and women whom I have known as his students or colleagues seemed as a rule to be on not much more familiar terms, though their impressions and anecdotes of him might be quite different from mine. McKeon was not a cold, unapproachable man, and he was a genial conversationalist most of the time, partly because he could talk about almost any subject without pontificating. He attended to business, however, and business for him was the whole universe of discursive knowledge.

Part of his reserve with students may have stemmed from his wish to avoid giving a hint of favoritism; he would not trade on his deanship or, later, his distinguished service professorship as a way of hustling pals over the rough spots on the road to a doctorate in the Department of Philosophy or in the various interdepartmental committees at the University of Chicago. I never heard any student boast that he had had an easier time because of his having asked McKeon to direct his dissertation. (The male gender is used here because in the years immediately before and after World War II women doctoral candidates were regrettably few in the department.) After the final round of examinations and defence of the dissertation, however, the relation often changed; letters from McKeon were no longer signed with his full name but with "Dick," and unless there was some cause for matters to be otherwise, the atmosphere remained throughout one of frank cordiality.

A certain wistfulness is inevitable in recalling McKeon's lectures, for although he was not a dramatic speaker, there was so much substance in his discourse that one felt a little surge of excitement almost every time he addressed a class. He was not colorful, and the much-used phrases having his personal stamp were far from incandescent: "A whole host of problems," "I shall want therefore . . . ," "the Platonic approach," "he worries about the negative form of a proposition," "a striking example," "It is much simpler than that," "to construct a theory in this fashion," and "Hasn't *anyone* read the text?" Not colorful, but highly characteristic. A lecture by McKeon, or even one of his grueling exegetic two-and-half-hour sessions on a page or two of some book, ancient or modern, was in many respects like a visit by a reasonably healthy person to a doctor. The tests were deftly performed, even if slightly painful, the probing was conscientious, one felt one's life to be for the time being at a critical juncture, but at the end one could emerge a little tired but greatly reassured, with a keen sense of being able to carry on the labors and participate in the enchantments of life with renewed hope.

I have deliberately shied away from looking to receive corroboration, approval, or criticism from my fellow students at Columbia University or the University of Chicago partly because other tales, impressions, and dissents would increase the book's length inordinately but chiefly because securing their editorial help might convert the work into one giving readers the impression of an official account of a man best approached, I am certain, from many sides, not one. Other persons with bigger stores of McKeon's letters, unpublished documents, and memories will be in a better position to write a biography. The planned republication of all McKeon's papers that first appeared in print in what are so often referred to as "obscure journals"—how their editors must delight in *that* characterization!—as well as some of the books, will offer opportunities for more detailed discussion of this thought than these pages can afford.

I have tried to achieve a balance that philosophic writing often desperately needs, a balance between personal and impersonal, between formal and informal, theory and practice, simple and complex, concrete and abstract, expository and critical. For those who would accuse me of unforgivable yawning omissions, dark errors, and perverse distortions, I quote McKeon's own response to a truculent elderly visitor to the first lecture in a course on advanced logic a couple of years after the close of World War II. McKeon was announcing that the four authors to be studied were Mill, Bradley, Bosanquet, and W. E. Johnson. Up spoke the angry voice from the back row: "You should have included Sigwart!" McKeon began to explain why his four made a clearer pattern for what he wanted to demonstrate in logical—the voice interrupted: "What about Sigwart?" McKeon dropped his eyes and smiled ruefully. *"I'm* giving the course," he said, with a mildness that barely cloaked other feelings but induced a roar of laughter from the rest of the class. Some of his students may have much to say regarding their own views, offering them by way of amplification, modification, or rescue. *Mögen andere kommen und es besser machen!*

The idea of universality in philosophy has usually been adapted to the range of topics that could be considered at the time. For the Greeks, heavy bodies fell and magnets attracted iron, but oxygen was beyond them and so were electric currents and the speed of light; nor did they have Shakespeare to theorize upon. A universal system was one in which the sciences and arts were dealt with in reasonable number and surprising variety. McKeon had mastered that in full measure, but he had also mastered another kind of universality—that of point of view. For he allowed, indeed demanded, a width of meanings of terms, interpretations of propositions, and construing of arguments that forced his readers to conclude that no one analysis was final, uniquely true, and ultimately verifiable by "the facts."

Because his writings were very tightly structured, the difficulty of expounding him is thus contained in a negative trilemma:

If one uses McKeon's principles of organization then one becomes a mere parrot, a not distinctively philosophical bird;

If one uses one's own principles of organization, the result is bound to falsify McKeon's thinking;

If one allows a certain amount of slack in either of the foregoing, it will give the lie to the way McKeon wrote and the account will again be falsified.

With these potential disasters staring at me, I prefer to combine some features of all three choices and hope for the best. The pattern of this book resembles a cycloid far more than a straight line; I shall return once or several times to some of the same topics, treating them each time from a different but perhaps consistent standpoint. This is also the best figure I can think of for McKeon's own way of returning again and again to problems that he put aside until he had expanded and deepened his own methods of treatment. My own returning will include the introduction of objections to various aspects of McKeon's philosophical analyses. Is it not true, however, that any important thinker is better served by someone who admires but does not worship him? McKeon's own impulse, revealed many times over, was to welcome contrast, intellectual opposition, debate. As I hope to make clear later on, however, the objections I raise are not peremptory and final but tentative.

At a meeting of the American Philosophical Association some years ago, the papers of one session were duly being read in a room of palpably increasing warmth and stuffiness. Upon their completion the chairman announced that the discussion from the floor would now be open, whereupon a sage, practical man in the audience was heard to say that it would be better to open a window first. I shall want to open the discussion, however, with the demurrer that it is almost beyond hope to lighten and freshen any further than McKeon himself did the myriad topics on which he talked and wrote so brilliantly.

It is an abiding pleasure to acknowledge the help of several persons. Some of the impetus for writing this book comes from Professor Walter Watson, and Professors Robert S. Brumbaugh, Charles W. Wegener,

Lewis E. Hahn, Hippocrates G. Apostle, Bonnie E. Flassig, Paul Grim-
ley Kuntz, and Jo Ann Boydston have furnished me with many insights
and much useful information. To Dr. Apostle I am grateful for permis-
sion to quote from his many fine translations of and commentaries upon
the major treatises of Aristotle. I am especially obligated to Dr. Zahava
K. McKeon for her frank, helpful letters and good will and for permis-
sion to use her husband's copyrighted material. Two persons have given
a great deal of their busy time. Dr. Franklin E. Robinson, not a classroom pupil of McKeon's but a devotee of much of his teaching nevertheless, has offered corrections and suggestions page by page of an earlier version of this volume. My dear wife Carolyn has taken time from
her own work to read critically every line—except this one—and to
help overcome obscurities and ineptitudes, those that remain being, of
course, the result of my own shortcomings. Beyond the help on details
of expression, and much more vital, has been her unflagging support in
this project, in so many ways a joint one.

1

Reminiscences of the Years 1932–49

Apart from the years when he served part of the time as administrator and councillor, the professional life of Richard McKeon rested upon two aspects of his work.[1] There was McKeon the author, magnificently erudite, incredibly versatile, honed to a surpassing sharpness for his dialectical assaults and defenses, and remorseless in the drive of his logic. Then there was McKeon the teacher, also magnificently erudite, incredibly versatile, honed to a surpassing sharpness in his dialectical assaults and defenses, and remorseless in the drive of his logic. As a writer, part of his task was to expound the opinions of others, which he did almost invariably with what might be termed a sympathy or sympathetic literalness, while another part was devoted to explaining his own complex views. In the classroom, much time was devoted to the delivery of his meticulously prepared lectures, the rest being given to discussion, nearly always directed to some doctrine or text, but with the same emphasis upon the method of interpretation. He stated flatly his theories at intervals; then he would defend them if attacked, though as a rule in connection with the expounding of other philosophers, so that it took patience to disentangle his original from his scholarly thinking. He did not, however, use the figures of history as buttresses for his own views.

I first heard of Richard McKeon[2] from an older friend who commented on the man's brilliance but gave me little indication of the directions in his philosophy. It was summer 1932, and I was about to enter Columbia College as a freshman; because McKeon taught no courses open to beginners, my enrollment in his classes would have to be postponed. I did manage to attend a noonday chapel talk that autumn and remember chiefly that he ended with a quotation from St. Bonaventura: "Plato spoke the language of wisdom, Aristotle the language of science, and St. Augustine, illumined by the Holy Spirit, spoke the language of both." McKeon talked in a low voice, deliberate in its rhythms. He was a stocky, muscular man of middle height in his early thirties. (He was born with the century.) I heard later that he was good in tennis, excellent in handball. The next year I was permitted to register for Philosophy 161–62, a required history course for all those intending to do graduate work in philosophy. The regular instructor, John Herman Randall, Jr., was on leave during that academic year (1933–34) and was replaced for the first semester by Irwin Edman and for the second by McKeon. Edman was a popular, entertaining lecturer, despite some physical oddities he worked hard to overcome. Tarrying a long time on Plato, whom he evidently enjoyed, and on Aristotle despite the fact that he did not, he brought the class no farther than Plotinus by the end of January. His interpretation of Aristotle's metaphysics was traditional and moderately clear, but he "covered" the entire *Organon* with a quotation from *Winnie-the-Pooh* about a bee and a buzz; that was all, and our feeling of dissatisfaction was not at all faint. It was left to McKeon to repair this and take the class on the drawn-out journey from Augustine to the present day, represented by John Dewey, who incidentally was then rounding off his great career at Columbia. The economical but comprehensive way in which McKeon led the class through the intricacies of the Middle Ages was remarkable. It was hitherto unexplored territory for almost everyone, and presented us the task, with lengthy readings, of virtually learning a new language, except for a few Jesuits in the class who already distinguished John Scotus Eriugena from John Duns Scotus. The texts for this three or four weeks were all from McKeon's own two-volume collection of the medieval thinkers.[3] He had selected, translated, and introduced very sizable passages drawn from Augustine through William of Ockham, chiefly on logic and epistemology, and had appended a hundred-page glossary to help stumblers. That glossary was as technically precise as the five- or six-page introductions to each philosopher were profound. It came as no surprise when McKeon later quoted G. K. Chesterton's dubbing of the Renaissance as the Age of Relapse. But we were taken through that period, too, with ease, making brief stops with Pico, Ficino, Peter Ramus, and others. When we came to Descartes, a good many students began to find themselves on more familiar ground and could compare McKeon's fine, straightforward account with others they had heard regarding the Father of Modern Philosophy, as the French regularly called Descartes. This was followed by a résumé of Francis Bacon, put forward by the British as the Father of that same epoch, and in turn by Gottfried Leibniz, Father for the Germans; the latter was discussed by McKeon in terms of the then untranslated Latin papers on logic. (Earlier, he had read to us from a book, a passage from Cassiodorus or Isadore of Seville, I forget which, and had come to a word he said was untranslatable. The class was startled to discover that he had been translating extempore. He did the same thing with French, of course, for he had already lived in Paris for three years. I doubt if he was quite so fluent in German, and although he taught many courses in Greek he read it aloud deliberately and with little evident relish. He expressed no avidity for the study of languages for its own sake.)

The famous trio, Locke-Berkeley-Hume, then some of the precursors of Kant, and the Sage of Königsberg himself[4] followed, and afterward came the other well-known trio, Fichte-Schelling-Hegel, as familiar in textbooks as Fitzgerald-Lorentz-Einstein in physics or Tinker-to-Evers-to-Chance in the wider, freer world. After that, McKeon had more to say proportionately about the French thinkers of the nineteenth century than one finds in most history books, though Mill and Spencer received their due as well. A respectful treatment of more recent Americans brought the course to a conclusion. It was a tight schedule, but handled with directness and dispatch. We read close to three thousand pages in four months, or at least that was the assigned list. Two long term papers were also required, and McKeon commented very carefully on all of them coming from a class of fifty or so, in his medium-sized, neat longhand. Occasionally his remarks were spiky. A friend of mine had to live this down: "Your entire last section is nothing but a stringing-together of Maritain's footnotes." During a visit to his office that spring, McKeon told me that a student of his in another course had turned in a term paper plagiarized from Joseph Ratner's study of Spinoza, with minor verbal changes made here and there: "This was an odd point of view" was altered to ". . . an exotic point of view," and more of the sort. If, said McKeon, this fellow had done a paper about someone the literature on whom was less familiar to me, I would probably not have spotted the deception. But I had written my doctoral dissertation on Spinoza, and this was the student's fatal choice. So I helped him by taking down the Ratner book and changing back his alterations to the original wordings, and putting in quotation marks and page references as well. I gave the paper an F-plus, and when I handed it back I told the student that the plus was not for him but against myself, because there were two paragraphs that I could not account for—he had either written them himself or copied from some other source that I did not know. And then he told me that he had never even *heard* of Joseph Ratner, so I said to him that in that case one of your fraternity brothers has played you a dirty trick.

McKeon was also teaching graduate courses in (physical) Science and Metaphysics, and History of Histories of Philosophy. More will be said about the first of these in chapter 5. In the second he distinguished—so I was told—between grammarian-historians, who seek to preserve historical knowledge, rhetorician-historians, who seek to marshall it to influence beliefs and behavior, and logician-historians, who test the truth of the ideas they encounter and expound. I was not permitted in these rather small graduate classes but managed to become acquainted with some of their contents through my agents in the field. It was a novelty for me to see headings for the medieval trivium turned to new account when they were applied analogically in ways stemming from and resembling the original meanings but by no means literally the same. This systematic reapplication turned out to be a regular device in McKeon's discourse, and one could interpret a term with significations that moved increasingly far from the original denotation. If one had a series of two or three or more terms, one could move in the same successive ways to the remoter meanings and thereby set up an array of them. One of the obvious differences between our two instructors in General History of Philosophy lay here; Edman merely put important words on the blackboard as they occurred to him, in no particular order, and with lines having no significance except to separate the words, whereas McKeon's blackboard was covered in his precise handwriting in diagrammatic style, and the lines always had some essential meaning: subsumption, correspondence, equivalence, or, again, these analogies, usually rendered in oblongs and squares. He was extremely visual-minded in his philosophizing, and his published work shows this, for the writings are almost invariably the working out in prose of these figures. He expected the reader to reconstruct the quasi-mathematical images in the mind of the author.

At the time of his teaching Philosophy 162 McKeon had been an assistant professor at Columbia for four and a half years, despite the very favorable impressions he had made with his book on Spinoza and his anthology of medieval philosophers, not to mention several journal papers. In the autumn of 1934, however, he skipped a rank when he was appointed for a year as visiting professor of history (not philosophy) at the University of Chicago. Those of us at Columbia had to change over to various other teachers, probably the best and most rigorous of whom was Ernest Nagel on modern logic.

Once in a while there drifted back to us chilling rumors that McKeon would not be returning to Columbia, though on vacation in New York at Christmas he allayed those fears, only to reverse the situation at Easter by saying that the rumors were now true. He was to be a full professor on the Midway and a dean as well. The first was as professor of Greek, but later he became professor of philosophy in addition. Chicago's Department of Philosophy was, to my mind, much more independent-minded and straightforward than the inbred staff at Columbia. (I am not sure what effect this apparent fact had upon McKeon's decision to leave New York, though certainly the opportunity to bypass an associate professorship and also become a dean must have been some inducement.) Hippocrates G. Apostle was one of the students who took a bus to Chicago the next fall, making that city and its most glittering ornament his home for many years. I followed in the autumn of 1936 (to be at the University for three academic years during that stint), and Alan Gewirth, a Columbia student who was spending a couple of years at Cornell, came to the Midway a year or so later. There were many others.

It happened that at Chicago McKeon's courses, most of them on the graduate level, were conducted very differently from Philosophy 161–162. Now the students, perhaps fifteen or twenty at most, sat in a quasi-circle round a large table; each person was required to read in turn a sentence of text and then to answer questions. Invariably nursing a pipe, McKeon sat or stood at the end of that ponderous blond wooden table in a homely white-walled, high-ceilinged room, lining up at table's edge the partly burned matches with which he had tended his smoking utensil. His questions were dreaded, and there was no escape, short of a desperate plea. If the questions seemed easy, that was deceiving for newcomers, who were not overtrusting for long. McKeon had a way of continuing his interrogations until the student, commencing bravely and with some small success, had finally to flounder and admit that he (or she—there were a few women in the classes, though never very many at that time) simply did not know. Try as we might, we virtually never came out unscathed. In the six years, all told, that I attended his classes at Chicago, I heard him praise a total of two recitations. Any one of us would have been glad to be included in that number, one of them a lady who was at the time on leave as dean at a prominent eastern women's college, the other a man later becoming director of classical studies in philosophy at one of the nation's great universities.

The questions had to do at first with translating each sentence of the texts, in courses devoted successively to the *Republic,* Aristotle's *On the Soul,* later his *Politics,* then Plato's *Timaeus,* and after that Aristotle's *Physics.* (I had been a year too late for classes in the *Nicomachean Ethics* and the *Organon.*) When translation problems had been settled (students of Greek in the class were dealt with slightly differently from those in philosophy), or it was agreed that a final decision on constructions was impossible because of corrupted text, the questioning would turn to definitions of the terms or to other devices, such as analogies, examples, and so forth, used by Plato or Aristotle to help fix their meanings or to offer reasons why they should be loose for the time being. The questioning might advert to the relation of the sentence under consideration to its predecessors, immediate or remote, its probable influence upon those to come, and whatever else seemed relevant. The structure of the argument was of supreme importance: what was the chief heading, what were the subordinate headings, how were the least parts related to the others, great and small? The most dreaded question, Why four (terms, modifiers, propositions, proofs, counterarguments, as the case might be), and why *these* four—or some other number that happened to fit the circumstances—was a query faced over and over. It was a strenuous discipline, but every other way of teaching philosophy seems in retrospect perfunctory by comparison.[5] Citing texts not immediately adjacent to the one under scrutiny was of course permitted, but the student had better have a good reason for so doing. One victim, having been backed into a corner, was silently scanning the entire contents of his memory for something helpful and finally brought forth a couple of lines from a text he considered obscure enough to awe the instructor. "Yes, I know the author said that," replied McKeon, "but then what does he say over on the top of the next page?" T. E. Lawrence said of the great General Allenby, in relation to his underlings, ". . . comprehension of our littleness came slow to him." I used to think this true of McKeon vis-à-vis most of his students; he seemed to think us capable of his own prodigies of application to so many subjects. When he handed out an extremely stiff take-home examination on the *Timaeus* and said that it could at most require three hours' work, this was greeted with nervous laughter, mingled with a few sturdy groans.

McKeon seemed to follow Hobbes's famous prescription to be sociable with them that will be sociable and formidable with them that will be formidable. The formidable moods, however, usually manifested themselves in coolness, not to say a kind of remote severity, and this was generally called forth in class by extreme inattentiveness or disagreeable combativeness, or else by repeated unexcused absences.[6] Outside of class, however, his manner was usually one of restrained friendliness, punctuated occasionally by puckish whimsicality or hearty laughter, head thrown back. McKeon enjoyed hearing a joke from time to time, but I do not recall his telling any that were not anecdotes of incidents in the academic world or in his many travels. His attitude from beginning to end in class hours was that comradeship was all very well, but there was much work to be done. Something similar was manifested in a remark he made in the nineteen-thirties about rural vacations. "Going to the country is all very well for a few minutes"—these were his exact words—"but there are no libraries."

There was a small difference between his way of conducting class and what I saw of his demeanor as host at his home. He taught *On the Soul* as an evening seminar, two-and-a-half hours at a stretch, and later we were usually invited to the McKeon's apartment, where Muriel, his first wife, was a witty, friendly hostess, who did much to soften the rigors of the earlier part of the evening (with which she was thoroughly familiar, having been enrolled in the course). She was a serious, able student, and later became managing editor of an excellent journal. Conversation at the apartment was generally rather lofty but fun, and much of it supplemented the classroom ordeals. There, McKeon had almost always adopted a favorable attitude toward the text at hand, assuming that if it made little sense it was our fault for misunderstanding its author. At his residence, on the other hand, one could ask what he *really* thought of the *Laws* or the *Treatise of Human Nature* or some book in modern logic and would generally receive a down-to-earth response, though not necessarily a detailed one.

The lively conversations were always intellectual in content. Persons who came to the classes all or nearly all the time, and who also repaired to the booklined apartment, were Paul Goodman, always arguing but quite goodnaturedly and often with tongue in cheek; William Barrett,

less flamboyant but every bit as keen, with strong literary as well as philosophic interests; Apostle, a devoted and learned Aristotelian, originally trained as a mathematician; Robert S. Brumbaugh, who went on
to become an outstanding Platonist; Gewirth, formerly concerned with
dialectical materialism and pragmatism, but now deep in late medieval
studies and later in much more contemporary topics. Many times international politics would obtrude, for Hitler was enjoying his rapid
rearming of Germany and the subduing of neighboring countries, and
was much in our minds and feelings. McKeon had been in the Navy
during the later months of World War I and had had a taste of its discipline and frustrations, though not of battle; it gave him a perspective
that most of us, who had grown up at a time of fervid peace marches,
did not then possess.

Although the conversations were free, occasionally spirited, and
often cordial, if McKeon ever learned anything about the substance of
the discussion from us or modified his opinions, this was a secret kept
sealed. He had already done the work, learned the texts almost to the
point of memorizing them, had the experiences, opened up the distinctions, and we were in fact opsimaths. McKeon might not convince us,
in fact he failed in this many times; but the assumption was that one day
we might at last catch up.

It was his great gift for seeing the relevance of one kind of concept to
another that enabled him to conduct a discussion so handily in the classroom, at professional meetings, or at informal gatherings. He could
help either party to a debate, and often did, though without adopting a
wait-and-see attitude. Frequently he would say, after a colleague's suggestion or objection to a speaker, "I think what Mr. X is trying to say
is. . . ." On occasion this kind of assistance would be showered with
gratitude, but not always.

Some students remained McKeon's steadfast friends throughout
later decades; others broke away for one reason or another—I never
cared much why. There can well have been right on both sides, but
though I had one or two differences with him I found McKeon almost
unfailingly kind and helpful, despite his occasional austerity of manner.
He had relatively little to say, at least to me, about his own life and
feelings, except for his professional experiences, and this may have been
taken by others as an unwillingness to share confidences. When he re-
tired from the deanship of the Division of Humanities after a dozen
years, I overheard one of the faculty praising him for his fairness and

willingness to listen, and this seemed to be the general attitude. His resignation came, he once told me, because the position had become so overloaded with meetings and directives and triplicates from above that he felt he could spend his time much more wisely.

One must remember that in 1935 when McKeon took on the work at Chicago he was scarcely more than a third of a century in age, but he seemed already to have pondered and clarified an enormous body of intellectual material and come to terms with many practical issues of life as well. A point in this connection: At Columbia he had worn a thin mustache, possibly because it would dispel the impression of youthfulness and at the same time by its sportiness avert the suspicion that its wearer was a mere bookworm. (A couple of years later, he dispensed with this decoration and remained clean-shaven until the last years of his life.) I think that above all he was unwilling to give others impressions that would encourage them to categorize him in some way; he wanted to be and to seem a man for all potentialities.

In the late 1930s, the Department of Philosophy at the University of Chicago was in one of its great periods. Several members, T. V. Smith, Charles Hartshorne, Charner M. Perry, Charles W. Morris, A. Cornelius Benjamin, and McKeon himself, were to be elected to high positions in the American Philosophical Association, which may not be the only essential touchstone of excellence, but these men were singled out for good reason anyway. Marjorie Grene had among other tasks the care of mechanics of the strenuous beginning course in philosophic history, Movements of Thought. Rudolf Carnap and two of his assistants, Olaf Helmer and Carl G. Hempel, had been signed on. Visiting professors for part of the school year were Morris R. Cohen, slightly acerbic and very penetrating, and Bertrand Russell, who brought his dashing wife Patricia, gave popular lectures, and also entertained in evenings at home for the graduate students.

McKeon's apartment was awash with books. I saw only those shelved floor to ceiling in the living room, though rumor had it that they were everywhere. One did not scrutinize, but my impression was that he owned very few lightheaded books in all the thousands of volumes, many of them leather-bound, that he had retrieved from estate libraries. (In the 1920s and 1930s there were very few edited, translated, or reprinted versions of the Latin classics, and of the Greek the Oxford and Loeb Library editions were the chief ones available in this country. To own a work by Grosseteste or Autrecourt or Nicholas of Oresme meant bidding at a special auction or downright good luck at some Parisian bookseller's.) McKeon confronted volume after volume of the most perplexing books to unravel their inmost structures and secrets. There was a tale that he read two hundred and fifty pages an hour, but when I once asked him he said his "normal rate" was "slow," he elaborated on this no further. Outlining texts occupied him frequently; he deplored the time he had to spend outlining the entire corpus of Francis Bacon. His class notes, typed on white paper folded once, were meticulously prepared, so it seemed; he guarded them zealously.

During the years before World War II McKeon was especially circumspect. As dean, he wanted to avoid siding with what was coming to be called "The Chicago School" of literary criticism, already associated in the public mind with Aristotle and St. Thomas Aquinas. Mortimer J. Adler had preceded McKeon to Chicago by a year or two, and quickly making it clear to everyone that Thomas held keys to the chief and enduring philosophic truths, had helped President Robert Maynard Hutchins acquire this view. Without having changed any of his own opinions regarding the intellectual acuteness and orderliness of the best medieval minds, McKeon nevertheless wished to dissociate himself from any movement to propagandize for them. He taught the courses on Aristotle, but it was a Greek Aristotle, he insisted, not one seen through the eyes of Latin divines. He had formulated a very independent, detailed interpretation of the Stagyrite and could have published profusely on him, but in general he contented himself with merely including briefer expositions in papers on a variety of topics. The exception to this was his publishing of a collection of Aristotle's texts, drawn from the multivolumed Oxford translations, to which he contributed a long introduction whittled down to some twenty printed pages. Otherwise, he seemed to shy away from his former topics. In the academic year 1937–38 he, Perry, and Hartshorne offered a course in Hobbes, Locke, and Kant, McKeon taking the first; he told me later that he had decided to teach Hobbes because this would combat the impression of involvement with the radically God-centered approach that teaching Spinoza would generate. The course on Hobbes was, like all the rest of his offerings, difficult, but discussions of *Leviathan* moved faster than with the Greeks and alternated with lectures on practically everything else written by the crusty, multifaceted Englishman.

In the early summer of 1939, having a thin purse, I left Chicago to teach for two years in New York State, and then had four years of military service, and returned to Chicago in the spring quarter of 1946. On furloughs, I had seen McKeon a couple of times, and he had done much to cheer me, and a good many others, by sending friendly letters and, on request, his published papers. My barracks mates in Yukon Territory were puzzled at my absorbed interest in "The Philosophic Bases of Art and Criticism."

Its author was on leave in the spring of 1946 but returned to the university that autumn, and those who had been in service set about trying to make up for the years lost from study. That there were changes at Chicago needs no explanation here. The department provided plenty of other teachers who gave excellent instruction, but to me McKeon was still the brightest star. Among the newcomers who had the Ph.D. from Chicago and had taken numerous courses from McKeon were Manley H. Thompson and Warner A. Wick, also Alan Gewirth (with a doctorate from Columbia). Kurt Riezler, formerly chancellor of a distinguished German university, was there, and Eliseo Vivas as well. Many of McKeon's circle of students had left, but a new group was coming on: Charles W. Wegener, Robert D. Cumming, Robert Sternfeld, William Sacksteder, William Earle, and several more.

McKeon's interests seemed to be shifting from the doctrines of individuals to the dialectic of systems, comparing one with another. The agonizing classroom exegesis of earlier years faded away, but the difficulties in grasping the recondite lectures were as severe; now he aimed at interpreting larger blocks of traditional doctrines in light of his own currently much more prominent theories. Questions were still asked in class and solutions argued, but it was no longer Plato at the center of discussion, or Aristotle, or anyone else. The elaborately-arranged rubrics into which the philosophers could be fitted held our attention. McKeon gave the old Science and Metaphysics course at least once again and in addition a successful offering that compared the logics of Mill, Bradley, Bosanquet, and W. E. Johnson and contained some remarkable insights into the nature of alternate formulations in philosophic logic. This was followed the next year by an even more impressive course on the ultimate theory of meaning, truth, and inference, in which McKeon expounded very painstakingly the square matrices he had hitherto kept hidden from our view.

This was the last, or nearly the last, regular class that I attended, for soon afterward I left Chicago for good to commence a new life with expanded academic obligations. Because this was a turning point, I bring these reminiscences to a halt, for after June 1949 I saw McKeon rather infrequently, mostly at philosophical association meetings. After that year much of my information about his life and work as teacher came secondhand. I can sketch a little more of his life from conversations with him over rare meals or coffee, or from public records. His chief honor at the university was his appointment as Charles F. Grey Distinguished Service Professor in the late 1960s, a chair he continued to hold for long following his retirement from regular teaching, though he kept up his almost incessant travels much after that. Some years after Muriel McKeon's death he remarried. As I said, Muriel was an editor; Zahava K. McKeon is a teacher of humanities and author. I have owed much to both of these exceptional women.

This chapter should conclude with one or two remarks on McKeon's versatility, which continually astounded the rest of us.

During his single adolescent year in the Navy, he had been given courses in marine and other engines and had indeed contemplated becoming an engineer; he later took a number of courses in fairly advanced mathematics in preparation for that profession. In addition he had studied languages and vast amounts of history and literature. Many years afterward, at Chicago, he taught a course in the school of law. The three different professorships that he held at one time or another could no doubt have been supplemented by some others. Always eager to discover and weigh, and if need be suggest possible refutations for what was currently being said in the philosophic profession, he attended large numbers of conferences, so many, in fact, that to us it almost seemed a weakness; at any rate it interrupted his scheduled classes. There was a story to the effect that on one occasion he was surrounded by an informal gathering of Near Eastern scholars wanting to hear all about James and Dewey, to which he responded that the almost-forgotten medieval Arab and Jewish traditions were of extraordinary strength and variety, and he sketched some points in Alfarabi and Avicenna, and of course Moses Maimonides. Upon his suggesting that they form an institute for the study of these worthies, the scholars replied that they would be glad to seek funds for this, provided that McKeon himself would consent to be its head. I once asked him if the tale were true, and he denied it but gave a corrected version so close to the other that I have always had a hunch that the original was not some concoction.

During World War II he was placed in charge of all the military instruction programs at the University of Chicago campus, as he felt it incumbent upon himself to do as much as he could to forward the war effort. I once heard him deliver an excellent lecture on modern short stories, after which, over some beer, he talked to friends about Stravinsky.[7] He had studied various works on physiology, and he also gave, so I was told, quite marvelous analyses of *Hamlet*. Through it all he made the unswerving effort to come to grips with inner meaning and truth, to illuminate with philosophy all things in nature and the arts, and make those things in turn broaden and invigorate the philosophic discipline.

Long ago, when I was a junior at Columbia and had taken just that one course from McKeon in the history of philosophy, I told a friend that I thought my professor was, for his breadth of mastery, clearness, penetration, and originality, a mind virtually on the level of Immanuel Kant. In the fifty-odd years since then, I have seen no good reason to change that opinion.

2

Conspectus

Writings and Publications

The expository chapters of this book on Richard McKeon's philosophy should commence with some superficial information regarding his publications and public stance. He was the author, co-author, translator, and/or editor of about a dozen books, depending upon the way they are counted.[1] These books, however, are not for the most part independent, unified statements of his major contributions, with one exception. *Freedom and History: The Semantics of Philosophical Controversies and Ideological Conflicts*[2] is the closest to a full-scale presentation of original materials not previously published between boards and intended to be complete in itself as a book. Still, it is short, and is constructed much like one of McKeon's extended essays.[3] Apart from his doctoral dissertation on Spinoza, published by a commercial house,[4] his works do not include any full-length studies focused on one occidental philosopher. Two volumes of selections from medieval philosophers were edited and translated by him when still a young man.[5] Two books of selections from Aristotle are provided with introductions hinting at the editor's highly detailed interpretation of the Stagyrite.[6] McKeon coedited a critical edition of the *Sic et Non* of Peter Abailard,[7] while he and N. A. Nikam also brought out a translation, with introduction and notes, of the famous *Edicts* of the Indian monarch Asoka.[8] *Thought, Action, and Passion*[9] selects three essays previously published and adds a fourth of considerable length and surpassing importance not printed before.

A listing of this sort reveals a surprising reversal of an author's usual emphasis upon large books: for McKeon many of these volumes could be termed scholarly incidentals. It is to the essays that the reader should turn for a sounder notion of the breadth and depth of McKeon's thought. They deal with an extraordinarily wide spectrum of topics, and like a spectrum the contents exhibit many carefully graded colors. The topics are connected in various ways so that almost any one of them could serve as the groundwork of a book containing several such treatments, with all manner of proofs, applications, refutations, and examples drawn from scholarship or observation. Lacking these amplifications, however, and lacking explicit announcements of their ties to each other, the essays, when read one by one, give a very different kind of sweep from that say, of Bradley's *Appearance and Reality* or Dewey's *Experience and Nature*. Despite this, it is mistaken to take the well over one hundred and fifty published articles and chapters as intended for sketches of books, just as it would be wrong to think of the *Gorgias* or *De rerum natura* as treatises in larval form. The essays are at once complete in themselves and yet form long chains, though not in any Cartesian sense. The painters who have executed the Stations of the Cross, or, on a more familiar level, Hogarth with his *Rake's Progress,* have painted individual works complete in themselves yet part of a yet more complete whole. McKeon's essays commence not with simple, indisputable ideas but rather with compounded forms in their own way indisputable, embracing all possibilities of approaches to a specific, circumscribed topic. Whether they should be called essays as units is another question, to which allusion will be made later.[10] Could one say that McKeon wrote essays but was not an essayist?

The strongest reason that McKeon has had fewer adherents thus far than he might have had, considering his marked effect on public gatherings, is that he never caught widespread attention with a masterly book that expounded and defended his views such as the two just named by Dewey and Bradley or *Process and Reality* or *Being and Nothingness.* Had he published such a book, general readers might have been attracted to it and then turned to his shorter writings. To subscribe to a journal on the chance that it would contain an essay by a particular author is uneconomical, and the uncommitted would hardly be expected to become habitual devotees. As it is, one examines the bibliographies and notes of book after recent book by others dealing with topics on which McKeon had much to say, only to find him represented by no more than one or two references, or none at all. This is true even for *The Encyclopedia of Philosophy,* published when McKeon was nearing his seventieth birthday.

Even if a multivolume edition of all McKeon's published works is issued (as is now planned), this may not remove misunderstandings al-

together, for the essay form virtually forced him to repeat certain fun-
damentals (I shall state them as theses in chapter 8) and the repetitions
will doubtless seem odd and be taken lightly by a new reader, who
would tend to skip to the accounts of what others had said on each
topic. In a great many of his writings, such as the longer articles on
Aristotle[11] and his address entitled "Symposia,"[12] McKeon offered the
results of careful, word-by-word analyses that were made explicitly only
in his classroom exegeses. Elsewhere there was little effort to give more
than a condensed version of doctrines and arguments pertinent to the
classificatory and other points being made. He said little regarding the
substructures that he invented and used throughout, but they are vital
to any interpretation of his writings nevertheless.

A classification of these writings might be something like this: the
basic distinction in all of his works, be they long, short, simplified, or
advanced, is between what I call the preservative and interpretive on the
one hand and the originative on the other. The books and essays under
the first heading can be divided into treatments of single figures and
plural. Of the single the chief example is the book on Spinoza, to which
the little volume on Asoka can be added. Each thinker in the two-
volume work on medieval philosophers is treated as a single figure as
well. Other examples are the brief study of Maimonides,[13] an essay on
Thomas Aquinas,[14] a much later piece on Duns Scotus,[15] an extended
account of Cicero,[16] a short but sensitive address in honor of Thomas
Mann,[17] and of course the essays on Aristotle.

As for the writings on more than one figure, there are three chief
kinds: first, those wherein the basic distinction is between two traditions, such as we find in "Literary Criticism and the Concept of Imitation in Antiquity"[18] and a few others; second, the three-term contrasts,
as in a piece on the Renaissance and methods in some predominantly
religious writers[19] and finally the four-term contrasts, in which McKeon
in later phases of his career analyzed a large number of problems, social,
linguistic, artistic, and others.[20] Certain of these studies heavily stress
historical aspects of their subjects.[21] but even so they are philosophically
organized so that the salient points and contrasts between them are
shown with great conceptual clarity; however, they are not always easy
reading.

The materials in these are held under such tight control that it is a
short step to the obviously originative works, where the chief doctrines
veer away from classifications of traditional answers and into fields in

which new ideas regarding current subject matters are explained, exemplified, and supported. Here the primary division is between monothematic and collational writings (I apologize for the neologism). Several of the collational essays bring together two, three, or four rival approaches to a problem, a discipline, or even to the whole of philosophy, allowing or not allowing minor variants to creep in but making great effort to find harmonizing principles between them. Of these collational essays there are two sorts, those dealing with a subject analytically and without emphasis on chronology or cultural milieu and those that are primarily historical. The monothematic essays, too, are of two kinds, either testing one other thinker or devoted solely to McKeon's own, uncompared views. Further subdivisions abound, but the lines between them become exceedingly hazy. The kinds of structures, however, can be more easily discerned. Some are what I call omnibus arrays, while others are special arrays. Of the second type, in which two or more kinds of thinkers are arranged in parallel but with limited lists of concepts ranged under headings dictated by possible divisions in the nature of things, the most elegant and clearcut representative is "The Philosophic Bases of Art and Criticism";[22] another is "Dialectic and Political Thought and Action."[23] Of those ordered under three main headings, I find no examples of an omnibus array, but of the special there are many: "Philosophy and Method,"[24] the little book *Freedom and History,* and a good many more, including the very difficult "Being, Existence, and That Which Is."[25] Of the four-term collational essays, a remarkable special array is the until recently unpublished "Philosophic Semantics and Philosophic Inquiry," about which there is much more to be said.

To give a better notion of the emphasis that McKeon may have placed upon different subject matters on which he wrote, I offer a rough quantitative measure, though publication does not always reflect a writer's intrinsic concern for his topics. Invitations to join a panel or symposium, suggestions from publishers, requests from editors of Festschriften—these and other encouragements, hazards, and vicissitudes with which authors are familiar everywhere help to determine the publications and even the written output of an author.

A tenth or so of the more than a dozen dozens of separate pieces are concerned almost entirely with Greek philosophy or literary theory, but except for a small number they deal with thinkers other than Aristotle or include him only in passing. A very few articles have Roman philosophy as subject matter, and another tenth take up medieval writers. A fifteenth, approximately, are about modern and contemporary thinkers, but such a statistic can be extremely misleading, since fully a fifth of all the essays deal with what may be called general philosophy, chiefly metaphysics, and most of these make extended reference to trends. Education and the arts account for about an eighth of the studies, and world peace takes up a like fraction. Two or three articles are on matters of law. There are many—a great many—that take up social problems overlapping with international differences. The rest are on heterogeneous subjects, and there is even a trio that are at least vaguely autobiographical;[26] a single collaborative essay deals with theory of numbers. By far, then, the largest portion of the essays treat of culture and social policy. To put matters otherwise, well over a third expound the author's point of view without reference to historical interests that have so frequently been attached to McKeon's name, while a similar number are chiefly expositions of the history of philosophy and of a truly prodigious collection of the practitioners of its special arts—grammarians, doctors of the Church, doctors of the body or mind, rhetoricians, political and legal thinkers, historians, men of a diversity of sciences, novelists. A small group of publications in which the classification and proper use of philosophic systems is the exclusive topic is equally rich in examples drawn from the history of the discipline, so that the essays remain partway between historical and analytical discussions.

All this poses a large problem for anyone surveying these works. The many strands make exposition of a single clean-cut organization nearly impossible. Simply to take the chronological order of publication would falsify issues, mainly because it often belies sequences in which leading ideas and even whole writings originated. Dates are important in his case, however, but I shall aim first at a dialectical order of connections between ideas as they seem to lead one to another. In general, McKeon gave greater attention to social problems after World War II; before it he displayed greater interest in epistemology, metaphysics, and the foundations of literary analysis.

Aristotelianism, Neo-Aristotelianism, and the "Chicago School"

Like all intellectuals with something to say, McKeon has frequently been misunderstood, sometimes grossly so. Laying to rest all instances, many of them flavored with disparagement, would, if it were comprehensive enough, require undue space, but a little can be said here.[27] Because he has often been termed a historian pure and simple, I repeat that relatively few of his papers are solely historical in character, even though most use historical materials, some of them recondite, and McKeon probably had as good a grasp of the general career of philosophy from Thales to the latest meetings of the various philosophical associations as anyone in the whole history of thought, Hegel and Ueberweg not excepted. He rarely paused in print to refute allegations against him, and let the general tenor of his published work speak for himself. In a sense, of course, it would be little disparagement to say that a philosopher is a historian, for the preserving, ordering, interpreting, and evaluating of knowledge constitute four important initial steps in the improvement of the philosophic position of thinkers, despite the fact that some of the best-known philosophers of our time are relatively untutored in the background of their chosen discipline.

A more specific criticism, sometimes leveled by the persons who made McKeon out a historian, has been that he was an orthodox Aristotelian or, a trifle more generously, a neo-Aristotelian. Because the only real Aristotelian was born in Stagyra, probably in 384 B.C., the first version comes to nothing. Barriers of time and language and culture would make it impossible to be anything but a follower, even if one were to espouse Aristotle's philosophy to the fullest possible extent, which McKeon did not. He made full and elaborate use of certain Aristotelian contributions, but literal adherence to the doctrines or even methods of the Colossus of Macedon was tempered by his use of a gathering of thinkers of quite different tendencies: Plato, Spinoza, and John Dewey (one of his own teachers) among them, along with Cicero. It must still be acknowledged that the man on whom he wrote most often was Aristotle, and unlike his book on Spinoza his essays on Aristotle were on several levels of elaborateness.[28]

I need first to lay to rest, if possible, the imputation that McKeon was a follower of "the bad Aristotle." Without question, if Aristotelianism means what many superficial histories have implied, then McKeon was no devotee at all: it posited a fictional personage of rigid doctrinaire type who "invented" the syllogism (so ridiculed by John Locke);[29] the Aristotle who defined man as a rational animal throughout, though we all *know* the facts are otherwise (a self-contradiction, by the way); the Aristotle who thought metaphysics rules the sciences and can solve all their problems; the Aristotle badly mistaken about the speed of falling bodies, possibly because Greece lacked any leaning towers; the Aristotle who had the audacity to lay down a flock of rules for tragic drama; and finally, the Aristotle who held science back for two thousand whole years.

McKeon carried on exacting studies that had the effect of reducing the bad Aristotle, alleged to be full of discrepancies, lacunae, and false confidence, to a chimera, a *Hirngespinst*. In addition, much of his scholarship expended upon the Dark and Middle Ages, regardless of whether he intended it for the purpose or not, verified the rather slight hold that Aristotle had, and could have had, considering the almost total absence of his texts from the ecclesiastical libraries of the western world until the twelfth century. Even the Peripatetic School founded by Aristotle adopted methods and principles that would have been rejected almost out of hand by the founder. That being so, the "reign" of Aristotle, if a reign at all, lasted for no more than about a hundred years and applied to relatively few men, Robert Grosseteste, Albertus Magnus, Thomas Aquinas, Siger of Brabant, and William of Ockham among them. Grosseteste and Albert, however, exhibited many Platonic tendencies, as did Thomas, a sizable selection of whose propositions were condemned; Siger was soon discredited; and Ockham excommunicated. By the middle of the fourteenth century several anti-Aristotelian movements, including some of skeptical bent, and a kind of pre-Galilean mathematical physics had become influential. This superficially outlines McKeon's picture of the history that he buttressed with all manner of textual proofs.[30]

So much for Aristotle as a blight. As for making him out a duffer who sought to reduce all thinking to one type, McKeon sometimes referred to the *Prior Analytics* (there should be a club for those who have read that dreary book through, start to finish!) to show that there are far more kinds of syllogism treated there than are retailed in modern texts, that some approximate ordinary speech, and where they do not the *Rhetoric* supplements them with its arguments akin to syllogism. The *Topics* affords much more latitude in the kinds of probable arguments than there is in the strict *Posterior Analytics,* with its requirements for scientific demonstration. The loose agglomeration of the other myths concerning Aristotle, such as the crazy-quilt theory of the corpus, were similarly punctured by McKeon in various essays and his classes.

This was the bad Aristotle. What about a good one, if such a thing could be? The exposing of the bad cannot prove the existence of a good, nor does the denial that one clings to the bad demonstrate one's allegiance to the other. The issue might be important, but McKeon never, so far as I can determine, used history to dictate his own principles. It made suggestions, certainly, but that was all. There was little advantage to fantasizing oneself back into an earlier epoch, in a remote country, writing in a strange language on wax tablets. McKeon was acutely conscious, as Dewey was, that changes in philosophy are pliant to changes in the culture of the times, and he looked to Aristotle's principles only to discover the kind of evidence for unshakable truths; but McKeon's own working principles were conceived in isolation from those of old. The Philosopher, as Aristotle was so often called in the thirteenth century, would have been dismayed by and would have vigorously assailed the starting points of McKeon's systematic thinking.

McKeon has many times been named a member or leader of a "Chicago School" of literary criticism. This has not always been intended pejoratively, though such labelings are often accompanied by a thin, toplofty smile. If there was indeed such a school, he was certainly a member and no doubt a leader; but the question is still open. The basis for the myth or the root of the fact, whichever you prefer, was a kind of seminar that met fairly regularly during part of the 1930s and early 1940s, in various apartments of its members, all of them teachers or advanced doctoral candidates at the University of Chicago. The membership, always very small, were chiefly on the staff of the Department of English, McKeon and one or two others being exceptions. Part of the work, true enough, was a close reading of Aristotle's *Poetics,* undertaken because earlier translations and interpretations by American and European scholars appeared to falsify the text and weaken the exceptional rigor of its analysis. But this was only one of the classics surveyed. Many years later, McKeon himself wrote an article[31] to prove that there was no Chicago School at all, that it was an informal gathering, nothing more, and he supplemented his thumbnail account with a detailed treatment of several other classical writers on rhetoric and poetic, a hitherto unpublished paper originally prepared for reading before the group. The motives for originally writing and then publishing the account nearly a half century afterward were evidently much the same: to dispel any notion of a monolithic doctrine held by all or even some of the "members." The impression each time was of the superiority of a pluralistic approach, regardless of whether each classical writer had a theory as broad, sound, and detailed as each of the others. The article by McKeon was followed by a friendly rejoinder regarding the situation by Wayne C. Booth of the Department of English, who set out to show that in his terms, at least, there *was* a Chicago School.[32] In Booth's terms, a school was a group of persons consistently seeking to understand one another, and he found six marks whereby this group could be identified, all having to do with processes of reason and intuition in general.

The most direct evidence lies in the chief publication enshrining individual writings of the persons attending most of the early meetings, *Critics and Criticism: Ancient and Modern,* edited by Ronald S. Crane.[33] The thread binding the essays together is far more a manner of tackling problems rather than a commitment to a doctrine or set of doctrines. There is a persistent drive toward discovering what poets, novelists, and other writers are about in their actual work, and a rejection of their *obiter dicta,* of psychoanalytical explanations, of a *Zeitgeist,* or of anything exterior to the work of art in hand.

To McKeon, the question of a "school's" existence was bound up with the striking revisions taking place throughout the college at the University of Chicago under the presidency (later called chancellorship) of Robert Maynard Hutchins. In the ferment of much communication and cross-fertilization between parts of the college, many thought it imperative to come to terms with processes of interpretation that would hold texts of all kinds up to clear-eyed scrutiny. The informal seminar in question was a kind of distillate of tendencies involved in reforming the college and the university as a whole.

There is, however, another side. To an onlooker, such a group would seem an entity, even had *Critics and Criticism* never been published. That responsible persons merely affirmed existence of a Chicago School would have given it some kind of real being, not so much because smoke is evidence of fire as because such an attribution, however false if interpreted literally, leads the outside world to expect and thus find a concerted effort to influence thinking.

It amounted to this: If McKeon was indeed a full-fledged neo-Aristotelian, he could not have spoken characteristically in or for a pluralistically oriented group, whatever it was. If he spoke pluralistically, orthodox Aristotelians would have had none of him.

Position and Superposition

A cardinal feature of McKeon's thinking is that the mysteries of being, cosmos, human nature, and meaning are all essentially soluble. Aristotle said that to be is also to be intelligible, and at another extreme St.

Thomas reportedly said that he had never read a page that he did not understand. In McKeon's writings I find no suspicion that ultimately the universe will withhold its secrets from the well-prepared inquiring mind. Nor did I ever hear or hear of a confession from McKeon that he could make little or nothing of a chapter in any authentic book of philosophy, even those by Hegel and Heidegger. This was not because he boasted of having universal understanding, but in practice he did feel that if one human being could write intelligibly to himself, another who dedicated sufficient energy could fathom what had been said. This assumption animated McKeon not only in his reading of others but also in his writing: if he could set forth his conceptions in precise, well-ordered prose, then any reader coming to them when prepared could be counted on to understand.

The complexities of individual essays and their many kinds make it extremely easy for critics to err in attributing or denying to McKeon any particular doctrine. He covered himself rather frequently with layer upon layer of recombined terms, modified statements, and extenuating arguments to build a technique and finally a science of observation, interpretation, and integration.[34] The reader must approach the writings with care, else he will come, against all intent, to conclusions that McKeon would have considered shortsighted or at best scattered. It is best to address the essays by endeavoring to reconstruct patterns, as he did with the classics, and at the same time try to preserve the intellectual independence that the author was looking for in his students. If Nietzsche was right that the pupil who makes no new discoveries is a poor pupil indeed, then to be a genuine McKeonian requires, entirely apart from this need to stand on one's own feet, a readiness to reinterpret the very same texts that McKeon had analyzed and eventually reformulate the theory of philosophic history and its intertwinings with cultural history. I cannot imagine how anyone could outdo McKeon in his ever-so-extensive researches and ever-so-intricate schemata and thereby fulfill Nietzsche's demand completely, but the attempt should be made within the limits of one's own powers. McKeon as teacher and author encouraged this, though he was not unready to note errors that a person undertaking it might make.

Pluralism is the only label I can think of that was not distasteful to McKeon, so its peculiarities should be scrutinized. It is one thing to believe in pluralism, quite another to demonstrate it. Those who consider it "a good thing" simply because they possess cheerfully tolerant natures or because they have tried unsuccessfully to resolve philosophic disputes usually do not aim at anything like the philosophic certainty that more than one system can and must be true to the same or nearly the same degree. There are, then, a "soft" and a "hard" pluralism, a naive and an adept. McKeon had much tolerance, but it was never easy-going. He invented what I call the machinery of pluralism, carefully erected to accomplish the twin tasks of discovering precisely what each philosopher meant in his assertions—and his silences—and then of finding ways to show kinds and degrees of equivalence between rival formulations. The machinery's use required that all the concepts, leading and subsidiary, in a philosopher's writing be carefully interpreted and along with them his method: a method to be followed if it was already set forth by him, or detected if it was not.[35] To bring this philosopher's utterances into line with those of other persons, it was necessary for McKeon to contribute certain concepts and certain methods of his own, in what amounted to a union of philology with philosophy.[36]

McKeon developed his theory of discourse quite steadily throughout his career, though not always in a predictable line, writing and rewriting from his student days up into an age when others as old could no longer consider themselves creative at all. Throughout, one might help to characterize his thinking by contrasting it to what he evidently believed could be properly modified among his typical contemporaries. I find it hard to cite exact references to published statements by McKeon indicating his explicit objections to the following; but his lectures and informal discussions furnished the contexts for voicing these indications:

Russell—that most philosophers, prior to the recent development of symbolic logic, had little way of detecting or remedying either the general confusions or their own special misreasonings. For McKeon, on the other hand, virtually all the responsible philosophers have set up their safeguards for thinking and doing and speaking, even if without such a symbolic outlay as is intended to replace customary language in the philosophical sciences.

Carnap—that the distinction between linguistically true and empirically true is final and exhaustive, and nothing intelligible can be said about existence as a universal. For McKeon, there are plenty of a priori propositions that are not mere verbal tautologies and plenty of "empirical" propositions requiring foundations of elaborate logical construction.

Wittgenstein—that there can be no uniquely philosophic doctrines, and accordingly philosophy is reduced to the activity of analyzing the grammar of what is said by scientists or by ordinary people. It was a cardinal point for McKeon that metaphysics can guide science and investigate problems that the special sciences cannot. Looking at grammar, furthermore, is but one kind of legitimate philosophic activity.

Ryle—that philosophic problems chiefly take the form of dilemmas that we resolve by exhibiting the supposed contradictions as resulting from conceptual confusions ("traffic jams") and mistaken categorizing of whatever is under discussion. For McKeon, misformed dilemmas are certainly one source of philosophic confusion, and they can be resolved by distinctions; but problems also arise out of discrepancies in our sensory reports,[37] conflicts between the order of nature and the order of understanding, and dubious moral choices. The oppositions found in the philosophic formulating of problems is not as a rule what Ryle thinks, because not only are the concepts given different meanings (ordinary ambiguity) but they are also arrived at and related by different methods.

Regardless of his agreement with other doctrines promulgated by these philosophers, opinions such as the foregoing are representative of the ideas McKeon set about to replace. The replacement was achieved not by refuting or otherwise shoving the older views out of the way but by finding means for locating a unique place for them in something—not a philosophic system in the usual sense—much broader and less controvertible. Much of his accomplishment arose through borrowing old concepts that he used markedly differently from the traditional ways. It is, for instance, very ambiguous to say that he used technical terms. Certainly it was in no more than a few cases, in which they were intended to be technical, fixed by definition and carried thus throughout a system, regardless of particular context. Instead, each of the terms gained a new and different meaning from the companions with which it was introduced, and again with the new contexts in which these limited sets were put through their paces. Again, and here too with few exceptions, nearly all were expressions that had already enjoyed long, distinguished, and therefore highly controversial careers in the history of philosophy, or at least in considerable stretches of it:

a. name-definition-thing (probably derived from Plato's *Sophist*)
b. knowledge-belief (from Plato's *Timaeus*)

c. material-efficient-formal-final causes (derived from Aristotle's *Physics* and *Metaphysics*)

d. demonstration-dialectic-sophistic (derived from Aristotle's *Organon*) (another version was demonstration-dialectic-rhetoric)

e. things-ideas-words, *or* objects-thoughts-symbols (probably derived from Aristotle's *Metaphysics*)

f. logic-physics-ethics (derived from Aristotle's *Topics,* from the Stoics, and from medieval authors)

g. grammar-rhetoric-logic (derived from the early medieval trivium)

h. knower-known-knowledge-knowable (derived from various sources, perhaps chiefly from Kant's first *Critique*)

i. method-concept (derivation uncertain)

j. theoretic-practical-productive (derived from Aristotle's *Metaphysics, Physics,* and *Nicomachean Ethics*)

k. holoscopic-meroscopic (probably original)

l. subject matter-method-principles (derived from Aristotle's *Metaphysics* and other treatises)

m. expression-communication (probably from John Dewey)

n. art work-artist-audience (from Plato's *Ion*)

o. proper places-commonplaces (from Aristotle's *Topics*)

p. invention-arrangement-diction-memory-delivery (from Cicero)

q. apodictic-epidictic (from Aristotle's *Posterior Analytics* and *Rhetoric*)

r. reason-sensation (from Plato's *Republic* and *Timaeus*)

s. method-principles-interpretation-selection (I know of no direct precedent for this very important quartet in McKeon's later work)

t. dialectical-logistic-problematic-operational (original)

u. whether it is-what sort it is-what it is-why it is (derived from Aristotle's *Posterior Analytics*)

v. political-forensic-epidictic rhetoric (from Aristotle's *Rhetoric*)

w. elements-causes-principles (from Aristotle's *Physics* and *Metaphysics*)

These sets are in no particular order and are by no means the only ones he used, but they are typical.[38] Later in his career he had a tendency to call less and less upon classical and other traditional sets, inventing his own instead. Among the traditional terms, one is struck by the number of distinctions directly traceable to Aristotle. Yet it should be concluded neither that these were entirely original with him nor that McKeon could not have found them in a dozen other places. Most of the Aristotelian pairs and triads are explicit or at least foreshadowed in

Plato, though often the terms are separately placed in the dialogues. In no location in the dialogues are the four causes expounded or even used together, but with a little patience one can discover that Plato was well aware of the possibilities of explaining things through mechanical sources of movement, the character of the bodies moved, their shapes or functions, and ultimately the purpose adduced for the movements. (I say this despite Aristotle's possibly biased remark that Plato used only two causes, the material and the formal [*Metaphysics* I. 6. 988a9–10].)

All the groups of terms served in two ways, as topics for explanation in modern, speculative terms, and as ordering principles, again not as Plato or the others used them but as regulative of discussions of problems arising in the course of contemporary philosophical inquiry. They could, of course, be employed in recovering and expounding the thoughts of others, but if so were modified in meaning so that they were not used as mere templates for interpreting the thought of Locke or Mill or Santayana as if they were sloppy or thin versions of Plato or Aristotle. They became, as it were, commonplaces for the invention of McKeon's own arguments, and this, rather than in a purely historical function, was where they were chiefly exercised. All the sets were incorporated into more elaborate arrays and thence into even more elaborate prose analyses. They were, moreover, capable of being turned upside down, so to speak: being was superior to becoming in some philosophers, but becoming could also rule over being, or they could sit side by side. McKeon could, in effect, as easily say that 3 is the Cth number in the integer series as that C is the third letter of the alphabet. Because most of the groups of terms had entered the history of philosophy quite early, they had eventually become common coin of philosophic speculation and debate and consequently could be made to fit more easily than neologisms and latter-day catchwords in the classifying and explicating of doctrines, sciences, and systems.

One of the most significant statements in the history of thought regarding method is also one of the shortest, and McKeon evidently set considerable store by it. The aim, says Socrates, is "that of seeing and collecting together the different particular things in one idea (*mian te idean*), to make clear in defining the thing one wishes to explain. . . . [and] that of cutting the things according to forms (*kat' eidē*) by the natural joints."[39] While one cannot separate McKeon from most system-builders by any single slogan, it may still be said that the emphasis of the latter is to grasp and relate entities by a single method, while that of McKeon is to divide and synthesize as required to make explicit a problem as it is elucidated—or ignored—by several alternative philosophic methods. Because he commences by assuming that most philosophers, when taken strictly on their own terms, make sense, it follows that whatever techniques he sets up for dealing with them must enable him to fathom their approaches, assessing carefully all respects in which these can be said to be true. His own method, while by definition independent of his concepts, cannot in practice treat the two as divided; indeed, most of his accounts of his method rests on showing the affinity of the concepts when presented in a philosopher's own order. Some distinctions and assimilations are obviously more compatible with one method than with another.[40] Nevertheless, McKeon sought a method that could treat other methods and other concepts in a virtually natural way, for otherwise distortions would creep in. His own concepts ground his method of taking in all methods, rather than grounding one more system. He is thus free to explore both the concepts—eventually he came to deal primarily with those considered to be principles—and methods whereby these are generated, linked, and justified in other systems. He could, within reasonable limits,[41] open up *all* systems to interpretation that will exhibit their internal consistency, their closeness of fit to obvious facts, their serviceability in whatever practical spheres they may treat, hence their ultimate truth. This is an article of reasoned faith, and full induction of a system into the roster of acceptable ones cannot possibly be allowed until its intricacies have all been explored. This is the opposite of establishing some interior illumination, some Augustinian truth whereby all other truths are true: yet in a loose sense the doctrine itself is just such an illumination, for it allows those other truths to be true. One can say, then, that the supreme truth whereby all truths are warranted is that these truths *are* true, when properly understood, and that they in turn reflect light backward upon McKeon's original assumption. Every genuine philosophy is at first a credendum, then an object of intellectual experiment, ultimately a compendency of legitimate assertions.

He frequently gave the impression that he was a cryptanalyst trying to crack a code unique to each philosopher or even to each text, or better, that he was an anatomist looking at the bones to explain the conformation of softer body tissues. To grasp this structure—something most other scholars have not tried with his persistence to do—he set great store by what the author hinted about his own methods and then, when the author did not quite follow his own prescriptions, would ask what had intervened. Was there an inadequacy of which the author was not conscious, or did he deliberately introduce a second method supervenient upon the first? If the text being examined provides no answer, then one looks at other writings by the same author, but mainly as a last resort.

Among Aristotle's most extraordinary performances are his *Parts of Animals* and *Generation of Animals*. What makes these extraordinary is their author's ability to notice not only single facts but correlations of facts, and correlations of these correlations of kinds, sizes, and shapes of organs with other organs or habits.[42] The correlations feed his wider schematism of the divisions of animals into blooded and bloodless and his still wider one distinguishing plants moving augmentatively but lacking locomotion from animals possessing both and the yet broader division between living things (having their own source of nutrition, growth, and reproduction) and nonliving bodies. The observations both contribute to a system as a whole and are guided by the system; Aristotle could not possibly have seen so many correlations and groupings had he not been looking for them. McKeon very early formed a habit of noticing facts about texts and their correlations in the presentation of ideas. A philosopher would customarily use such and such a characterization for certain kinds of entities, in certain contexts, for reasons not explicit but anyway internal to the character of the philosophy. What, then, would be the limits of application of this expression? The answer could only be in terms of the author's own principles and methods. Finding gills of a special sort in a species of fish would stimulate the search for a specific number of fins.

The noting of marks and their correlating was not, however, the whole of the enterprise, for McKeon's chief premise was that *any* well-made system would fit into his more comprehensive pattern into which other systems would also fit, but two systems were never *directly* translatable one into another. The pattern is, however, capacious and flexible enough to allow for many alterations and even mixtures of types, and at the same time radically defective systems can be shown up for what they are by exhibiting their disconformity to any acceptable combination of rubrics in the main array. This approach strikes me as having a disadvantage and an advantage. One comes away from reading many of McKeon's major papers with the impression that there is almost nothing new to be said in systematic philosophy, and yet that everything well said is somehow, and in its own terms, perfectly true, that later systems do not overturn the earlier except in the choice of problems and manners of expression. But the enterprise differs from the construction of one more system even so.[43]

Another likeness comes to mind. Jay Hambidge was the hope of art students for some decades earlier in this century.[44] Basing his theory mainly upon careful measurements of Greek vases and sculptures, Hambidge sought underlying principles of symmetry, not static but dynamic, that could in turn be used both for analyzing all more recent paintings and other artistic fabrications and also in the creation of fresh pieces to be taken from easel or kiln. The similarities and dissimilarities to McKeon need hardly be set down. He began with principles loosely derived from the Greeks and applicable to whatever could be put into writing or speech that bore upon communicating philosophic ideas. It is a formal theory, as he himself expounded it, with a maximum of order in the posing of questions and arranging of topics, yet the order deliberately accommodates individual cases all the same. I cannot say how many of his pupils and other readers have set about following to the letter his procedures, but with trifling exceptions there is little reason to condemn any of their writings that I have seen for being overly routine, uninspired, or mechanical. McKeon's own hand is of course not there; but by the late 1980s many and varied articles and books have been published, works showing unmistakable evidence of his teaching. Its benefits seem manifest.

Style and Arrangement

Despite the regard that most of his students had for McKeon—some of it this side idolatry—and despite his indefatigable speaking at philosophic and other conferences over the world, his effect upon scholars, teachers, and creative thinkers who form the usual public for philosophic writings has been somewhat less than one would expect. He was by no means neglected. He was talked about, argued about, what he said made a difference; and yet his printed works never quite received their due. This is bound to change in the future, with publication of his previously printed essays collected in book form and with other plans afoot for collecting the *Nachlass* of various sorts. All in all, however, there were aspects of his writing that may have been responsible for the spotlight's shining less brightly than he deserved.

The list given of leading terms in his distinctions, no more than a part of his rich vocabulary, was prescribed by the subject matters in hand. The words in that list and in the rest of his choices are chiefly interesting for the specificity of the meanings he gave them; even "true," "thing," "good," and other transcendentals are used to satisfy a definite purpose and are often set off *against* each other. The sturdy old English words are there, but they often seem outmaneuvered by the many Hellenisms and Latinisms. He had learned his style partly from his teachers Woodbridge and Dewey, and relatively little from the chapters and papers so dotted with neologistic intrusions by Peirce, Whitehead, and Heidegger in their most inventive and abstruse moments. The occasional little flashes in his writings come not so much from turns of phrase, wry humor, or metaphors as from little clumps of epithets, duos and trios of shrewdly chosen nouns or adjectives. The epithets are not timeworn (for instance, McKeon does not use the expression "timeworn epithet"), there are many polysyllables in succession but no unneeded ones, almost no colloquialisms, there is no faltering or groping, no apologizing for his phrasing. But of memorable phrases one cannot hope to make a sizable chrestomathy as one could of Whitehead in his less technical passages, or Bradley, Russell, or many others. At one point in his career he succumbed to a temptation, but not for long; it was in his *Selections from Medieval Philosophers,* a work of his comparative youth,[45] where he wanted to avoid excessive capitalization, referring as he had to very often to nationalities, concepts, and other notions often or always accorded uppercase treatment. It would, he said, have looked like German; so instead he wrote "german" throughout. One can wring this out of St. Bonaventura: If Plato spoke the language of wisdom and Aristotle that of science, McKeon, inspired by the muse Erato, wrote the language of lowercase letters and semicolons.

Just as he invents few words, except for the now-famous "holoscopic" and "meroscopic," without which no graduate student in philosophy at Columbia or the University of Chicago could long survive, McKeon does not consciously return to words long in the vocabulary of British and German writers. There are one or two aspects of his style stemming from the masters of the eighteenth century, nevertheless McKeon is up-to-date; it is a twentieth-century style, but sober. The age-old terms or their translations and transliterations were much employed in the first half of our century—substance, proposition, justice, art, dialectic, semiotic, analytic, semantic: words still common in philosophic talk. As a rule he begins a long succession of points by using these terms in meanings as close as possible to their original significations but gradually alters them so that by the conclusion they are broadened in his peculiar manner and can enter into multiple new connections.[46]

His words are often perforce long, but his sentences are long by choice. They tend to be periodic, but often containing pairs and triplets of balanced phrases, though lower in key than those of Dr. Johnson and ordinarily less acerb than those of Gibbon. Modifying phrases and clauses abound, and this makes for a complex rhythm, with patterns not immediately apparent to the ear until the last phrase, just before a full-stop. With his theory of evenly matched choices, his tendency to anaphora is very evident. Special elegancies, conceits, allusions, tropes, "artistry" of any sort, never long detain him, though he does notice these adornments in others; and when a reader starts upon a sentence in the essays he can, as a rule, count a length of four or five lines, without flourishes. Nor is there possibility of finding a non sequitur. The balance in phrasing is achieved by antitheses, for few modern writers display more of them, but they grow from the subject matter and give proof of McKeon's method, which is both differentiative and encircling in due proportions.

Like his sentences his paragraphs are long, taking up a single aspect of a topic, dealing with all of it, dropping it at the end, never any sooner. If one were to outline his works with ordinary dendritic charts, one could cover pages upon pages with little branches that merge into bigger branches to indicate the distinctions, subordinate and then principal, contained in his packed but fine-cut paragraphs. I do not remember a single one of them that left me wondering why he had bothered to retain it from a draft; each slice of his prose carries forward the argument, proves it, illustrates it, applies it, explains it in some way, and none of the parcels of sentences can be brushed aside.

The essays were cut from the same stylistic cloth throughout the sixty years of McKeon's adult career, though there was a gradual, all-inclusive change and many minor deviations within that long stretch. Sentences of many of his later writings have more balanced rhythms than the earlier ones, true enough, but this is only because there is a growing balance in the arguments and arrangements of structures that is reflected very closely by the balance of the phrases. The author becomes more concerned than ever to be correct and complete, to leave every stone turned face up in full view.

Yet McKeon often varied the order in which he listed important items serving as headings for his discussions. Thus at one point A, B, C, D becomes A, C, B, D and then B, A, D, C, and though there are doubtless dialectical reasons for this, rhetorically it would have been simpler to follow the alphabet.[47] In addition, he sometimes commences an essay section with a summary of preceding materials or a longish transitional passage, so that it is now necessary to read a couple of pages before lighting upon the topic of the section in hand. One usually finds a program there—sooner or later—but it often requires a second reading to be clear.

Some essays show evidence that McKeon had a wider audience in mind—fewer footnotes, fewer (though still a great many) distinctions, a smaller technical vocabulary. At a guess, one article in ten or a dozen is of this kind. The easier articles normally contain references to major figures who seemed to be his favorites not because he always agreed with them but because they illustrated highly characteristic points of view: Democritus, Plato, Aristotle, Cicero, St. Augustine, St. Thomas, Francis Bacon, Hobbes, Descartes, Spinoza, Hume, Kant, Mill, Dewey, and perhaps some more. But there are many names in the longer essays that are not part of the everyday luggage of most philosophically-minded readers: Porphyry, Hincmar of Rheims, Lully, Nizolius, Baumgarten, Herder, Renouvier, and others who appear and await more general recognition.

I know of no instances where a shorter, more readable article is a mere popularization of the same lessons, omitting details of a longer one, though there is often considerable overlap. The essays on rhetoric have many general points in common, and this is true also of those on politics. Otherwise, the directions of the respective arguments in the essays are never identical. McKeon speaks of the words in Plato's dialogues as fitting a "vast matrix,"[48] and something of the sort obtains here in the terms, statements, and proofs McKeon arranges. Now it is the clarification of lines of historical development, now the resolution of philosophic conflicts, now the concordance between seemingly opposed opinions of physicists, now the agreements between discordant nations, peoples, or cultures, now the silencing through mutual understanding of warring literary critics, now the establishing of grounds for world peace: the search for resolution and harmony is ever present.

Almost no paper of McKeon's remains within confines of a single traditional discipline, not because he was, to use an old phrase from an advertisement for a course in mental training, "the man with the grass-hopper mind," but because the problems he chose almost invariably cut across the lines laid down in scientific studies. He seemed in this respect far more at home in fields other than the Aristotelian, wherein, as he never tired of pointing out, the sciences were carefully differentiated in terms of their subject matters, methods, and principles.

If one reads McKeon's books and papers chronologically, as early ad-herents had to for many decades when his writings were appearing in various journals and on bookshelves, one receives the impression of a county fair, a subdued, decorous fair to be sure, in which the papers follow each other in somewhat bewildering succession with a surprising variety of subject matters. If, on the other hand, one is in a position first to collect a set of papers all concerned with the diversity of cultural structures, or with rhetoric, or with the Middle Ages, or metaphysics, it soon turns out that there is a close correspondence, an interlocking such as I have already suggested, even between papers composed two or three decades apart, McKeon's methods being sufficiently flexible and all-embracing. With a trifle of pruning and rearranging, each of these collections and several more could well be made into separate books, and these in turn could be so selected that they conformed to favorite distinctions of McKeon himself: theoretical-practical-productive would be one, historical-literary-scientific another, and thing-thought-word still another.

McKeon once complained in class that a student, whose full name I happened to share, was treating a topic as if its organization depended upon the matter of the text under discussion rather than its form. He himself found it almost impossible to speak of any subject in philoso-phy, the special sciences, or the arts without making at least one root distinction and then relating some other distinction to it, thereby giving even the most elementary treatment the beginnings of a formal aspect. The difficulty of expounding his work is that either one must stick to his principles of arrangement throughout, in which case one is parrot-ing, or one must apply a diverging and even contrary set of distinctions; the result then would be to falsify or at least to overcomplicate the orig-inal. If as a third try one introduces a loose topical sequence, dictated by popular conventions, one runs the risk of bringing chaos out of order. I can scarcely believe that with the means now at any writer's disposal the keenness and pervasiveness of selection of ordering principles in Mc-Keon's essays can be outdone, and these will be put into a better integrated, more comprehensive system of ideas. Most persons will, I think, be content, and properly so, if they do not unwittingly introduce confusions, forgivable or unforgivable, into his life work.

3

A Learned Apprentice

As an undergraduate, I happened one day to run across Richard Mc-Keon's M.A. thesis on file in the yawning, somber rotunda of Columbia University's Seth Low Library and for curiosity's sake thumbed it through. The year of authorship was 1920, when McKeon received both his bachelor's and master of arts degrees. In his thesis he dealt with theories of art and took up, if my memory serves, Benedetto Croce, George Santayana, and Leo Tolstoy. At the time his style was direct and slightly hyperbolic, and I recall the last page, which contained a line that would never—not *ever*—have found its way into his later writings: "Not art for art's sake should be the cry, but art for life's sake." Many years later he referred privately to the whole thesis as "damn bad."[1]

Although he also had reservations about his doctoral dissertation in later years, he made no such sweeping condemnation. *The Philosophy of Spinoza: The Unity of His Thought*[2] was its title, and the work was dedicated to Frederick J. E. Woodbridge, whose seminar had provided its initial stimulus. It was published the same year that McKeon was awarded the Ph.D. (1928), although he once said that it was substantially finished before his sojourn in Europe (1922–25). The only part betraying a later touch is the densely packed bibliography, which lists a few papers and books published as late as 1927. At any rate, its author once gave credit to Woodbridge for having underlined the great importance of a "slight point" that McKeon had contributed in the seminar, and later incorporated into the book: "If thinking could be conceived which did not reveal and know itself, there would be no grounds or opportunity for knowing God" (p. 233).[3] For Spinoza a further step was required: to know all things it was necessary to know God, the ground of every mode, finite and infinite.

Part One of the dissertation traces the many currents leading up to Spinoza's synthesis: medieval Jewish and Christian traditions and the Cartesian philosophy that Spinoza set about to expound and rearrange in an early work, his *Short Treatise,* as well as his controversy with Robert Boyle on the reliability of experiment for science. Part Two traces Spinoza's system, chiefly through the *Ethics,* but with much attention to *The Correction of the Understanding* (McKeon's own rendering of the title, *De emendatione intellectus*), the *Theologico-Political Tractate,* and the unfinished *Political Tractate,* as well, of course, as the few dozen letters remaining. McKeon said to me (it must have been about 1972) that he planned to make some rather radical changes in the book, and I have been told by Zahava McKeon that notes for these changes are now being used to bring forth a fresh edition of the work. (Meanwhile, the original version has been reprinted by a small press.) McKeon mentioned in particular the first chapter, on the medieval background, where he had conflated several varied traditions, summing them up as a largely homogeneous influence in a way not at all characteristic of his later work. Among other improvements, he planned to bring the bibliography up to date—but what a bibliography it had been in its original form! Occupying pages 319–37 in six-point type, it listed works (many of them also quoted in the footnotes) in Latin, German, French, Italian, and Dutch, as well as English, with the entries classified under eleven headings.

The principal contention of the book bears out its subtitle: Spinoza was seeking a method that would bring together metaphysical, theological, physical, and psychological truths, all of them intended to bear together upon the analysis of the passions, their great and frequently deleterious strength, and the power of the intellect to inquire into the nature of God and to receive a cool beatitude from its love of Him. This, the highest good of man, can only be understood and attained if man's connection to the whole of existence, both the universe and what lies in thought apart from the universe of bodies in motion, can be seen as an interlocking system. The basic feature of the Spinozist method is its reflective character: Method is an idea of an idea, and this is as natural an activity of the mind as is the original simple idea of any finite mode. If an idea is adequate, the mind has produced it solely through its own activity, whereas every inadequate idea results from joint causes operating in mind and in the world of bodies. Because of the strict par-

allel between idea and body, changes in the human body are directly
mirrored in changes in its ideas, and as that body reacts to bodies,
whether living or not, outside itself, there will be corresponding alterations in ideas; and because of this reactive character, these will be inadequate, tinged with emotion. The mind is the source of the virtues as
well, and these are emotions generated solely in accordance with one's
own nature; the passions are the way one suffers from the impact of
alien finite modes. But the laws of causation themselves derive from a
universal source beyond bodies, namely, God or Nature.

As chapter 4 will show, McKeon was persistent and adept in his use
of diagrams as aids to philosophizing. As I have said, when teaching, he
almost invariably covered the blackboard with comprehensive charts,
and these found their way into his publications—only in prose form. As
a foretaste of his own uses I present in figure 3.1 what seems the truest
representation of the primary structure underlying his account of Spinoza's theory of man and God.

The Philosophy of Spinoza carries through this pattern but ends with a
statement of a distinction between unity in the sense of consistent recourse to the same set of principles and unity in the sense of completeness of the texts in which the application of self-evident starting-points
is enshrined. A passage (pp. 315–16) affirms the former but points out
that none of Spinoza's short works was ever finished, and even Parts 4
and 5 of the *Ethics* are "open to criticism from the point of view of both
organization and comprehensiveness." An unusual remark for McKeon,
and although he spoke this way privately many times, in print and even
in class he rarely criticized a book on such grounds.

This was a doctoral dissertation of exceptional scope, erudition, and
clarity, and the author made good almost all of his intent to show how
the highly diversified traditions that had fed Spinoza's thought emerged
in a unified if complex system. It was an effort to show how, examining
a work in its own terms, we must at least take seriously its own tests for
meaning, truth, and validity. In so doing we can grasp its wholeness and
possible correctness, even where it departs most from previously existing and rival systems.

The author published but three subsequent papers on Spinoza.
(Chapters 1 and 4 of Part 1 of the book had already been printed as
journal articles.) The first new article supplemented the book,[4] the third
in order of time altered its exposition of Spinoza's background,[5] while
the second, a very erudite paper on possibly authentic opuscula on

Institution	Persons	Discipline	Kinds of Knowledge	Communication	Purposes
PHILOSOPHY	choice spirits	intellectual love of God	intuition	teaching	to see oneself in relation to eternal things
RELIGION	prophets and communicants	obedience to God's laws	revelation, imagination	commands	love of neighbor piety toward God
STATE	citizens	obedience to laws of nature and human ordinances	reason, experience	legislating	enforce respect for rights of others: justice, peace, security

Figure 3.1   McKeon's Conception of Spinoza's System

probability and the rainbow,[6] adds little to the understanding of the philosophy as a whole. I turn my attention to the first, "Causation and the Geometric Method in the Philosophy of Spinoza," in which Mc-Keon tries to show first that the mere influence of Descartes is insufficient to explain Spinoza's adoption of a geometric method in the *Ethics;* the real reasons lie much deeper. Truth for Spinoza must take the form of a system; no truth can be isolated from the totality of true propositions, even when it is juxtaposed with them. A set of true ideas must be sequential, and an adequate idea is indeed one dependent solely upon a principle that itself is beholden to no further principle for its support. A true idea (defined as one corresponding to its ideatum) gives the reasons for the making of a thing and thus moves from its cause to the effect it has. To this progression the geometric method is exactly fitted. Through its deductive chain we can explicate not only what is known but also the knower, that is, the understanding, which is no random assembly of ideas but the most orderly possible selection of them, each successive member of which depends upon all its predecessors. The dependence is that of deducing properties of the thing from its essence as defined by its proximate cause. Since the geometric order is an order of ideas, the causes it presents will be the causes of ideas, but then the question becomes one of explaining how the causal connections of one idea with others can be the same as the relations of the ideates with other things. Even if a true idea is one from which the properties of the thing it defines may be known, that idea is simple and is not one associated fictively with some other. The simplest of ideas is that of God, Who must exist because the mind can make deductions from particular affirmative essences through the formation of definitions, which is to say, because the mind is capable of understanding.

Definitions and deductions stemming from them deal neither with individual finite modes nor with empty universals but rather with these affirmative essences, which are fixed and eternal things. A particular body, well defined and of known proportions in both its dimensions and its quantities of motion and rest, may be deduced by supposing its proximate cause. The prime source of error, however, lies in supposing that any one causal explanation necessarily excludes all others except, of course, in the unique case of the deduction of all things from God.

To discuss here the correctness or incorrectness of McKeon's interpretation would divert from the chief purposes of this study, but perhaps it has been a misfortune that much subsequent writing on Spinoza has followed directions quite contrary to this effort to see method and concepts as inextricably linked. Whether McKeon was right or wrong, it was wise to ask whether Spinoza could interpret both nature and man using the single conception of what understanding really is and yet allow for the unchanging character of nature as much as for the ever-changing bodies that owe their very existence to a unitary origin.

Quite apart from this, both the book and "Causation and the Geometric Method" exhibit certain themes, certain aims that loom large in McKeon's later works. First, a fair judgment of the thought of another man requires the expenditure of intensive scholarly effort—the mastery of the philosopher's native language (in Spinoza's case Latin was chiefly a late-adopted, almost artificial language), the reading of authorities great and small, the outlining and charting, the finding of connections and contrasts even where these are not fully explicit but left for the careful reader to elicit. Second, an understanding of a philosophy cannot be gained without a thorough grounding in its principles, traced through the main body of the thinker's logic and metaphysics (where these exist), then in their many applications in ethics, politics, art theory, and so forth. Third, a grasp of a philosophy's true purposes does not necessitate filling one's mind with the biography and social background of its author; these can lead one astray.[7]

McKeon's next major publication, a remarkably mature work—the author was not yet thirty—expounded, assessed, and finally quoted long passages translated by him from doctors and saints of the Christian Dark and Middle ages, St. Augustine to Ockham.[8] This large book (over 900 pages) appeared in the early dawn of a more widespread American interest in medieval studies—Harry Austryn Wolfson, Charles Homer Haskins, George Sarton, Lynn Thorndike, and a few others were learned exceptions—when almost nothing but serious misconceptions and silly clichés dominated the prevailing impressions of the period: (*a*) medieval philosophy was wholly based on authority; (*b*) medieval logic was almost totally concerned with realism versus nominalism, with conceptualism thrown in; (*c*) there was no freedom of thought in the medieval universities, and this was reflected in the dogmatic thinking of the time; (*d*) there was no interest in science; (*e*) all medieval logic was sterile, a mere set of devices for winning debates; (*f*) all medieval philosophers engaged constantly and exclusively in logic-chopping; (*g*) all medieval philosophies upheld the same basic doctrines; (*h*) Ockham's Razor somehow put a timely stop to all this; (*i*) the medieval theologians seriously debated the number of angels able to dance on the point of a pin.

McKeon, who had received far the greater bulk of his training in medieval studies in France, tarried very little over such issues, feeling that the richly diverse texts would, if carefully read, speak for themselves. The only point of any genuine philosophic concern to him was (*g*), dealing with the degree of likeness and difference between the philosophers.[9] In his introductions to individual authors, he was able to show occasional equivalences that were not a matter of the ordinary translation of terms into supposedly exact replacements in adjacent systems but of a careful adjustment of terms, principles, and directions of movement in what is stated. If, for example, a philosopher has begun with God's illumination of the human mind and moves downward to our awareness of particular things, no simple verbal change could help make the transition to another philosopher who holds that truth derives from reports of the senses arranged according to logical principles for setting out the warranties and conclusions of rational discourse. The adjustment would require a broader view in which all the doctrines, together with differences in the respective theories of their meaning, would have to be taken into account.

Until the second half of the nineteenth century, European philosophers and historians alike had accepted the fancy of the Renaissance and seventeenth century that the Middle Ages had been a period of logic-chopping carried on by men in bondage to theological authorities.[10] The English-speaking nations harbored this notion somewhat longer than others, so that McKeon and his early successors in medieval studies found that any literal translation that used cognate expressions rather than analogues or paraphrases would be widely misinterpreted. McKeon avoided so far as possible alternatives to the most literal renderings consonant with decent English, however, but supplemented his renderings with a glossary of terms, many entries containing very sharp distinctions; a large number were from the thirteenth century, and most of those from St. Thomas's works, so replete with definitions. This glossary is no superficial help for those hopelessly at sea; it makes representative parts of the medieval treatment of theory of knowledge intelligible in considerable detail. The same comment holds for McKeon's introductions to each philosopher, which again offer next to no biographical or cultural particulars but explicate something of the problems as individually stated and the methods used for clarifying and solving them.

The two volumes afford insights into the deeper layers of thought between the fourth and fourteenth centuries, and if they ignore the political colors of the period or the variety of incidental topics dealt with, all told, by the sages of that thousand years, we must remember that McKeon always aimed, as did Kant and many others, at a conceptual rather than imaginative history of philosophy.

Publication of these volumes was preceded by a short piece on William of Ockham,[11] a longer essay on St. Thomas,[12] and a brief account of medieval empiricism.[13] McKeon's later essays were aimed not so much at exposition as at general interpretation: a paper on utility and medieval philosophy,[14] a long study, "Renaissance and Method in Philosophy,"[15] and then studies of rhetoric and poetic, property, Duns Scotus, and other topics that will be noticed later in this book, as well as a collaboration on a scholarly edition of Abailard's book collecting arguments for and against over one hundred fifty propositions.[16] One reason that McKeon wrote relatively little, considering his mastery of the period, was that medieval authors concerned themselves less with the topics in which he became intensely interested later in his career: the possibility of world government, the extension of rhetoric, social adjustment between groups, the theory of education, the foundations of science.

Anyone familiar, however, with McKeon's later writings will be struck by the number of portents of explicit teachings and general tendencies that were heralded by the book on Spinoza and the anthology of medieval thinkers. The vocabulary that eventually appeared in his writings and made them easily identifiable is not in evidence in either work, but the introduction and final chapter in the volume on Spinoza betray many concerns that came ultimately to characterize McKeon's entire approach: the strong emphasis upon method; the stress on the need to see a system as a whole even though it should also be interpreted part by part; the distinction between theoretical and practical knowledge and the latter's tendency to rule the former; the attention to the order of entities, that is, grades of power or excellence, and the order of their presentation; the stress upon goals or purposes in philosophy; the concern for the interdependence of the sciences, even where a full unity cannot be established. In the two volumes on the Middle Ages, one finds over and over an impulse to state precisely the relations of opposition and agreement (sometimes bound closely together) between philosophers; the need to read each thinker separately to discover and account methodologically for his uniqueness; the distinguishing of types of influence running from one thinker to another.

So much for these two outstanding books by a prodigy. There existed a fairly early manuscript by McKeon, "Philosophy in the Middle Ages," referred to in a footnote by a distinguished pupil of his[17] in connection with a specific point; the manuscript has never been published, and the only reason that comes to mind is the guess that McKeon wished to be identified as a medievalist no more than he later wished to be viewed as a neo-Aristotelian. I once asked him if his book would ever be issued in print, and he replied that it would—in the footnotes of books by other people.

4

The Structural Dialectic of
Philosophic Discourse

By turning the pages of Plato's dialogues one soon confirms that dialectic for him is not merely the art of adroitly querying an opponent to force him into concessions he had never dreamt of making. Now and then the master dialecticians whom Plato conjures up—Socrates, chiefly, but also the Eleatic Stranger, Parmenides, and the Athenian Stranger—do that with dispatch, but their tactics are by and large constructive, and the respondent who begins by thinking that he knows but soon finds that he does not is matched in many dialogues by one who begins by confessedly not knowing and coming finally to realize that now he does know. Inherent in this dialectic is Plato's demonstration that content cannot be divorced from the manipulations of contraries, contradictories, analogies, step-by-step proofs, images, and his myriad other devices.

Turning to another exploiter and expounder of dialectic, Aristotle, one just as quickly finds an entire aspect of this art manifesting itself as rules—rules devoid of the content of the sciences, theoretical or practical. By far the longest treatise of the *Organon*, the *Topics*, is devoted to the ways by which, using honest, straightforward means, one can win arguments and avoid impeding oneself in disputes. I shall follow Aristotle's lead in this chapter, so far as McKeon's dialectic would be amenable to it, and Plato's in the next. Here I shall relate some details, at least, of the many and increasingly complex schemata across which McKeon laid text after text from the history of philosophy and point after point in his ceaseless efforts to find certainty or an alternative.

The Early Versions

After his *Selections from Medieval Philosophers,* most of McKeon's publications referred to and often expanded other men's thoughts, though never their complete systems, and always with a teaching of his own integrated with them. As time passed his own views became far more explicit than in earlier writings. All-important alternative statements, their possible equivalencies, and generalizations linking the cited approaches could be combined, and his many writings bore different emphases upon each of these three. His massive erudition could support first his accounts of the thoughts of others and second his own dialectical syntheses and discriminations.[1]

In this examination of pluralism's machinery he regularly though not invariably used three kinds of schemata as essential supports. (There were others, more unique, that cannot be brought under convenient headings here.) The first I call omnibus arrays, the second special arrays; the third is more subtle, difficult, and original, and his usual name for it, matrix, should be preserved here.[2] All three played important roles in his writings at different times, though no description of them entered his publications. The first two might or might not take shape as squares, but precise limits were prescribed in one of their dimensions, while the third *had* to be a square.[3]

PLATO   ARISTOTLE
many items listed   many items listed
                             (the contraries of Plato's)

Figure 4.1   The Earliest Dichotomy

At Columbia University McKeon first gave his course, Science and Metaphysics, and at the outset made an overall separation between two well-known philosophies. This structure exemplifies an omnibus array because the lists in both columns are not limited in number and are only required to correspond with each other; in application it is timeworn and relatively primitive, reminiscent of Coleridge's famous remark that everyone is born a Platonist or an Aristotelian; it was soon discarded in favor of one slightly more anticipatory of McKeon's later style (fig. 4.2). In a sense, this is still an omnibus array, being headed by names of philosophers found in history; each philosopher covered a wide range of topics, and the number of concepts is unlimited, as in figure 4.1. In another sense, however, it is a special array, as "holoscopic" and "meroscopic" (commencing from wholes and parts, respectively) are intended as contraries, and "concepts" and "methods" supposedly exhaust the contents and structures of the systems of physical science. In this case the columns are curtailed. The items under "concepts" are presum-

PLATO	ARISTOTLE
holoscopic physical concepts (several listed)	meroscopic physical concepts (several listed)
holoscopic method (defined)	meroscopic method (defined)

Figure 4.2   Concepts and Methods Divided

ably relevant to the problems discussed and chosen in an order that brings out a common principle illustrated in opposite ways by the items lying in the same horizontal line. In each case the method is merely defined, and since there are many concepts connected by each method, the number of concepts is much larger than the number of methods, which in each case cannot be more than one. The concepts would not need to be physical if the subject matter were different; mathematics, rhetoric, poetic, or any other discipline would fit in this pattern on different occasions.

This array could be modified or enriched in two ways, the first by fitting in philosophers who resembled Plato sufficiently to be classed with him because their systems used enveloping, overlapping concepts linked by a single all-inclusive method that Plato himself called dialectic or who resembled Aristotle through their use of limited concepts literally defined and of a method whereby parts are selected, examined, and set together to make a whole, whether an inanimate substance, a cosmos, syllogism, living organism, poem, or *polis*. The Platonic method, McKeon used to say, was applicable to any system, the Aristotelian to specific subject matters, and the method varied accordingly. This is the earliest distinction between "holoscopic" and "meroscopic," and examples will be given in chapter 5.

The second type of modification was more perplexing, resting as it did upon the diagonals when a philosopher sought to unite holoscopic concepts with meroscopic method, or else meroscopic concepts with holoscopic method. Either way, the fit of method to concepts was less sure to be sound than with "pure" holoscopic or meroscopic approaches. A holoscopic method that could range anywhere was better adjusted to concepts that could vary in meaning from the extremely narrow to the extremely broad, from a squeal of a pulley to a cosmic creation.[4] Throughout the 1930s McKeon explored a number of thinkers who assumed the risk of mixing types, always, I think, with his reserved attitude toward their results.[5] The meroscopic method, linking as it did concepts as subjects and predicates in the same and then in successive propositions (thereby forming a syllogistic or quasi-syllogistic chain of reasoning that tended to narrow rather than broaden the subject matter in hand), was adapted only with difficulty to holoscopic concepts; a similar problem arose with a holoscopic method and meroscopic concepts, whose popular and technical meanings received a critical examination at the outset but afterward were bound to special definitions whose every part was in turn defended. The two methods promoted different conceptions of science: The holoscopic method divided sciences temporarily for specific purposes, the meroscopic permanently.

Threefold Distinctions

As time went on, the range and exact meanings of holoscopic and meroscopic altered in McKeon's thinking, and for many years he never committed them to print, probably with good reason. His students were more inclined than he was to apply these two coinages to various texts,[6] and some of them even took "holoscopic" to be a label for loose thinking, an interpretation their teacher deplored. But the basic dichotomy was proving unsatisfactory. Such atomistic philosophers as Lucretius, Hobbes, and Hume (with his unitary impressions joining together by an associative power resembling gravitational attraction) were considered a subset of the Platonic on the ground that they used their terms in an analogical, generalized way, despite their abjuring of forms beyond sensible things, beings beyond changing bodies. This awkwardness disappeared when the atomists were later (in classes in 1946) accorded separate status, with a method all their own attuned to working with their special concepts (fig. 4.3). This schema involved a radically new orientation. It was proper that Democritus become the meroscopic philosopher, grouping his simple concepts much as he grouped atoms together to form perceptible bodies; the method was exactly suited to the selecting of the least parts as the starting points of philosophic demonstrations. Yet this array, too, seemed awkward, for it left Aristotle compromising between two philosophers of opposite tendency and thus unduly bound to them, and although this could be partly justified by looking at certain references in his texts, it paid no honor to his great originality; and it left him compromised as well, since there is no substantive mediating notion between whole and part to characterize his concepts and method. Perhaps "balanced" would do, rather than "mediating" or "intermediate."[7]

PLATO	ARISTOTLE	DEMOCRITUS
holoscopic concepts (many listed)	[intermediate concepts] (many listed)	meroscopic concepts (many listed)
holoscopic method (defined)	[intermediate method] (defined)	meroscopic method (defined)

Figure 4.3   Threefold Division between Types

In all versions of this early columnar device, method is not directly commensurable with the concepts, since a method is the justified and deliberate movement of the mind from one concept or set of concepts to another. The concepts, although representing stations in that progress, are not simply mile markers; they possess distinctive content and character of their own, especially after being rendered as unambiguously as possible in a given context. The movement from "form" to "matter," for example, in an analogical system might be virtually the same as that from "ruler" to "ruled," yet the concepts differ in their references. How, then, can a particular method and set of concepts fit together yet retain their diversity? Purely abstract intellectual concepts, such as "being," "contradiction," or "essence," cannot be properly manipulated by a method intentionally limited to empirical findings. It is equally clear that literally defined terms should not—I refrain from saying cannot—be intelligibly ordered by a method using a potentially infinite number of alternative analogies (as does the holoscopic) rendering it as a single topic shown in infinitely varied contexts. Yet a certain latitude is required, as history demonstrates, otherwise the entire succession of systems would be a choice of methods, nothing more. A chain of analogies can be elaborated with God at the summit, or mind, being, energy, or the state, and the method as abstracted from its actual embodiment in one of these systems may well look like that abstracted from another. But the fitting of method to concepts both brings about and rests upon the meanings developed for *all* concepts in the system. The method, if a good one consistently employed, would no doubt prevent a mistaken assortment of concepts and their meanings from creeping into the philosophy.

Because a system must be constructed with two chief aims in mind, that of keeping each part of it true to the way things are and that of making each part cohere with all others, it is easy to violate one of these requirements while attending to the other. Not only that, but philosophers have often used more than one method—I would hate to use "submethod" here, but that is what I mean—even when they advertize their choices. Plato names his method dialectic, but despite this he gives many differing descriptions of it and moreover allots to almost every speaker in the dialogues his own particular dialectical procedure. Again, Aristotle uses a variation of his method for each science, sometimes even between parts of the same science, despite his also requiring that the standards of his demonstrative logic be upheld so far as possible— strictly for mathematics and physics, less so for politics. In one aspect, the method becomes an ordering of the problems to be attacked successively in each of the sciences. Most philosophers of the seventeenth and eighteenth centuries sported an analytic or synthetic method, or both, but these did not interfere with their using Democritean or Platonic or Aristotelian methods in a wider sense.

We turn to advantages of the three-columned array (fig. 4.3) over those with two. Fewer systems had to be counted as variants and deviants from Plato or Aristotle, or from the nine possible pairings of methods and concepts (to mix two kinds of concepts, or two kinds of methods, would result in serious inconsistencies). The mixtures could be stated both more precisely and more flexibly than with the 2×2 arrays, it being possible to find some errant philosopher who combined features of all three original systems. In the two-columned versions, the Platonic tended to become a catchall simply because the terms were conceived as analogical and subject to radical transformations.[8] When Democritus was added, his column tended to become the catchall, though it was likely to contain fewer entries than had Plato's.

The value of an omnibus array is chiefly to the historian or the beginner in philosophy, and the corrective seemed to lie in a special array, structurally a slight departure from the omnibus. Such a chart could begin from common statements drawn from history of philosophy, or common labels narrowly designating the disciplines or doctrines. One starting from the trivium of the Dark and early Middle Ages was implied in the long essay "Renaissance and Method in Philosophy"[9] and can be charted as in figure 4.4. This special array does not start from whole systems identified with putatively universal thinkers who have carried enormous weight in almost all subsequent speculations and analyses. A special array is limited, each column being closed by some name, individual doctrine, or term, whereas the omnibus could be extended downward as far as one pleased. The special array, however, no less than the other, derives its only strength from its closeness of fit to historical

Logic	Rhetoric	Grammar
seeks to establish truth of propositions by showing their connections with others	uses expressions, clear or unclear, to influence belief and action	preserves rules of clear expression
discovers grounds of truth in historical texts and estimates validity of conclusions	uses historic ideas to give impetus to actions in society	preserves historic ideas and orders them conveniently
Abailard	Nizolius	Erasmus

Figure 4.4   The Trivium with Applications

facts; it suggests but does not explicitly present criteria for evaluating systems or doctrines, unless its prose exfoliation includes materials not specified in the array.

Several observations can be made in regard to figure 4.4. First, the headings of the square can be made factual by quoting Hugh of St. Victor or some other writer in support of the top-row formulations of the trivial arts, the second-row concrete instances of the historians who write in the ways suggested, or again, the bottom-row men who have explored the separate possibilities recommended.

Second, the merit of this 3 × 3 square (or of the 3 × 2 oblong coming shortly) is its suggestiveness: it encourages one to make connections between known types of thinking and to distinguish them from other types radically different, and it also leads one to seek ways to fill up places (i.e., commonplaces) by improving one's own deficient learning.

Third, assuming both that this square is historically accurate and is useful in suggesting to an author a point of view or in persuading a reader to adopt it, we still wish to know if philosophic truth can be obtained from it. The answer is affirmative—up to a point. Even if it could be shown that the distinctions between grammar, rhetoric, and logic were not those actually held by the early encyclopedists and others, still the distinction as given is instructive as regards the uses to which language can be put, or the arts for exploring it.[10] Even if the three men chosen were not the happiest examples, it is still true that some thinkers are distinguished in these ways and the analogies between the three listed disciplines and the several methods employed in texts can hold with fair exactitude.

Fourth, there is a limitation to such an array. The number of approaches to history or philosophy is controlled by the number of arts of language (or other headings) alleged, probably quite independently of the historians and philosophers considered in the outline. The bed thus tends to become mildly procrustean, if such a piece of carpentry is conceivable.

Fifth, there is another difficulty, for the purposes of the columns are thought to be mutually exclusive, whereas in point of fact they can interweave with each other, if not in the writings of the men included at least elsewhere (as can be seen in Peter Ramus). The analogies are rigid; that is, one must remain in a single column throughout if the efforts of an individual man are to be successfully described. If Abailard, starting from his stated principles, ever considered chiefly rhetorical purposes, such as pleasure, this would become manifest as an inconsistency in his thinking, and would be an anomaly in the chart, or require an entirely new supplementary square, on the ground that his original theory had been discarded.

This special array is too good precisely because it is too narrow, requiring careful selection of examples; too clear, recommending one single purpose only; and too rigid, making it impossible to depart from one fundamental classification already taken as true. A possible cure would be a larger array, say 4×4 or 4×5, to allow slightly sharper distinctions in greater variety; but the historic trivium would have to have changed or been entirely dispensed with. The omnibus arrays lack a way to show original specificity of doctrine, as well as any conception of a philosophic problem before the columns have been filled in; so it is a matter of good fortune to find Plato differing in various concepts and features of method from Aristotle. By itself, this is quite insufficient for any analysis of systems. Such arrays are instructive as summaries, but they lack form.

The essay on the Renaissance and its methods as contrasted with those of Abailard was a fairly early composition, and most of its subtleties came from the material itself. A far more elaborate 3×3 array was presented in a paper published in McKeon's middle period, "Philosophy and Method."[11] It had become clear by the late 1940s that the distinction between types of methods and of concepts in terms of part and whole was inadequate, though not altogether false. McKeon set out on a radical rethinking, not in his selection of the chief root-philosophers, *Urphilosophen,* I shall dub them, but of the ways to characterize and distinguish them. In the new essay he did not commence with names of these men (although they appeared early in the exposition) but with

METHODS

DIALECTICAL	LOGISTIC	PROBLEMATIC (INQUIRY)
a. treats organic wholes	a. traces knowledge back to elements and processes composing it	a. solutions of problems and advancement of knowledge
b. transcends contradictions of nature, experience, knowledge, action	b. —	b. univocal definitions, but meanings not arbitrary
(Plato, Hegel, Marx)	(Democritus, Descartes, Leibniz, symbolic logicians)	(Aristotle, Francis Bacon)

PRINCIPLES

COMPREHENSIVE	SIMPLE	REFLEXIVE
sought by reconciling differences, conflicts, contradictions (subject-object, etc.) with final overarching synthesis (being, reason, God, matter)	decomposing wholes into indivisible elements and simple relations stated in definitions and postulates	results of analysis of problems or subject into a whole to permit solution; wholes are things, thoughts, operations, symbols

Figure 4.5   Three Approaches to Methods and Principles

formal aspects of thought (see fig. 4.5). The treatment of each item is detailed and orderly, but the lists are not closed at the bottom, though the principles are in fact discussed under four specific headings; "holoscopic" and "meroscopic" are gone, and the tripartite division could be made neither on historical nor on logical grounds alone but rather by a keen insight into the very possibilities of sound methods and principles, history afterward bearing out the intuitions.

The logic of the array changes from column to column as the terms are altered in their meanings and thus in relation to each other. Asserting that the logistic thinkers rejected the dialecticians' holistic totalities is very different from saying that the problematic thinkers also rejected them; problematic thinkers have different conceptions of what they are denying and quite different notions of how much of the wreckage should be salvaged. This new array, basically but not altogether a special rather than an omnibus array, presumes far more careful separation of methods and the newcomer, principles, than did the older ones.

The chart here (I am following McKeon's prose account, which prints no diagrams) seems to imply nothing more than separate headings, independent kinds of philosophies, but if the problematic method is placed second and the logistic third, it again appears that Plato and Democritus are mediated by Aristotle, giving a whole cast to the history of philosophy when the three men are treated as *Urphilosophen* from whom all systems spring forth. It must be owned that Aristotle himself viewed his work *in part* as a mediation, at least in metaphysics and physics, between Plato with his striving toward forms and Democritus with his reliance upon matter (*hulē*), though he did not quite say this.[12]

The choice of three horizontal headings is dictated now by divisions within philosophy itself, irrespective of historical priorities and influences, and the assumption that the three are the only ones possible is also supplied by the essential discipline. Could the history of philosophy give us a fourth, or even a fifth? So long as the answer is not definite—and "Philosophy and Method" does not explicitly address this question, though anyone can surmise what McKeon's answer would have been—the array cannot claim to be a priori in this respect.[13]

The columns are likely, but no more than that, to be structured and thus limited, as the account of principles in the essay is regulated by a four-part distinction that treats successively of starting points, materials, forms, and purposes of principles, Materially, again this is an improvement over the methods-concepts distinction simply because concepts lack limitations, whereas principles may be identified, grouped, and accorded special status. The task, however, of showing completeness remains, because with the three columns it is difficult without using mediation to find any logical relation between them and hence to prove either exclusiveness or exhaustiveness. This mediation by the problematic method is ruled out when one column is headed "dialectic" and the other "logistic," two epithets differing from each other but not necessarily in total opposition. (Or is it that the *problematic* method is the end term?) If there were four terms instead of three, one might set up a tetrad (with X and its contrary and Y and *its* contrary paired), and with ingenuity one could then find the terms under these headings related in much the same way. This would give a formal limitation, structurally a priori.

So far as *historical* considerations go, one or two remarks will have to suffice concerning the scheme underlying this essay, which is one of McKeon's most brilliant and authoritative pieces, having a sweep and vividness making the efforts of most other writers seem a bit pale. Certainly the logistic method, calculative in essence, placing least parts in conjunction and combination and then noting the new kind of entity that emerges, is widely used in symbolic logic, from Leibniz and Boole to the present, and in all types of atomism, what with Lucretius postulating little hooks to hold his units together, Descartes his swirling motions, Newton his gravitation. Dialectic is described or at least mentioned, usually in contrast to some imposter method such as eristic or poetry, in thirteen dialogues of Plato. Some descriptions are figurative (e.g., dialectic is the art of good butchering—*Phaedrus* 265e), while others are more nearly literal definitions (*Statesman* 258b; cf. *Sophist* 240a). In the same way, both Hegel and Marx claim the effectiveness of the dialectical method, though like Plato, they insist upon certain conditions. The problematic method, too, seems almost immune from objection, though in a more searching study a few questions could be raised. The word *aporia,* "difficulty," "problem," dots Aristotle's treatises, as well as various words for inquiry and its synonyms. Certainly his principles are not comprehensive; they carry their own baggage of justification with them in the form of succinct statements defending their constituent terms and their applications rather than spreading it retrospectively over an entire subject matter as Plato often does; nor are they simple, invisible bodies or indefinable impressions or primitive propositions.

In McKeon's earliest divisions, Plato and Aristotle were made different, reciprocally contrary, and if read literally, mutually cancelling. This is still true in the 3 × 2 arrays where Aristotle seems intermediary between Plato and Democritus, though here the distinctions are finer. Yet with all the emphasis on conceptual and methodological distinctions, McKeon never tried to keep the two thinkers totally separated. He said more than once in class that Plato was occasionally very literal when erecting a hierarchy such as the Divided Line or the Ladder of Love or the kinds of goods (in the *Philebus*). Aristotle, for his part, used "pedagogic" analogies, more especially when dealing with the higher reaches of his system, for example the soul and the arrangement of the heavens. But in the main, both authors respectively employed analogies between fluid terms and inclusions and exclusions between fixed ones.

McKeon's Plato was no ordinary run-of-the-mill author whose dialogues merely reflected his recording of opinions common in the idler classes of ancient Athens or uniquely held by philosophers of many persuasions traveling to Athens from far-off islands. Nor did he interpret Plato, as do many, as writing a kind of textbook and concealing this by literary dressings-up having little to do with the march of propositions.

Nor again did he view Plato's dialectic as a way of exhibiting clashes of opinions and then giving the victory to the most persistent and embarrassing questioner, snub-nosed and homely, with little effort to find the many indications of a powerful and very subtle method. Because he did not always resolve issues as a modern treatise would, Plato is thought vague, inconsistent, lighthearted, or, more generously, to have repeatedly changed his mind and forgotten what he said a little earlier.

McKeon's Plato, expounded in his exegetic courses on the *Republic, Timaeus,* and other dialogues (late 1930s) was a strong thinker of uncommon sensitivity to words and to the manner in which those words changed their meanings, not at random but systematically in the contexts of carefully constructed arrays, hierarchies, and other structures. Oppositions and agreements were based on inharmonious or harmonious multiple relations between the constituent elements of discourse. Opinions, furthermore, were not uttered by chance persons, one of them a "hero" or a "mouthpiece," but were the true-to-life expressions of men carefully chosen by Plato to put them forward to match opinion and character; the tendencies and stresses in one invariably corresponded with those in the other.

In this dialectical milieu, elusive at first but plain once the keys had been supplied, Plato's thoughts took on the shape of an open system that always, in the hands of his aptest dialecticians of whom Socrates and Timaeus were two, elevated its concepts higher, toward a collection of permanent forms and ultimately toward pure unity and being. Whatever fell short of that might in its way be good, but never *the* good.

This Plato could take his seat as one of the great originators in history, not a dweller in the hinterland who was a gifted doxographer with a turn for inflated romantic mysticism. The old philosopher, so well communicated in the classroom, never quite revealed himself in McKeon's published writings; in them Plato affirmed what was indeed put forward in the texts, but the feeling that the reader was himself participating in a dialogue conducted by Socrates and Plato and, in a novel sense, by McKeon, was lacking in the accounts committed by the latter to the printed page.

In the array from "Philosophy and Method," mixtures of segments of the columns could easily be adopted so that a philosophy could be, say, dialectical in method but logistic in employment of principles—such mixtures (of which there could be eight others) are prevalent in history. Some of their characteristics will be glanced at in chapter 5.

The Three Matrices

Instead of trying to improve upon the 3 × 2 or 3 × 3 arrays simply by enlarging them, McKeon embarked on something (winter 1949) quite new. A column can offer a mere list, its items not ordered to make the list closed at both ends; if there are two such columns, the items answering in position to each other are not necessarily logically related. Second, there can be plural columns in which each item in one answers as closely as logic can make it to an item in the adjacent columns. A third possibility is a column whose items are so grouped under traditional philosophic headings that it can answer its partner or partners. Last is a new array in which all headings are limited by root principles ordering the successions of terms; this is closed at both ends. McKeon did not offer the first kind and gave up the second rather early, except in some of his more casual moments in the classroom when using the blackboard to record the contents of student recitations. The third requires more insight and learning to make it operate cogently, and the fourth is founded upon careful analysis and planning. And arguing thus, we arrive at a matrix.

This device for classifying doctrines more precisely and definitively had to bring out the most significant terms used in framing doctrines and their priority and posteriority, their affinity and disparateness. The bare positions that these expressions occupy then play host to the leading terms of any other system or part of it; hence refined comparisons and contrasts can be made more easily than with the old arrays. One begins in this not with systems as wholes or types of systems but with their least parts, the individual statements: the humeri and ulnae, not the skeleton, and certainly not the entire corporeal frame.

The unfilled positions—I call them nodes—are given generic labels and pairs of labels in advance; a node is then filled by a kind of species label that in turn is narrowed to a doctrine contributed by a text to be analysed. If the investigation is not historical but represents inquiry of one's own, then this impaling on the nodes is to assure oneself that the theory being constructed is not obviously defective in a very general way. When several texts are compared, their sets of terms and propositions will one after another occupy a line of nodes so that likenesses and differences are easy to see. McKeon suggested too that in framing one's own philosophy it is also sound policy to contrast one's formulations with those of another system. A succession of different occupants of a

1	2	3	4
5	6	7	8
9	10	11	12
13	14	15	16

Figure 4.6   Numerical Translation of the Matrix

single node is usual, and its utility lies in the precision obtained by singling out doctrines and the flexibility allowed both in multiple applications and in other ways shortly to be explained. To achieve the desired results, McKeon began by using a square 4 × 4, but this is its most superficial feature. He based his matrix rather loosely upon Leibnizian determinants, though taken over for conceptual rather than algebraic interpretation. The simple basis is a square in which the top row and left side (called the major of the matrix) were made to represent conceptual summating principles, supergenera one might say, of the items appearing in the 3 × 3 square (called the minor or submatrix) comprising the remainder of the figure. Let me introduce this first in numbers, something McKeon never did in the classes I attended, though it simplifies his cryptic, complicated oral accounts; see fig. 4.6.

In the omnibus arrays, the verticals were the pure, uncluttered versions of each philosophical system, while in the matrix it is the diagonals; but this is owing not to a rearrangement as much as to a whole new conception. There are two summating lines, indicated by the integers 1, 2, 3, 4, and again 1, 5, 9, 13. In this square eight different diagonal lines can be drawn, two to each of the top-line integers; hence eight basic approaches rather than two or three (columns) are representable. For help in identifying the lines, I reproduce the original square, duplicating some of its numbers on each side for ease of reading the diagonals (though this duplication can be made unnecessary with the help of hairpin instead of straight lines, as Leibniz conceived it); see fig. 4.7. The diagonals built upon the integer 1 thus run to 8, 11, and 14 and again to 6, 11, and 16; on 2 they run to 5, 12, 15 and again to 7, 12, and 13; on 3 they run to 6, 9, and 16 and again to 8, 9, and 14; on 4 they run to 7, 10, and 13 and again to 5, 10, and 15. It is easy to see a number of pairings of individual numbers.

Two philosophers sharing all four nodes of a line would have all general characteristics of their relevant doctrines somehow in common, however much they might differ in detail. Total divergence would obtain when two philosophers occupied parallel diagonals, or crossed lines not intersecting at a node (e.g., 3, 6, 9, 16 and 2, 7, 12, 13. Otherwise

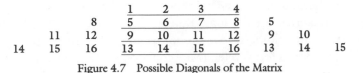

		8	1	2	3	4			
		8	5	6	7	8	5		
	11	12	9	10	11	12	9	10	
14	15	16	13	14	15	16	13	14	15

Figure 4.7   Possible Diagonals of the Matrix

two nodes or four would be held in common, since both one in common and three in common are impossible.

So much for simplification. McKeon used a trio of letters at each node. The matrix therefore needs recasting, introducing these letters signifying logical concepts and operations, their specifications and combinations. To grasp this a small glossary is needed:

A or a = any unit or element (for example, a term)

B or b = any combination of two such elements (for example, a proposition)

C or c = any combination of the immediately preceding, the last element somehow implied by those coming earlier (for instance, a syllogism or other argument)

M = the theory of truth, a summation of three other elements on a row, column, or diagonal

Σ = the theory of meaning, a way of interrelating what is said in its various parts; this too sums the expressions in any straightline set

W = the contrast between analysis and synthesis

O or o = objects, i.e., things (capitalization confers priority upon any letter, as does placing it before another)

P or p = persons, i.e., thoughts or ideas

S or s = symbols, i.e., words or other linguistic elements

X = a matrix giving the theory governing interrelations of logic forms (elements) A, B, and C, with kinds of real entities O, P, and S

Y = a matrix offering material interpretations of the logical forms, that is, how they are used, the method

Z = a matrix offering a theoretic interpretation, that is, a theory of logical theories

The major and minor have already been defined; the summating symbols, M, Σ, and W appear in the major only; the rest, O, P, S and A, B, and C, can appear in the major and minor.

Note that although A, B, and C are forms used in logic, as so used they become materials for the logical theory to consider. M and Σ are the summating principles, M for the forms and Σ for the ontic types to which the logical forms refer. (McKeon took it for granted at this time that there were three and only three kinds of possible reality that could enter into a matrix: things, thoughts, words. Each one of these could in certain philosophies do service in some way for the others. A fourth kind of reality, action, was added later, but to my knowledge was introduced into the matrix only by being absorbed into one of the first three.) There being three matrices, X, Y, and Z, each with sixteen nodes that house philosophic commonplaces (generic expressions, headings for arguments), there would be forty-eight possible points on which to compare and contrast any two proposed logics; and the number would be further multiplied by various manipulations of the order and capitalization of the letters filling these nodes.

The X matrix that emphasizes the relations between common logical forms and the three ontic types, together with both of their summations, M and Σ, can be seen in figure 4.8. The letters MΣ placed on the intersection of the column and row containing summations are in effect a summation of summations, and any philosopher who happens to occupy node 1 (MΣ) together with three others has thus but one summating principle, though it is double in significance. So much for the construction, though not the explanation, of the X matrix.

As for the second, the Y matrix, which offers material interpretations of the logical forms coming from the X matrix, it is the same in shape but differs in nodal designations in two ways. Here are materials determined by scientific theories; that is, they relate to the formal aspect of regulated discourse or in short to the method proposed not only for the generation of other sciences but for the creating of logic itself. The letter W is introduced to specify that the matrix exhibits the contrast between analysis and synthesis, and it occupies all four nodes of the left-hand column. Meaning, Σ, heads the top row, while M, truth, drops out temporarily. The Y matrix continues to use O, P, and S and again A, B, and C, but in orders and combinations different from those of the X matrix. Not only are there different orders, but the individual letters change meanings, not at random but by analogy with those adopted in the X matrix. In the Y matrix, A stands for the single undivided essence or cause of something, B for the proposition as a substrate for truth or falsity, and C for what is valid or invalid. The values O, P, and S change

1. MΣ–connection between systems of propositions and their subject matter effected by principles	2. MA–connection between constants by symbolic or ideal representation of existing objects	3. MB–connection between systems of subject matter by laws true of subjects-inductive	4. MC–connection of terms within a matrix
5. OsΣ–meaning attributed to symbol by noting characters of things symbol must express	6. OsA–elements in things given expression	7. OsB–propositions having conjunctions of terms justified by things	8. OsC–derivation of characteristics based on rules; judgments of causes and effects
9. PoΣ–summation in terms of grounds of credibility; wholes of logical elements isolated by principles	10. PoA–categories as ideas having at least phenomenal interpretation	11. PoB–justification of connections of ideas by rules of thought	12. PoC–derivation or relation based on rules of thought
13. SpΣ–summation of symbols manipulated under rules of operation	14. SpA–elements as simple symbols, their kinds determined by rules of operation	15. SpB–justification of truth in rules of operation	16. SpC–derivation or relation based on formulas of inferential operations

Figure 4.8   The X Matrix

in harmony with this, and one sees the primary subject of the matrix, namely method, as an emergent from this alteration, for O is now some individual or universal nature, P is not a random thought but one reflecting what is real, and S is the symbol as properly defined for specific use.

The Z matrix, resulting from a kind of "multiplication" of the X and Y matrices, uses the summating M again, down the left side this time, while those headed by W lie across the top. The other letters are again enlisted, but once more with new significations. The Z matrix deals with the general theory of disciplines, emphasizing the variety of principles required for each.

For all the accumulation of headings to be combined at each node, the result is still not a doctrine but a broadly defined place where a doctrine can be located, filled in, and connected with others. This holds for all three matrices.

We recall that Gilbert Ryle spoke of "traffic jams" in philosophic formulations where confusions arose because of misunderstanding of the real intent of symbolisms. The newcomer to these matrices might excusably term them veritable gridlocks. The application of the matrices to follow may persuade him that these vehicles can be made to run more smoothly than he suspects.

Although McKeon did not point it out explicitly, there must be differing ranks of definiteness in the matrices. (1) The most general, totally undirected positions lack any significance other than their status in the major or minor of the matrix and therefore are summating or not. These nodes are strictly speaking not philosophic at all, they communicate no message, no assertion. (2) The most general headings, O, P, S, and so on, to be placed in nodes are metaphysical and are used in many of McKeon's essays, sometimes directly. (3) The metaphysical headings may also be filtered through terms significant in politics or other sciences. The terms descriptive of kinds of freedom are made to form a species, narrowing as they do the application of the metaphysical terms (2) to a specific field of inquiry. (4) Falling under these species would be the individual writers who exemplify—rather neatly—the classifications arrived at in this matrix. Here the line between theory and practice begins to show itself.

Reverting to an explanation of the X matrix (fig. 4.8), we find the top row signifying four different kinds of summation, that is, the most general but alternative principles whereby various elements subordinate to each of them (in the columns below) could be determined as having common character. The second row would represent whatever is referred to real objects taken independently of mind or symbols, whether these things are generalized or are single terms, propositions, or arguments. The third row assumes the priority of the person (or mind), again referring to its characteristic logical operations as being generalized to include all meaning or more specialized to include terms, propositions, or arguments. The fourth deals in the same way with symbolism. No philosopher worthy of the name, McKeon claimed, has succeeded in constructing a coherent logic lying on a single vertical or horizontal line; such a performance would take away the proper scope of the discipline, making it a mere exercise. Somewhere the logical must deal with terms *and* propositions *and* proofs, somewhere with these in relation to things *and* thoughts *and* language. A bent line would betoken inconsistencies. Incomplete logical theories would be revealed where one or more of the needed four nodes had been left unfilled on a diagonal. Philosophers who invert the order of treatment of the elements (material inversion) would show up as leapfrogging on a single line, for example (2), (12), (7), (13), and those inverting the priority of objects (formal inversion) would show up in the same way. As an instance of material inversion, consider W. E. Johnson's statement: "A systematic treatment of logic must begin by regarding the proposition [not the term] as the unit from which the whole body of logical principles may be developed."[14] C. S. Peirce at one point makes the inference primary: "The law under which a sign must be true is the law of inference. . . . Hence the illative relation is the primary and paramount semiotic relation."[15] These writers, however, would doubtless be reluctant to admit that they had inverted anything.

The X matrix is thus meant to show that and how, at some level of compounding, an acceptable theory of logic must handle ontic and epistemic aspects as well as symbolic, and levels of integration implied by term, proposition, and argument along with them. One of the easiest theories to map in this way, because it is so directly expressed, is Aristotle's; he indicates in the *Categories,* chapter 1, that it is individual simple expressions that must be attached directly to things through signification (6) OsA; that sentences are (*On Interpretation,* chaps. 1–2) signs of mental operation (11) PoB; and that syllogisms (*Prior Analytics,* Book I, chap. 1) are to be taken as symbolic, verbal constructions (16) SpC. The summating principle, (1) MΣ, is outlined at length in the *Posterior Analytics,* (Book I, chaps. 1–3), in a description binding together scientific (as opposed to other) syllogisms and their constituent terms and propositions in a unit in which language becomes a vehicle for exhibiting the exact conformity of thoughts to the forms of things, when very exacting conditions are met in the formulation.[16]

So much for exposition and exemplification here. The matrices suggest some questions, so obvious that only their answers need to be recorded:

First, only in the context of all methods taken together can any one of the disagreements between any two of the philosophers upon any point be finally resolved, though they can be detected and, as it were, catalogued with the help of but one other. Two positions, contrary though they may seem, do not exhaust the possibilities for all conceiv-

able positions upon a given topic, and unless this is done, no more than
tentative solutions can be found.

Second, if a disagreement arises, it is symptomatic of differences in
method, of different tests for truth, of different grounding in even more
fundamental principles than those being examined; and with all these,
different meanings have been assigned for the terms in which the original statements were made.

Third, if a resolution is formulated for two opposed doctrines, it
takes place first through the detection of the simple apparent opposition, necessary as it is during introductory stages of analysis to keep the
issues sharp. Since the chief two, three, or four methods that McKeon
distinguished are inharmonious with each other in every simple sense,
they cannot be combined in some conflation that includes every answer
and coalesces them into one while still preserving anything of the originality of the *Urphilosophen* who gave them life to begin with.[17] Progress
results from showing that none of the original statements is final but
that in its own context each can withstand the assaults made from other
points of view. If no one philosophy can be proven finally true, no one
philosophy is shown to be ultimately false unless it is clumsily devised.

Fourth, if one attached designations of the great systems to the ma-
jors of the matrices, listed either by philosophers or else by types (dialectical, problematic, logistic), an approach would merely be summed
up by its name, whether personal or designative, and would become a
cheap catchword. If instead one were to use either the top row or the
left column, the matrices would be useless, for no longer could so many
ways of conceiving elements or aspects of methods or selections of principles (on the X, Y, or Z matrices respectively) be included and given
the flexibility they must have.

Fifth, it is harder to guess why McKeon had three (later four) prototypical philosophies rather than the eight that the matrices, with their
diagonals, would permit. I can only suggest, with misgivings, two possibilities. The history of philosophy seems to show the clearest divisions
between these four—the quartet that McKeon selected makes for a better way to read history than other groups (for instance, St. Thomas,
Duns Scotus, William of Ockham, and Nicholas of Autrecrout or
Fichte, Trendelenburg, James, and Quine—though each group is almost wildly heterogeneous). The Greeks, of course, possess the advantages of having been not only originators, or probable originators, but
also of having had considerable influence, bumpy and uncertain as the

paths leading from them to their successors most certainly were. Those might not have been the chief reasons for the selections, however; it is the purity of each method and its appropriateness to the corresponding concepts that the four men entertained.

Furthermore, if all eight lines were made fundamental, the complexity of the analyses of problems would be so great as to baffle any reader. As it is, the obstacles to keeping all the twists of argument in mind are forbidding enough, and this is especially true when the four are crossed with three foci for conducting philosophic inquiry of any kind: things, thoughts, words. Mixtures of the four (and they are legion) make the list still more complicated.[18]

Sixth, the three matrices could, in the hands of some hardworking but perhaps misguided technician, be joined together in one grand cube, yet its faces would convey no more than they did when separate, and the inside nodes would be virtually incapable of suggesting any new doctrines, so complicated by the multiplication would they be. There is no theoretical limit to the complexity of a plane or solid figure, but philosophic sense demands that it be kept as simple as possible.

Seventh, the flexibility of the scheme balances but does not destroy its fine-cut precision. If each node of the minor contained but one letter, say P, one could work out rigid, simple interpretations; but using two, Po and Op, for example, makes a difference based on the standpoints from which these two elements are viewed. In Lucretius a start is made by speaking of the thing seen and then the seeing; the setting up of the discourse follows this order. In Bradley, the emphasis is on perception and cognition, and what is seen is in important ways secondary, experience being the Absolute. The nodes are less like squares on a checkerboard, where at the game's opening every square except those at the remote end is a possible host to the same kinds of pieces having the same values, than they are like the chessboard squares, whose values are constantly shifting because of tactical changes implied by positioning of the varied pieces.

Eighth, the most striking difference between a matrix and the preceding arrays is not that of greater flexibility. The arrays began with the history of philosophy, taking rise from men (or schools) or commitments to methods and principles, whereas the matrix commences from an analysis of what logic must in its most general aspects contain. The closeness of fit in the first group is of doctrines (in a broad sense) to men or to established patterns under which doctrines find their proper places. With the matrices one must, of course, possess in advance some notion of what logic is by being well-read in its history, though such preparation lies outside the structure and actual use of those matrices. A matrix is so broad yet allows such precision that it is independent of any interpretations of logicians or coteries of them.

Ninth, in his early career McKeon did not concern himself much with psychological and social reasons why philosophy, a fairly late arrival on the world's rough-timbered stage, became as diversified in methods and principles as it has become. The fact of diversification is evident, and it is no sign of weakness in philosophy itself, or neurosis in philosophers, but rather is one of health, showing as it does the mind's willingness to venture into parks and pastures hitherto occupied by poets, historians, and scientists. Because of this venturing, however, the philosophers have been ready to model their styles and methods after those of other creative thinkers. We see this perhaps most of all in Plato, whose *Phaedrus* owes much to poets and orators, whose *Critias* and *Laws* owe much to mythmakers, historians, and town planners, and whose *Timaeus* is in part patterned after the work of astronomers and biologists of the day. As a result, there are so many apparent—I repeat, apparent—divergencies between these dialogues that a very large number of dialectical adjustments must be made to show any harmony between them. If one can find these differences in the writings of one man, how much more likely it is to discover wider diversities between several!

Tenth, beyond commenting that the Z matrix can be used for matters of equal metaphysical and logical interest (see chapter 5, below), little need be said here except that, like the X and Y matrices, it shows that consistent theories *are* consistent, though only in a very general way. The advantage of all three matrices is not that they deal with all elements of a system, or all stages of a method, or all referents in reality in exactly the same way, but rather that there are different grounds for meaning and certainty accorded to different elements needed for the logical aspects of the system. McKeon once said that in those cases where thinkers had attempted a wholly uniform, vertical-line profile in a matrix, they could "produce not logics but parts of logics." The metaphysical basis of this is, I believe, that reality is no homogeneous totality, apprehensible fully by one kind of cognition and represented by symbols all of the same kind. Even if there were but one inquiry ever made (hence neither a diversity of systems nor a semantic comparison of systems), it would still be impossible adequately to present in thoughts and words a simple, homogenized world.

Eleventh, this account, going back to the earliest arrays, will perforce give a wrong impression concerning a different matter, an impression that there were several easily marked stages, few in number, in the evolution of McKeon's thought and that one need only count the side and top of a rectangle and then multiply the numbers to determine at what stage the paper or chapter was penned. I doubt that McKeon tried to cover his tracks to frustrate such attempts at simple arithmetic, yet it is true that the chronological and structural sequences do not exactly run in tandem. Terms playing some part but not really essential in a 3×3 array become integral in a larger array later on—or they are dropped, even when seemingly quite relevant. The question then becomes, Was this term important in the first place? There are, of course, two opposite answers, both acceptable when sufficiently qualified.

The Arrays of Semantics and Inquiry

The old 3×2 and 3×3 arrays, allowing choices from either pure vertical lines or pure diagonals or even bent mixtures, were circumscribed, static, a defect that the 4×4 matrices were designed to correct. The latter were not ways of classifying systems as wholes but only doctrines extracted from systems; if the classifying could be extended to a whole system, this would be a point external to the matrices. The chief difficulty with the old arrays was that in addition to being stiff they were also vague: to offer a heading no more specific than "Method," "Concepts," or "Principles," let alone "Platonic," was to invite a democracy of data to come tumbling in. The principal defect of the 4×4 matrices was that despite the diverse interpretations of a given node, there was a certain rigidity built into the very structure; the stage had to be set almost from the very start for an entire elaborate theory of logic or whatever else was being investigated. Any two points on the X matrix would determine a diagonal (assuming a consistent theory), thus requiring that the other two points would also lie on that line; McKeon then asserted that the diagonal of that theory of logic would be the same for the Y and Z matrices as well, so that the diagonals of all three if superimposed would coincide. Hence a new level of rigidity of the general headings, and the only possibility for restoring the required flexibility was in the plurality of letters in the nodes and the possibilities for formal and material inversions. It was time to devise something new that would have advantages drawn from both of the older ways but without their shortcomings.

McKeon often repeated certain contentions about the nature of philosophy and the facts of its history, but always with fresh applications and, on occasion, radical innovations. The advance from the three matrices to an even more sweeping, directly applicable, and immediately, vitally relevant machinery came about in 1966, or at least was first heard in that year. In March, McKeon presented a paper before the Illinois Philosophy Conference, held at Southern Illinois University—a paper densely packed and bristling with novel terminology, though still using many old expressions. The number four is again prominent, but this is no matrix like that of 1949, but a group of four new arrays, two of them shaped as 4×4 squares and the other two again having four columns. The paper is "Philosophic Semantics and Philosophic Inquiry,"[19] and these two expressions give their names to the squares. (The other two squares are called "Philosophic Problems" and "Divisions of Philosophy," both of them having four heads, but because the very brief lists under them are homogeneous and suggest no special manipulations, I would call them 4×1 rectangles. At present they can be put aside; they merely list four interpretations of the customary threefold divisions of philosophy of classical and early medieval days, and the problems inherent in four pairs of contraries suited to each kind of philosophy are also treated in the far more important squares.)

These squares of semantics and inquiry suggest all manner of searching questions to ask of history, present all manner of acute observations, enable all manner of solutions to be found, bring about all manner of difficulties, and introduce a flood of new distinctions, none of them having directly to do with the character of the squares themselves.[20] Hence the glossary of labels and multiple operating instructions for the matrices are no longer needed. Although many terms in the 1966 arrays derive from McKeon's earlier papers on the history of philosophy, their present arrangement is one of signal originality. In some respects the essay is an expansion and refinement of "Philosophy and Method," but it changes the three *kinds* of philosophy as labeled by three methods to the methods found *within* any system and adds a fourth, the operational,[21] and with it a fourth kind of Principle, the actional, to the comprehensive, the simple, and the reflexive earlier employed. The stiff diagonals give way to exploratory connections, but most of the contents of the X, Y, and Z matrices reappear: they had been elements, interpretations, and methods before, but now Interpretations is a new line in the semantic matrix; the elements are at least partially embodied in what are now called Selections; and the Methods have already been named (*FHOE,* see chart, p. 253).

The square of inquiry takes up what McKeon calls the four modes discriminating systems: modes of being, thought, fact, and simplicity, matching each one of these with all four types of approach listed under semantics. The semantic square seeks out formulations already made in the history of philosophy, detecting and resolving their differences, while that of inquiry charts the proposing of new and independent ways to set up and state problems and their solutions. (Previously, both functions were combined in one array.) Because the chief commonplaces of the new arrays are traditionally metaphysical terms, I will postpone a more detailed account of these until more of McKeon's own metaphysical thinking has been surveyed in chapter 5. Suffice it to say here that whereas the three matrices were capable of dealing with a single discipline only, and one had to construct entirely new ones in order to deal with other sciences (I am excepting the overlap between the Z matrix and metaphysical commonplaces), the new squares deal primarily with whole systems, even though the terms are in good part metaphysical in character. Any discipline could be analyzed in their purview with little addition, except for some obvious applications of terms peculiar to art, history, ethics, or whatever. For in this 1966 paper, metaphysics is treated not so much as an entirely separated subject matter, like logic, but as constantly present, underlying the entire range of sciences and arts. The new arrays both remove the isolation of metaphysics and show positively how it penetrates the other fields of endeavor. The matrices did not of themselves deal with systems, unless they were multiplied far beyond the trio X, Y, and Z; the new arrays could deal with systems as wholes or with the many subject matters comprising them, but not with the elements of the subject matters.

It need scarcely be said that the combinations possible in this fourfold division of modes of inquiry, multiplied by the fourfold division between types of semantic approach, allows—indeed enforces—combinations that would put Polonius's account of the manifold offers of the Players to shame. The addition of the column devoted to the operational approach (more broadly conceived in this square than the definition given by P. W. Bridgman) may raise some eyebrows because it seems to have been forced upon the Sophists. Really, the conflict seems resolved in taking the strict operational approach in the sciences, and the sophistic and rhetorical as a tool for the humanities. But this can be left to one side here.

These, then, are the structures, the weapons, that McKeon constructed in his program to solve the question of the differences between thinkers and between the possessions of which they were proudest. How these many structures were used will form one of the main concerns of the next three chapters.

5

Metaphysical Bearings

Richard McKeon did not limit the subject matter of metaphysics to the science of objective reality alone but insisted that it deal with the ways we know reality in general and the ways our knowledge of it can be communicated. Historically, this unique (positivists would say bogus) science had been pursued from one of these standpoints or another. There are short cycles in history, and metaphysics as a study of conditions of knowledge replaced the Platonic and Aristotelian concerns for reality outside the mind and was in turn supplanted by an approach holding ideas to be too vague and too fugitive and suggesting that we should examine symbolic means whereby knowledge can be isolated and structured.

This chapter will present samples of McKeon's efforts to state a more comprehensive outline of a metaphysics in which reality per se can be selectively studied so the truths of being are alternately or even alternatively expressed as truths of intellect or of linguistic formulations. Structures of language can be held over from the previous chapter and applied more concretely, if that is the right expression, in metaphysical problems, old-fashioned or new.

Of the tasks traditionally metaphysical, McKeon most frequently addressed that of showing how this discipline examines scientific principles. That it is the science of being qua being, or of the grades of being, or of a Supreme Being—all this McKeon freely acknowledged to be vital, yet he had less to say about these aspects except to remark that they could be made harmonious with his own interests. I shall accordingly give little attention to whether he was a theist in theology, a pluralist in cosmology, a rationalist in epistemology, or to other questions of this sort.

His earliest publication in the metaphysics of scientific principles is a largely historical piece, "Spinoza and Experimental Science,"[1] later incorporated into his book on the philosopher.[2] For metaphysical reasons Spinoza thinks motion and rest explain the extensional aspects of nature, and other notions, such as hot and cold, are of little use; unlike motion and rest, they are not amenable to mathematical treatment and hence lack certainty. In his famous but often misinterpreted controversy with Robert Boyle,[3] Spinoza contends that no heaping up of experimental evidence can ever prove what Boyle had sought to prove, the heterogeneity of niter (potassium nitrate or saltpeter). It is the other way round: truth for Spinoza forms a system derived from simple, clear axioms and defined terms combined and recombined to form a quasi-geometric chain of reasoning. What is reported through the senses reveals almost nothing of what things are.

McKeon himself did not adhere to so stringent an account of knowledge. In a brief essay printed a few years later,[4] he distinguished between empirical and rational science, giving approximately equal status to both. They manifest (1) generality to their constituent propositions, that is, generally going beyond the immediate evidence; (2) determinate validity, as resting upon definite evidence, be it a set of principles or a set of facts observed; (3) the formal characteristic of stating a relation between variables; (4) the compendency in a set of propositions. Although there are several implied concessions to an empirical outlook here, the other requirements would scarcely have been unacceptable to Spinoza.

One of McKeon's most successful monothematic essays was one of the first, "*De Anima:* Psychology and Science."[5] Employing a unitary rather than bipartite or collational approach, it deals with the question of whether a science of the soul is possible. Evidently this involves the prior questions, Is there a soul? and Exactly what is the soul, if it exists? A twist characteristic of McKeon's thinking is this search for more fundamental problems. Whether or not the soul actually exists is less important than the implications of the answer, given either way. He remarks: "In respect of the philosophical consequences to which they were intended, Ockham's repudiation of the doctrine of the soul as held by his predecessors is identical with the affirmation of the soul by Aristotle: for Ockham meant to emphasize that the soul is nothing over and above the activities of knowing and moving that are attributed to it, and Aristotle wished to emphasize that no entity, harmony, number or principle is necessary other than the principle of such actions and motions as an organic body can encompass" (pp. 674–75).

One should begin with the principle dividing into two others: the principle of sensation is reason, and that of reason is the soul (p. 676). This flies in the face of virtually all modern psychology, accustomed to tracing the genesis of ideas from sensations or more generally, of complexes out of simples. If this is turned around, and higher functions are made to explain powers of the whole human being, and finally those powers are examined in order to arrive at a definition of the soul, then a scientific formulation will be possible, despite the fact that the psychology of reason is but poorly understood; yet it is needed as a faculty responsible for such a science. Of the three chief problems of psychology, namely the organic bases for functions, the relations of those bodily organs to the soul, and finally the soul itself (pp. 677–78), the first has been far more avidly pursued and dexterously treated than have the other two.

When the soul attempts to state a science of itself, knower and known become identical. Thought has a content, and behaviorism, to take an extreme example of the attempt to reduce mind to bodily functions, in this case movements of the larynx, would find it troublesome to explain how these movements could be about laryngeal movements (p. 679). If, instead, the mind examines itself, it can best proceed by considering the propositions that the mind forms. But this subject matter is all possible propositions (p. 681), which immediately (1) involves us in a paradox of the whole, call it one of the *insolubilia* of Jean Buridan and his contemporaries or a violation of the Whitehead-Russell theory of types (ibid.). An insoluble puzzle here is a proposition exhibiting in itself the fact that the mind, if it can make propositions at all, can fabricate them about things because they must not apply to themselves. Or (2) it involves us in a self-justifying situation, in which a proposition formulated and then doubted is nevertheless thought to imply a necessary truth, as in Descartes's famous formula (p. 682). Here, evaluating such a statement is attached to the fact that both affirmation and denial of truth always involves its affirmation; if truly there is no truth, then this proposition is true, which thereby falsifies this same proposition (p. 684). However, any proposition about the totality of propositions requires that it must itself be added to their number, along with whatever proposition is needed to apply this general proposition to all the others. Although propositions about the class of all propositions are logically impossible, still such propositions can be formed and understood; they indicate themselves. Propositions stating *what* all propositions are must be fallacious; propositions stating *that* given propositions exist are necessarily true (p. 685).

The inference from propositions yields the realm of all possible ones; that from thinking yields the existence of the individual thinker, as Descartes held. Rational psychology is the sum total of all possible propositions, and the rational soul formulating it is potentially all things. The upshot is that a completed science of the soul is impossible, for knowledge of all things (which would include knowledge of all propositions) is out of the question (p. 686). Although no science of the soul exists, paradoxically no science is possible without the soul (p. 688), which is potentially all things, including all propositions about propositions. But because science is of the actual, not the potential, it cannot be a complete science of what the soul is, marked by its limits, for the limits are simply not there.

Psychology taken as the science of an organism operating among data of experience will be a collection of propositions generalized from experience. Psychology taken, on the other hand, as a science of functions of a soul at bottom unknowable is a science concerned with propositions deduced from self-evident truths (p. 689). In either case the impossibility of a science of the soul is again demonstrated (p. 690).

This monothematic essay argues a single case, start to finish: McKeon would have called it an essay in philosophic inquiry, exploring a subject matter with a single and, so to speak, self-made method, with a set of concepts to match. Comparisons with other methods are absent, and its solution is not a compromise or transcendence of differences between opposed theories of equivalent value.

This early work is not McKeon's last monothematic study, though more of his papers adopted other patterns. It is speculative, but several other monothematic papers are not, one of them being "The Relation of Logic to Metaphysics in the Philosophy of Duns Scotus."[6] Technical and highly concentrated, it suggests no fixed parallel columns delineating alternate approaches, except for a prefatory passage on the distinction between different historical trends in logic running from antiquity to the fourteenth century. The rest of the essay (pp. 526–50) is also historical but devoted step by step to the logical and metaphysical doctrines erected by Duns to deal with "that which is" (*ens*) and "being" (*esse*). Most, but not all, of the Scotist distinctions are dichotomous, and McKeon follows them through to bring out the fact that Duns had created "a logic of relations and a logic of the concrete" (p. 549). To do this, Scotus had shown, among other things, how categories of existence, that is, substances and their attributes, could be a foundation for operations of the understanding and forms of signifying. Scotus was no Aristotelian in any orthodox sense, but like many others made use of Peripatetic distinctions to erect an elaborate theory of his own.

Dichotomies, Physical and Metaphysical

In fleshing out the development of some of McKeon's metaphysical ideas, I must repeat the order of chapter 4. In his early course Science and Metaphysics at Columbia prior to 1934 and during the first half of that year,[7] he pointed out four possible levels on which theories of space, motion, and so forth can be presented: as matters of opinion, which cannot stand against philosophical doctrines once the latter are well established; as matters of empirical science, which hold only to the extent that such a science can supply the facts for grounding a rational science; the rational science that correctly describes the propositions defining such concepts and describes their properties; and finally the metaphysical truths (whose contraries are self-contradictory) that underlie scientific formulations and into which they can ultimately be translated to clarify them in terms of the most general principles, conceptual and methodological.

In a brief but all-important aside portending his later distinction, McKeon remarked that metaphysical truths could be expressed as truths of the nature of being, as truths of the structure of ideas, and as truths of grammar. It is this tolerance that distinguishes McKeon from such thinkers as Rudolf Carnap, although McKeon's own espousal, as opposed to his tolerance, is a slightly more disputable matter, to be discussed later. The earlier arrays of McKeon's throw some light on the *Scheinprobleme*—the illusory or pseudo-problems described in Carnap's earlier writings. Carnap condemns all questions demanding answers lacking means for direct empirical verification. McKeon would restrict this condemnation not to any general list of problems but to those not fitting the requirements of a particular method and set of principles. What is false in one approach may easily be proper in another, and problems significant here can become worthless elsewhere. A dialectician convinced of the continuity between physical and mental would think Carnap's own separation shallow and unnecessary. McKeon would say this was true, but only in certain contexts.

Perhaps the differences are best explained by this, that to Carnap the reality existing outside of linguistic facts is a matter-in-motion reality that can and must be observed and measured; otherwise it is unreal. For McKeon, this takes no account of the nature of things that underlies the matter and the motion; but he admits, indeed he insists, that reality can be investigated in the two other ways.

In 1934, McKeon presented metaphysics as a science of real things, not ideas or words. The chief kinds of real beings he treated were space, time, infinity, motion, and (briefly) categories of things. He told a friend of mine that he planned to publish a study of one concept each year, so he could dispense with it in lectures and add a fresh concept from a list including cause, matter, laws of nature, and number. I never saw the promised publications in any form, though it struck me that he must have put much of this material into near-publishable shape, so thorough was his oral account.

He dealt with space from two standpoints typical of most of his early work: concepts and methods. In each he found two leading kinds, whose headings were posted in chapter 4 (see fig. 5.1). The Platonic is a method of search for an all-embracing concept, while the Aristotelian is one of progressively (syllogistically) linking subjects and predicates. As for the concepts, Plato evolved a theory of space as a formless something, known by a bastard type of reasoning (*Timaeus* 50a–51b, 52b), while Aristotle projected a theory of place (*topos,* not *chora,* "space" or *to kenon,* "the void") which is a kind of containing envelope or limit of a body and is in turn in its place (*Physics* IV. 1–5), and so on up to the extreme outer limit of the cosmos, which obviously cannot be in place (*On the Heavens,* I. 8–9).

PLATO (HOLOSCOPIC THROUGHOUT)	ARISTOTLE (MEROSCOPIC THROUGHOUT)
concept: amorphous space	concept: physical place
method: applicable to any physical system	method: applicable to this solar system

Figure 5.1   Contrasting Theories of Space

McKeon then analyzed two of the most prominent mixtures in modern times (fig. 5.2). Newton uses a method of likenesses, in which sets

NEWTON	EINSTEIN
holoscopic concept: amorphous space	meroscopic concept: physical place
meroscopic method: applicable to the solar system only	holoscopic method: equations applicable to any system

Figure 5.2   Mixed Approaches in Physics

of purely physical relations are held to be kinematically similar when similar (or homogeneous) formulas describe them. In his formulas, space becomes dimensionality and length is taken as a function of time. Aristotle, who upheld the primacy of substance and dealt in physics chiefly through not solely with inanimate bodies, conceived place as absolute ("the innermost motionless limit of a containing body") and held absolute distinctions—up-down, right-left, forward-back—all of them inseparable from body's motions. For Newton, space is absolute, unmoving, filled with an ether, with mathematically determined dimensions. Place is but a part of space, perceptible to the senses. Bodies bound this latter space, whereas for Aristotle place bounds all bodies and is only incidentally amenable to geometrical measures. Were geometry to be wholly, simply, and immediately applicable to place, geometry would have to embrace physical principles; for Aristotle this was out of the question, for Newton not. Einstein still has elements of Plato and Aristotle, but differently combined. Space is "grained," it has structure, it gains character from bodies in it. Gravity is no longer a pull exerted through empty space or resisting mediums but results from features of space as conditioned by moving bodies. Einstein's formulas for uniform and accelerated motion are generalized to fit any system, not merely our universe.

As McKeon pointed out, when a body moves, space or place remains motionless, and when bodies are at rest, space is a principle of their order. Time distinguishes motions when bodies are moving differently, and when they rest time is the continuous, for the interval of rest will still be a tract of time. Time is related to body. For Plato, space is explained by reference to (1) the model: the eternal, mathematically perfect pattern; (2) space itself: the formless somewhat that is neither change nor body but enters into both; (3) the changing copy: namely bodies, celestial and terrestrial. Time is treated similarly: (1) the eternal: the same perfect pattern; (2) the soul, primarily world-soul but also the human soul; (3) time, the moving image of eternity. The soul that both knows and perceives mediates between eternity and time.

For Aristotle, change must be either in a thing or else in the place where the thing is. Time is present in both, hence cannot be motion, yet there is no motion without time, so the latter is an accident of motion necessarily. Time is the measure of motion with respect to before and after, whereas for Plato time is the image or imitation of an eternity and is measured by motion. Aristotle gives little consideration to the eternal in his physics but much in his astronomy and metaphysics.

In connection with these two, McKeon expounded the theories of Plotinus, St. Augustine, Galileo, Newton, Whitehead, and C. D. Broad, not to mention the Fitzgerald Contraction, the Lorentz Transformation, and Einstein's Relativity, all of the latter three being stated, where appropriate, in terms of equations.

The motion (McKeon's third concept) in Plato's universe is at least as regular as a slightly frustrated effort of the creator (*dēmiourgos*) could make the motion of the stars, and partly irregular, being that of structures compounded of bodies formed from triangles behaving not unlike atoms, randomly moving on earth. Physics is not perfectly exact, since even the most regulated natural movements do not quite match an ideal mathematical model. Aristotle distinguished perfect, eternal sidereal motions from terrestrial which like Plato's could move in six directions. Aristotle's physics is full of distinctions: substantial change (coming into being and passing out of being) vs. quantitative, qualitative, and topical (local) motion; motion per se vs. motion per aliud (where some body is carried along by another moving body); natural motion vs. force (violent or impressed motion); natural motion of inanimate bodies (straight up or straight down) vs. plants growing upward and downward at the same time. In Descartes, treated here as a moderately consistent holoscopist, the effort, rather like Plato's, is to mathematize all of kinematics; this can be done if Aristotle's substantial and qualitative changes are dropped, leaving only locomotion and quantitative changes. Through a geometry for solving algebraic equations, Descartes could deal directly with questions of order and quantity, which for him comprised all mathematics. Physics differs from mathematics only because it deals with motion, whose quantity in the universe is maintained fixed by God. Most other Aristotelian distinctions are discarded, and seven laws of shock (impact) based upon seven sets of contrary determinations, such as heavy-light and so forth, are substituted. The world is a machine, and man's body is a machine as well, one into which a soul of totally different substance has been inserted. For Newton, too, the world is a machine, but here the emphasis shifts back to space (which Descartes had rejected in favor of extension) and time as the framework for any grasp of motion's nature. Forces take on a larger role in Newton, impact a smaller.

In the 1934 course, McKeon expounded and evaluated theories of the continuum and the infinite, contrasting chiefly Aristotle with Russell, two authors with most to say of scientific interest regarding these, and concluding with categories (Plato, Aristotle, Kant, Peirce, and others), making a point of the distinction between philosophic issues from those purely scientific.

In the winter of 1938 he offered Science and Metaphysics at the University of Chicago, this time stressing a totally different set of concerns, about which more in the following section: alternative approaches to the same problems but through a distinction between things, thoughts, and words. In subsequent years he examined several mathematical instead of physical concepts, and then metaphysical terms ("actuality," "substance," etc.) as they tend to sift into the special sciences. I cannot report on these last two.

Threefold Distinctions in Metaphysics and Science

Let us return to the winter of 1938. McKeon greatly admired John Dewey for teaching the same course many times over, varying it each term, recasting his notes almost from start to finish, and the lesson had not been lost on McKeon himself. He now worked out a prefatory structure, a 3 × 3 array, but with a difference that illustrates and also forms a subtle involution in use of the structure. The list of headings for types of philosophic approaches is exactly duplicated for the list of topics they are expected alternately to discuss. This means that there are three ways each of analyzing things, thoughts, and words, so that a philosopher committed to a metaphysics of symbols, for instance, can talk not only about the symbols directly but also, and indirectly, about thoughts as seen through the symbols and about things similarly viewed.

I have said earlier that the difference between the approaches is chiefly a difference of emphasis, and this is true, but it is the very cause of different interpretations of these major subject matters that McKeon later came to call Selections. That any credible philosopher ever flatly denied the existence of things, thoughts, or words is very doubtful, and the old pleasantry popular in London in the days of Berkeley and Hume, "No matter, never mind," is just that, a joke that both philosophers would have disowned. Each, then, of the three had to make at

SUBJECT MATTERS		PHILOSOPHIC APPROACHES	
	THINGS	THOUGHTS	WORDS
THINGS	primary	posterior	intermediate
THOUGHTS	intermediate	primary	posterior
WORDS	posterior	intermediate	primary

PRINCIPAL PROBLEMS

What is metaphysics?   Is metaphysics valid?   Is metaphysics meaningful?

Figure 5.3   Involuted Threefold Approaches to Things, Thoughts, Words

least *some* room for the subject matters and issues of the other two, however much of an effort was made to reduce those others to a total assimilation.

In one sense, but only one, McKeon's decision to teach this material
in terms of a linguistic approach was arbitrary, for he had been skeptical
of G. E. Moore's accomplishments in this vein.[8] Hence his commitment
fell a little short of absolute adherence to language as can be found, for
example, in the linguistic studies by Wittgenstein or Austin. Metaphysical problems, no matter how linguistically interpreted, are still as different from purely grammatical problems as are scientific ones. Yet in the
distinction between nouns and verbs, or between words and sentences,
it is possible to draw some positive conclusions not only about thoughts
but about things (see fig. 5.3).

The reason for hesitations regarding the third column and its priorities is that in adopting this approach most of its adherents allow the
cosmos to fade to mere gossamer, undifferentiated almost as radically as
the epistemic approach of Kant reduces the thing-in-itself to even less:
a characterless somewhat hovering between existence and nonexistence
because deprived—or *perhaps* deprived, for Kant is tentative here—of
unity, causality, reciprocal relations, and all the other properties of exis-
tent things except bare existence.

Partisans of the linguistic approach as a group have been rather less
than keenly interested in the history and contrast of doctrines, for there
is no need in their eyes to survey the cultures of mankind and the philosophic systems that many of these support as examples of gross error
or nonsense—if the errors can be banished or the nonsense made rational with one stroke by attending to what is in essence most intelligible: signs. Alternatively, a variety of cultures breeding varied grammatical patterns attest to the hopeless relativity of all truth that is so
contingent upon these paradigms. In this linguistic approach, meta-

physics is reduced to so slender a role as to consist merely of the assertion that there can exist no metaphysics. What is left after this impoverishment, McKeon pointed out, is the special sciences, commencing with mathematics and physics, together with the grammars appropriate to them. Being is now nothing more than an article of faith for which no demonstration or experiment could possibly be forthcoming.

All three approaches honor the structural possibilities of combinations of words. Put these together properly, they all say, and then one can arrange signs in wholly intelligible relations with one another, and since signs essentially point to something beyond themselves (an idea or a stovepipe, say), what is pointed to has some sort of established relation to its indicator. Thus the subject-predicate relation implies both some distinction between thing and property and also that thing and property are intimately related in at least one instance. Again, if some signs indicate transitive relations and others intransitive, these can be meaningfully attached to different kinds of things or ideas exterior to the signs.

The adoption of tripartite schemes also held for publications, and of a very different sort. In one example, historical references all but disappear, except as confirmatory asides. "Being, Existence, and That Which Is," the presidential address to the Metaphysical Society of America in 1960,[9] surveys problems and possible solutions offered by a thorough science of metaphysics, a survey so forbidding, so abstruse, that one might turn after hearing it to parts 3 and 4 of *Process and Reality* for mental relaxation. It is an essay divided between the collational and monothematic types, for although different approaches to the problems are assumed, there is no attempt to divide them according to the *Urphilosophen* or any other designated schools of philosophy. The few thinkers mentioned—Avicenna among others—are introduced quite incidentally and accorded but a line or two apiece. I am not sure why the title was not "That Which Is, Being, and Existence," for the essay seeks to prove that metaphysics should accord priority to that which is, taking up existence as last in erecting a competent, complete science.

High though my respect is for the Metaphysical Society of America, I am inclined to doubt that every member could have grasped and remembered all details of the tight-packed reading.[10] The address is no plea for a science of metaphysics or a criticism of past efforts to arrive at such a science; it makes no suggestions regarding what neglected sources to exploit for improving metaphysical speculation. Instead it outlines the order and types of problems of constructing a suitable theory of all reality, making no assumption whether this has ever been followed or will be followed. Probably the best way to present it is in the form of a 3 × 3 array in prose.

Three considerations govern approaches to metaphysics (those same three would do for other sciences as well): starting points, distinctions, and unities. Three orders can be detected, according as one begins with that which is, or with being, or with existence. (Six orders are possible if one reverses the second and third items of each list, but the essay ignores this, probably for economy's sake.)

Wisdom considers what McKeon calls ontic questions grouped around the most general inquiry into What Is. Wisdom seeks principles, looking for general modes to determine that which is, beings, entities, things. The knower, in order to recognize the known, must determine What Is, and this involves as starting-points the transcendentals (being, thing, something, one, true, and good).[11] These terms provide grounds for distinguishing physical entity from logic, and both from value entity. These then divide philosophy into physics, logic, and ethics, and the unity of all is rooted in the fact that what is cannot be isolated in the known but reveals its characteristics in connections of knowledge and perceptions of the knower. This section ends with the recommendation for a broader conception of "thing" to include things said and sought as well as known.

The second question, which relates to being, can be framed as, What is it that is? and is explored on a level of knowledge, not wisdom, and requires that categorical questions be so asked as to encourage answers stressing connections.[12] There are now special, not general, modes determining being, nature, and essence. The knowledge is directed to establishing the truth of statements about what is in connections, sequences, and consequences; this is science itself. Looking to natures and essences calls into play causation, responsibility, and communication. The distinctions are no longer between physics, logic, and ethics but between the theoretical sciences, which deal with what is asserted, the practical sciences, which deal with what is done, and the productive, which deal with what is made. Here unity will result from the broader use of categories to include natural institutions affecting action and creation.

In the third set of modes generated when one begins with that which is, McKeon asks, Under what circumstances is that which is what it is?

This is a question of existence, and the epistemic level of its pursuit is no longer knowledge but experience. The circumstantial modes here determine the existence, occurrence, or factual determination of things: What agglomeration of characteristics constitutes a fact or event? The circumstantial questions relate to the probability, possibility, or necessity that a fact may exist or an event be brought about. The types of inquiry distinguished are history, poetry, and philosophy (each of them with its own concerns with all three modalities of existence). The unity sought will be found when it becomes clear that the probabilities of history, art, and science are distinct, not identical.

So much for beginning with That Which Is. I leave out the remaining two choices, which are treated by McKeon less fully but with no more concessions to the hearer or reader. Thus pruned here—indeed gutted—of its many interconnections, ancillary interpositions, and modifiers, not to mention two whole sections, this address must still impress one at second hand that in its fifteen pages an outline of the task of the metaphysician has been shrewdly and profoundly stated.[13]

The Matrices Once More

Chapter 4 showed that change to a 4×4 matrix from a 3×3 array involved much more than merely one from nine nodes to sixteen; the matrices were more nearly prescriptive of a necessary form any theory of logic (or metaphysics, or ethics, for that matter) should take than were the classificatory arrays of earlier decades.

The two metaphysical aims of comprehensiveness and precision are nearly opposite standards, together with freedom from distortion, and they multiply the difficulties, for among philosophers there are not only differences in doctrines on which compromise is possible but also many ways that these authors believe their doctrines should be stated and ordered. Philosophers holding, for instance, the unity of compounded discourse to be propositions have been countered by those upholding sentences or judgments or other acts of the mind. Many who deemed it impossible to discover truth in any one statement, thinking that truth is developed painfully and skillfully throughout long sequences, or even sets of sequences, will counter those championing individual propositions as the vehicles for truth. If, then, one is to make out some clear matrix node, it may clarify the fixed statements but inevitably falsify the others embedded in sequences. One must not draw up a matrix offering multiple entries to compare and contrast one node against many. Any-

(1) MW	(2) WA	(3) WB	(4) WC
(5) MsS	(6) AsS	(7) BsS	(8) CsS
(9) MpO	(10) AoP	(11) BoP	(12) CoP
(13) MpO	(14) ApO	(15) BpO	(16) CpO

Figure 5.4   Reconstructed Z Matrix

one using a matrix must make a stand *somewhere*. McKeon seemed most to want to create matrices containing the best definitive statements of the philosophers themselves, for instance, Plato's Divided Line, rather than preliminary sequences leading up to it.

In the course in advanced logic that I attended (winter 1949), McKeon referred in passing to the Z matrix but did not expound it in detail. It is possible to reconstruct it from hints he offered, but I cannot claim invincible authority for my results. Using the same symbols explained in chapter 4 and again numbering the nodes to conform to the earlier ones, I would hazard a reconstructed Z matrix like that in figure 5.4. The Divided Line begins with (14); Plato refers to this as images, simple visibles such as shadows and reflections. The letters ApO stand for just such objects that can become objects of thought on its lowest level. The next step for Plato is natural and artificial things in great variety; node (11) BoP stands for compounded things, things naturally or physically real as compared with their shadows. As objects of thought, they are firmer than the umbral reflections of ApO. Plato's third stage is arbitrary hypothesis in reason seeking not unity but some ad hoc truth; node (8) CsS stands for complexes existing in symbolic form. Lastly, above all the localized reasonings so to speak closed, there is the one: node (1) MW is a doubly overarching concept, arrived at by the analysis Plato calls dialectic and presaging the one truth by which all other truths are true. So much for a hierarchy made explicit, one famous in the history of ideas.

Some may feel that chapter 4 deals with what Rudolf Carnap calls philosophic syntax while the present one is semantic in character. The difference between the two chapters can be better stated using McKeon's terms rather than those of Carnap, who began with a bare structure, *Aufbau*, of a logic rendering a given sentence entirely in the terms found in another sentence. This is a syntactic principle that McKeon never thought appropriate to philosophic propositions. It might be that some statements in one context could be translated (transformed according to rules) into others within the same approach—in fact Carnap's own would be examples as long as one introduced no new philosophic foundations. But to translate the expressions of one system directly and simply into those of another McKeon thought to be out of the question. Even if the words happened to be the same—"life," "evolution," "expression," "truth," "experience"—their exact meanings would only be made to develop in light of methods and sets of principles wholly at variance with one another.

Later in his career, Carnap supplemented his theories of syntax with several contributions to semantics. McKeon, on the other hand, had never put aside semantic questions and for all the structuring of concepts that he performed, he never thought in terms of such structures alone. An array simply ordered meanings *already* conferred upon words or sets of words. A matrix displayed possibilities that any sort of logical (or other) commitments would possess but did not directly determine what those commitments should be, only that they had broadly a consistency and range of topics. Again, from the standpoint of semantics, there were no rules or even means of transformation. (My only reason, incidentally, for separating the discussion of the arrays into two approximately equal and parallel parts was rhetorical—for ease of handling. It appeared wiser to try to simplify the account by splitting it in a way falsifying McKeon's theory less, I believe, than would a logistic split on Carnap's grounds.)

Inquiry in Relation to Semantics

Although he lived nineteen years, almost to the day, after delivering an extraordinary address, "Philosophic Semantics and Philosophic Inquiry," at Southern Illinois University in March 1966, McKeon, as I pointed out in chapter 4, never published it, though he used many of its insights repeatedly in essays and occasional pieces issuing steadily from his hand in the last two decades of his life. These latter writings seldom treated metaphysics directly but extensively employed the metaphysical distinctions embodied in the two chief arrays labeled by his title.

This account will resemble an attempt to show a living body by giving the skeletal structure of about half the torso and perhaps part of a skull: an unwarranted diminution and distortion. The address-essay is probably the most densely packed of all McKeon's writings, with every part closely interlocked with every other. His own chart, which he mercifully supplied to his audience, could only suggest: it contained two 4 × 4 forms replete with new terminology and recondite juxtapositions, subordinations, and pairings of concepts. "Philosophy and

Method" of 1951[14] was, let us say, like Beethoven's Archduke Trio, or the Symphony No. 7, with subtleties of their own yet as wholes fairly straightforward and clear of intent, while the 1966 lecture resembles one of the last five quartets, each a work endlessly involuted, idiosyncratic, puzzling, and wonderful.

I begin with the square of inquiry appearing second in the essay title, for it forms the basis, as McKeon affirms, for deducing the square of semantics. Inquiry concerns the creating of a philosophic system without extended reference to others, and is stimulated though not fully determined by the common issues of philosophy; it provides what McKeon calls modes, so arranged that he could relate different solutions based upon different formulations of the common problems. Inquiry, the mother of a system, seeks to make new connections within a subject matter when this is treated by a single philosopher (*FHOE*, p. 243).

An inquiry is at bottom a question and divides into the four questions that Aristotle posited (*Posterior Analytics* II. 1. 89b21–25) as the basis of all inquiry into scientific subject matters. McKeon himself varies the order originally given the questions, for reasons of his own, asking Why it is?—answered by Being; What sort it is?—answered by That which is (Thought); What it is?—answered by Existence (Fact); and Whether it is?—answered by Experience (Simplicity) (*FHOE*, p. 255). Under the modes of Being (which are four, as suited to the square) are being and becoming, phenomena and projections, elements and composites, and actuality and potentiality, fitting, respectively, the dialectical, operational, logistic, and problematic methods. The modes of thought are: approximate englobing truths; interpreted arbitrary formulations; least parts assembled; and problems solved (pp. 244–45). Although the square of semantics can be deduced from any of the four modes, it suffices to use only the modes of Thought (p. 245). Details of his deduction are left open, though hints—slender ones—are supplied. The modes of Fact are reality and approximation; process and frame; object and impression; and substance and accident, while those of Simplicity are categories of thought; of language and action; of things; and of terms.

This is the outline, which is so laconically expressed in the original that it would be fruitless to invent fuller explanations here. It can only be said that much of the mystery is cleared up in the working out of applications in subsequent essays on politics, history, the arts, and more.

The aim of inquiry is truth while that of semantic comparison of systems is clarity. The entire semantic enterprise rests on the fact that common problems as formulated in inquiry have diverse solutions; these may well use words in common, but ambiguity always intrudes (p. 243). Semantics is then invoked to restore univocal meanings by showing that different authors intend different kinds of discourse to express themselves. One cannot, from a Platonic principle, construct a logistic argument much like Hume's theory of impressions and ideas. Once we learn to differentiate philosophies in this way, elimination of dubious meanings becomes possible.

Two of the four headings (p. 244) of the square of semantics are old friends (Methods and Principles), two are new ones (Interpretations and Selections). There are four subtypes of each. Each method has for its aim the answering of the question, Does a predicate inhere in a subject? Each looks for a different kind of predicate and a different kind of subject:

The *dialectical* method is a dialogue by assimilation and exemplification dependent upon changeless models;

The *operational* method is debate by discrimination and postulation dependent on theses and rules of action;

The *logistic* method is proof by construction and decomposition dependent on indivisible elements;

The *problematic* method is inquiry by resolution and questions dependent upon discoverable causes (p. 245).

The dialectical and operational methods are universal, applicable to all problems and subject matters, and are thus called holoscopic—the word held over from the distant past and now reapplied; the logistic and problematic methods are particular, requiring distinct procedures for different problems or subject matters, and are meroscopic.

Principles falling under the semantics of comparison are differently arranged:

The *comprehensive* assume a whole to which successive statements more and more closely approximate and assimilate all things, thoughts, symbols, and actions into an inclusive whole;

The *actional* postulate distinctions for discriminating into kinds what is said, done, or made;

The *simple* decompose things, thoughts, symbols, actions into atoms, simple ideas, undefined terms, or unconditioned impulses;

The *reflexive* resolve problems into a plurality of wholes formed by principles reflexively instances of themselves.[15]

Like the others, Interpretations are derivable from any of the four types of modes of inquiry, though here again the steps are lacking. Interpretations are the ways reality is approached: either (the dialectical and logistic) as something transcending or underlying all appearances, correctable by reference to that reality, or else (the operational and problematic) reducing reality to aspects or consequences of phenomena. The dialectical is termed ontological, the operation is existentialist, the logistic entitative, and the problematic essentialist. Note the different pairings from that of Methods.

Selections, while not exactly banished to the sidelines, are still less amply noticed than the other three headings. Their kinds stem primarily from modes of simplicity listed among types of inquiry and attach to the same question, Whether S is P? which is now answerable in terms of experience. Simples of assimilation are categories of thought set forth in hierarchies; simples of discrimination are categories of language or action expressed in semantic types; simples of construction are categories of things set forth by matters or objects to which others are reduced; simples of resolution are categories of terms dealing with natures and dispositions, set forth as functions whereby the natures may be defined (p. 251).

If we ignore pairings under the headings of holoscopic and meroscopic and two other divisions omitted here, we can rearrange and simplify the chart (p. 253) as in figure 5.5. I have little or no idea which of these caused McKeon to hesitate to put the array before the public, and were I to try to divine his reasons one or two doubts of my own would be sure to intrude, making the guesses doubly risky. As I have said, he used parts of this square in a number of his subsequent writings, and some of his followers have used virtually all of it in theirs,[16] but he evidently did not intend that it be taken as a set of spikes upon which to impale all the systems of our long cultural heritage. A sign of this is that he supplemented his outlay with a number of listings of philosophers who mix the *Ursysteme* just now displayed—these men being of first, or nearly first, rank (fig. 5.6). I might venture to classify the early Wittgenstein as being logistic, simple, and existentialist, while the later is problematic, actional, and existentialist, although McKeon apparently felt that once a philosopher had chosen his "profile" he adhered to it; but Wittgenstein is never an easy subject for analysis.

One wonders how the semantic square differs from ordinary semantics, whether of common speech or philosophy, and why this machinery

PRINCIPLES	METHODS	INTERPRETATIONS	SELECTIONS
comprehensive	dialectical	ontological	hierarchies
simple	logistic	entitative	matters
actional	operational	existentialist	types
reflexive	problematic	essentialist	kinds

Figure 5.5   Simplified Square of Philosophic Semantics

	ACADEMICS	AUGUSTINE	DESCARTES	SPINOZA
METHOD	dialectical	dialectical	logistic	logistic
PRINCIPLES	actional	actional	reflexive	reflexive
INTERPRETATION	existentialist	ontological	entitative	ontological

	KANT	HEGEL	JAMES	DEWEY
METHOD	operational	dialectical	problematical	problematic
PRINCIPLES	reflexive	reflexive	actional	actional
INTERPRETATION	ontological	entitative	existentialist	essentialist
				(pp. 254–55)

Figure 5.6   Mixtures of Pure Approaches

is required. No one knows quite what a Pickwickian sense is, but it is universally recognized that reference to it in respectable books of logic is a banner held aloft to indicate that a word is being used in something other than its most literal meaning. But Mr. Blotton and Mr. Pickwick did not trot out dialectical as opposed to problematic methods or simple as opposed to actional principles to settle their differences. McKeon has specified that his proposal is for *philosophic* semantics; the persons involved are thinkers of the high rank rather than—may I say?—nitwits who long ago investigated the origins of Hampstead Pond. McKeon's semantics analyzes the conditions under which thought, often abstruse and abstract in the highest degree, becomes efficacious or inefficacious. While the major problem of inquiry is ultimately to frame a system to fit the ascertainable character of the universe, not just the local grass-is-green facts, that of semantics is to frame questions to be asked of each philosopher's writings so that they may be read in light of contrasts to others. The discrepancies can then be adjusted, for hidden differences in vocabulary and discordant relations of words can be harmonized by recognition of all the assumptions of method and so forth that animate a philosopher's thinking. Unexamined likenesses are less likely to fester and lead to hostilities than are hidden disagreements, but it is too much to expect that these likenesses will of themselves be sufficiently strong to win over a thinker with an opposed point of view.

Richard McKeon's Preferences and Reasons

So much for the extraordinary, perplexing essay which I think of as a culmination and at the same time a roughed out torso. Its implications are made to reach far beyond metaphysics into the entire fabric of philosophy, as all metaphysical considerations must reach. This very universality, however, leads one to ask, How is this schema applicable to itself? More individually, Where does McKeon himself fit? I tried to lay in a grave—admittedly a shallow one—the talk about neo-Aristotelianism and the fugitive "Chicago School." Were he orthodox in his neo-Aristotelian affiliations, he could not have said, as he did in 1934, that he analyzed the meroscopic method holoscopically and the holoscopic method meroscopically, or that he was Aristotelian in his attachment to principles and Platonic in the generality and fluidity of his approach. Years later in Chicago, it struck me that because the interest in what others say is chiefly a sophistic concern, McKeon was the greatest of the Sophists. Yet this could not be right, I felt, because of his concerted effort to find many-sided truths with little thought of deriving personal advantage. I was unready then to acknowledge mixed affiliations as being on a par with pure ones, so could not ascribe the sophistic method to him without assuming that all the rest of the operationalist approach must accompany it.[17] The real question of his subscribing is a dual one, psychological and philosophical, though two such answers must not conflict with each other. I assume that McKeon was in earnest in saying that one picked an approach "that feels most comfortable"; yet he also persisted in his attempt to discover more and more ways that philosophy itself comes to be and the way it "works," as an electric motor works; and here we move from preferences born of early influences or pleasing styles and the like to objective reasons, to which I shall now attend. We can rule out the notion that somehow McKeon embraced all four types of systems—that is, all sixteen nodes of his rows and columns. He was a philosopher, not a chameleon. We can also rule out that he put himself above all the *Urphilosophen* (whether two, three or four) and above all mixtures with some mysterious, undefined metaphilosophy, thereby exempting himself from involvements with ordinary concepts and methods. In class he rejected this suggestion almost brusquely. Not only did he rule this out for himself, but I doubt that he would have conceded that anyone else, using McKeon's premises, could provide such a universal analysis, floating high above all the rest. Nor was it likely that he would find a fifth system, irreducible to the other four but on a par with them, into which his own activities would fit. Such a fifth system would be subject to the same old strictures and would possess defined capabilities and limitations as did the others: distinction but not a difference.

There are no printed statements of McKeon's own affiliations that I can discover, but fortunately there are oral traditions having excellent authority for what he considered his central adherences. These are buttressed by reasons, but the reasons, of course, are slowly and painfully arrived at, being part and parcel of the very arrays being exploited. The most painstaking method for showing how McKeon fits his own schematism would be of course first to evaluate again his procedures and commitments in light of his descriptions of the *Ursysteme* and then, after it became evident that not one of them quite fitted his case, to explore possible combinations. An entire volume would thus be occupied with this exploration if it were carried out conscientiously, for the possible combinations of Methods, Principles, Interpretations, and Selections— ruling out some that might obviously be so jarring that no one could espouse them—would be extremely large. Some of the nodes might not be difficult to reject. I see little trace, for instance, of an "englobing" principle, an inexpressible Idea that informs and enlightens every other doctrine in a system and whose clear conception is always just beyond reach save in some rare moment of intuitive insight. But the other three types of principles are not so easily dismissed. Nor do I see McKeon as a kind of atomist, holding onto small pieces that are joined to make bigger and more complex pieces; but this still leaves three other Methods. And so for the rest.

The fact that McKeon liked to begin by laying out his principles should hint of the Aristotelian character of this phase of his thought. That he thought of his principles as self-evident showed his use of the reflexiveness of those principles. Essay after essay of his begins with some variation on the theme that there are great discrepancies in the traditional philosophies, and it is important to lay them out in order to resolve them. If you disagree, he is saying in effect, then you and I are enunciating pieces of different philosophies, and if *this* be true, we shall never reach an agreement merely by standing pat on our respective opinions. This is his own reflexive principle. He was also an essentialist in his Interpretation, holding reality to be not a light and airy thing, blown about by winds of doctrine, but having structures to render it stable though not static. His Selection, in turn, was linguistic, not cognitive, nor was it based chiefly on things in this phase of his work. (There were throughout his career portents that the attachment to verbal structures, chiefly found in the army of texts that he had mastered, was actually a propaedeutic in that career, and that the devising of ways to enable men to talk without letting ambiguities dangle and spoil communication was a mission. Once this machinery was set up he could revert to what he all along had thought of as the better approach— through things, not thoughts or language. He vigorously confirmed this impression in a conversation I had with him in the spring of 1949.)

It remains to say that his Method was not dialectical, for although he was, like Socrates, sick with love of speeches (*Phaedrus* 228c; cf. 227b, d; 230e; 236e), he did not direct them toward a single, all-embracing truth. Second, it must be said that Aristotle himself did not want to, nor using his principles could he even with all the modern libraries at his disposal, arrive at the kinds of comparisons and contrasts that McKeon regularly made. McKeon wished to dispose systems properly to penetrate to their common truths by resolving their differences, whereas Aristotle wished to dispose *of* other systems as wholes and by simply picking up terms and propositions from them and then reformulating these arrive at his own statements of truth. McKeon was an operationalist in his Method, seeking to apply it universally (as with dialectic), discriminating very carefully the significances in what others have said, and laying down rules in the form of the arrays and matrices for their interpreting. In summary: McKeon used reflexive Principles, essentialist Interpretation, linguistic Selection, and operational Method: two Aristotelian and two stemming alternatively from the Sophists and the Operationalists.[18] What I have taken to be his animadversion on the linguistic approach—or rather his lukewarm tolerance of it early in his career—was an attitude that had to be overcome when he had settled upon making a contribution in world politics some years later. But there may have been no real change in attitude; it is hard to say, for like Immanuel Kant he could hold more distinctions in the palm of his hand than his hearers or readers could inspect and assimilate at any one time.

If neo-Aristotelian be taken to mean that all four entries in the semantic square pertaining to Aristotle must be subscribed to, then McKeon was not an Aristotelian or neo-Aristotelian; but if only two of the four characteristics of Aristotle's philosophy are required, and the other two do not unduly obscure the affiliation, then he was indeed a neo-Aristotelian. As a subsidiary point, had he ever been satisfied that he had finished with exegetics and communications theory, he might have altered his profile in philosophy; but it is an open question whether he would have adopted the other two Aristotelian modes. We cannot judge a philosopher by all that he does not say.

I do not know how closely "Philosophic Semantics and Philosophic Inquiry" ever represented what McKeon really wanted to say about the inner workings of his magisterial discipline. Evidently he entertained a mixture of feelings, though his refraining from ever publishing the essay may have been intended to carry a hint—not taken very seriously, I think—to his followers. He set the highest standards for ultimate testaments of this kind. Henrik Ibsen writes, "The songs unsung are ever the fairest," but again, McKeon cannot be judged by what he never said.

6

Discourse, Controversy, and Resolution in Society

The first of Richard McKeon's papers devoted solely to broadly political matters was a long piece on property.[1] This mainly historical account was a prelude to a copious, elaborately conceived flow of essays, of which there are nearly five dozen appearing in learned journals or as chapters in books between 1940 and 1966. (A handful of studies in law and in education would add to this tally.) These essays are with some exceptions the least heavily documented of the writings, relying instead upon solid argument bristling with distinctions between and transformations of his concepts. When concerned to do so, however, McKeon could freight his papers with erudition: In "Philosophic Differences and the Issues of Freedom,"[2] he uses seventy-two footnotes to cite or quote (in his order) Hobbes, Hegel, Marx, Mannheim, Laski, Croce, St. Augustine, Rousseau, Kant, Plato, Cicero, Epictetus, Marcus Aurelius, Ralph Barton Perry, Spinoza, Mill, Aristotle, Dewey, and Herbert Read, not to mention some UNESCO reports.

It would be easier to expound these papers if all showed a settled tendency, moving from one subject or set of questions to another, or if one could show their adherence to a single, all-embracing matrix. It is unlikely, however, that in the thirty years' work of a subtle and far-ranging intellect one could map a single line of march or collect a small number of principles serving as warranties for conclusions traceable through several groups of deductions. If, however, there *is* one principle in McKeon's writings on politics, it comes perilously near to outright paradox: no single doctrine can be formulated to establish any set of statements regarding economic, social, or political relationships, or once for all define freedom, right, justice, well-being, or others terms of this kind. This is a monistic foundation of a radical pluralism envisaging that peoples of any two cultures or even members of one cannot be brought to single-minded agreement on substantive principles or concepts, nor should they. The right method would instead clarify the differences, so that the originally opposing parties could soon grasp and respect the opinions embraced, sometimes obsessively, by each other. They would then make adjustments in common to live harmoniously with this modest, indeed minimal, resolution of conflict. This principle of concordant pluralities within larger concordant pluralities would hold between philosophers, between statesmen, between everyday men and women, between cities, regions, states, empires.[3]

How McKeon passes from this principle as a matter of linguistic interpretation to one of an objective world of nations in flames, seeking to moderate the warring parties before mutual destruction overtakes them, seems a desirable line to trace. In doing this one cannot always follow McKeon's order of publication, and certainly not his order of private thinking.

Communication and Dialectic

It soon becomes apparent that the distinctions between McKeon's ways of approaching language were ways familiar to the Greeks or Romans. Whitehead, Russell, Wittgenstein, Austin, Sartre, and Chomsky were all expounded in McKeon's classes and occasionally in his writings, but one searches long and hard in the essays for substantive uses of "presentational immediacy," "denotation," "family resemblances," "performative utterances," "nothing," "strings," and other common coinage of twentieth-century discussion. Instead, "dialectic," "ambiguity," "refutation," "paralogism" "rhetorical," "commonplace," "grammar," "argument," "signification," and "term" seemed to him better adapted to his ideas, though they did not match but could only overlap the modern terminologies. This might impart a slightly antiquarian flavor, but one soon realizes that it put his authorship more solidly in traditions that over many centuries had accumulated a serviceable vocabulary.

Between any two persons the same words are ambiguous—so runs McKeon's argument—so what appears to be a single proposition is in fact two. Refutation takes place only when by dint of clear-sighted perception one party apprehends the intended meanings of the other and applies devices only to demolish those particular meanings. What devices there might be would vary from philosopher to philosopher, and each would need to justify his own tactics. Lacking all this, the refutation is apparent but unreal, though it would be as annoying and perhaps inflammatory as if it were genuine. Persuasion often uses the soundest, most irreproachable proofs, and this is dialectical or, more narrowly, logical if the grounds rest at all points in the nature of things as apprehended by a combination of inductive reasoning and intuitive insight. If, when analyzed, the proofs are found vague or faulty but are somehow still persuasive to the audience for which they were originally intended, this is rhetoric, not dialectic or logic, and here the power of the proof rests less upon its structure than upon other aspects and accompaniments of what is said—the coincidental associations of principal terms, the voice and bearing of the speaker, his reputation for honesty, and the social milieu at the time of delivery; all of these are extraneous to logical structure and factual content.

McKeon's exploration of the ways people have talked and the ways they ought and ought not to talk is twofold. He sees grounds for adjustments of alternative sequences of doctrines that permit the historian to group them, traditional or novel, and show their points of difference and agreement. On the other hand, he examines reasons why philosophers, presumably a tolerant lot, are soon, and without necessarily intending to be, embroiled in battles and even wars of words, echoing Newton's complaint that philosophy was an "impertinently litigious lady." McKeon addresses this question in "Dialogue and Controversy in Philosophy,"[4] which he commences by showing that controversy replaces dialogue when a philosopher, fearing misquotation or misunderstanding, excitedly restates his position or has it restated by a disciple; this is followed by jurisdictional disputes over rights of participants to deliver the interpretation. Synthesizing of opposing arguments, the usual way in systems such as Hegel's, breaks down when "dialectic degenerates into sophistic or skepticism by neglecting content or into subjectivism and mechanism by neglecting argument" (p. 146; *FHOE,* p. 107). In our day, controversy has decisively won out over dialogue, yet the latter, were it attainable, would not be wholly desirable.[5] It would best be concerned with coordinating means of communication rather than with issues relating to truth. The severity of the problem is increased by two facts. Each term means something different to all parties, and all methods of connecting terms to each other differ, and even the methods of interpreting families of terms are so disparate as to require much adjudication before the problem can even be reached.[6] To alleviate this, McKeon suggests we drop the demands for strict logic in politics and turn our attention to communication making use of rhetoric instead (p. 162; *FHOE,* p. 124; for more on rhetoric see chapter 7). This may provide a method for lessening tensions between whole cultures. The philosopher thus occupies a unique though ambivalent position respecting the use of words, for he is probably more carefully trained than other intellectuals to detect and root out ambiguities, deliberate or inadvertent, casual or rigorous. Yet he has the dubious honor of being abstracted from immediate experience in politics, including dilemmatic polarities and the actual consequences flowing from practical decisions. The philosopher both is and is not the person most suited to directing the fates and fortunes of states and world-embracing leagues. One difficulty is that philosophers are notoriously unhabituated to working together, at least in their composing of theories as opposed to writing textbooks, translations, encyclopedias, and the like. McKeon was much impressed with the way physicists have sometimes worked together, especially on nuclear energy. In "Symposia" he laid down four stages or levels on which cooperation among intellectuals of any stripe can be achieved of which the first three are cooperative in a loose sense. They are (1) using someone else's information or ideas, obtained over the telephone or in a book; (2) solving a problem requiring several kinds of information and yielding a composite result; (3) discussing a common problem, by men of different backgrounds, but experts specialized so that one person is unaware of implications that a second may use in a totally different way; (4) attaining a result exceeding not only what any member of the group has thought but also the sum of their individual thoughts (p. 35).

Written under the auspices of UNESCO, an article, "Dialectic and Political Thought and Action,"[7] discharged McKeon's part of a task (described in a long footnote, pp. 28–29) of preparing a dictionary of approximately one hundred and fifty ethical and political terms, detailing those meanings considered ambiguous or difficult to resolve but of central importance for understandings between nations. Beside "dialectic" he undertook to write of "power," about which more in a later section of this chapter.

The essay on dialectic begins with a history of the art from the Eleatics to Hegel, continues with a discussion of its varieties, and concludes by relating it to practice. (Its first two sections expand and specify some parts of *Freedom and History,* published two years earlier.)

The nondialectician[8] makes distinctions that to the dialectician are unwarranted, so the terms of the argument change meanings as they

Dialecticians	Nondialecticians
1. Application of thought and science is dialectical, requiring either a transcendental logic or a science of the history of society.	1. In applying thought one must look to noncognitive elements and communicative elements as well; this results in sciences of society that are slightly different from physical sciences.
2. In any organic universe, the nature of things and their development are inseparable, and proof becomes in a sense the same as history.	2. The history of science has been cumulative, but the history of society has been "spasmodic and intermittent."
3. Freedom is the essence of man, history traces its progressive realization, but freedom is choosing what is dialectically determined.	3. History is not the progressive attainment of freedom; democracy prevailed in the nineteenth century because of fortunate circumstances. (Pp. 21–22)

Figure 6.1   Oppositions of Dialecticians and Nondialecticians

change sides. Yet irreconcilable courses of action often exist that depend upon differing hypotheses; action follows from thinking, not from nothing at all, but thinking is not fixed and unassailable, and the actions to which it leads are often accompanied by force (p. 21). The opposing camps and their views may be seen in figure 6.1. McKeon makes clear that theory and practice differ and that if they are confused then reason will be used only destructively to demolish opposed positions. The resolution of disagreements concerning common actions depends neither upon reaching agreement on principles of action nor on agreement on justifying meanings, nor on doctrines (p. 23). Reason has three practical functions: first, in forming and undertaking common courses of action when power is not being used against oppositions; second, in inference, though not from propositions to predictions but rather to the reliability of statements as made by their upholders in a given situation (p. 26); third, in establishing communication, association, community:

The emerging world community has been the result of many mutually supplementary influences—the advance of science, technology, and industry, the emergence of interdependent economic needs and opportunities, the recognition of comparable social and religious ideas, comparable artistic expressions, and comparable philosophic tendencies (p. 27).

Philosophy and Society

Contrary to the impression produced by many of his writings suggesting an aloof intellectualism, McKeon was a man of wide experience and much practical accomplishment. As we have seen, he served in the Navy for a time, lived abroad and traveled extensively in western Europe in his early twenties, made adjustments in moving from a small New Jersey town (his birthplace) to New York City, thence to Chicago, and married and started a family well before these political and ethical publications had appeared. He had already served as dean of one of the four divisions of the University of Chicago for some years, had become university director of the military program there during World War II, and was now becoming a member of numerous commissions, national and international, including UNESCO.[9] He lived on solid ground.

From many essays one gathers that for McKeon there are two levels in the human being which always can and sometimes do work toward harmony. The higher level is reason or understanding, where genuine insights and supporting arguments are generated that see all relevant sides of an issue to achieve a harmonious solution. The lower level is a hodgepodge of passions, dreams, irrational choices, and destructive impulses tending to cloud every issue, including those that reason can deal with successfully. These swarms are intruders in a world never perfect because of accidents of fate but that could be far better were reason able to overcome the lower feelings. (I know of no writing in which McKeon fully analyzes these parts of the human psyche; he seemed to take this unusually simple dichotomy for granted.)

There is a rider to this claim that reason invariably works for truth and justice. Even when it holds fullest sway there will be differences of formulation and context conferring widely different meanings upon terms, principal and subsidiary, and this holds even when thinkers are persons of good will and strong resolve and intellectual prowess. When they are not, the differences are still less likely to be erased so that common actions advantageous to all warring parties can be undertaken. The philosopher's task, then, is the second—but not secondary—one of trying to settle the strife between opposed philosophies, which are really opposed, or apparently so because of superficial differences in language.[10] No difference in kind is implied when this second task is pursued; it is merely a change of theme or subject matter, for the devices and methods needed are identical with those used in formulating principles and their consequences in carrying out the first task, that of producing a systematic statement of one's own convictions.

Nowhere is this better seen than in the concern McKeon evinced for ways that philosophy could relieve tensions leading to possible war, as partly expressed in "Discussion and Resolution in Political Conflicts."[11] It would be amusing, he says, to examine the stumbling efforts to base practical affairs on philosophy or to reduce philosophy to the practical, resulting in "countersenses, sophistical refutations, and sublime inconsequentialities," were it not that practical results are genuinely involved (p. 236). The many books on planning for peace are largely irrelevant to each other, and both the objections to their plans and the replies to the objection are ready-made.

The problem is metaphysical, for one must approach questions of practice primarily in its relations to theory; this adjustment of kinds of knowledge is chiefly one of principles, hence metaphysics enters willy-nilly. Either theory is made superior to practice, as abstract is related to concrete (Plato argues this way), or there is a horizontal relation (found in Mill) where the two kinds of knowledge are coordinate or, again, practical wisdom is the summation of all philosophy. In the long history of debates running through Cicero, St. Augustine, and Hume to Dewey and others, several senses of "practical" are encountered: as knowledge applied to particulars, as relevant to moral and political action, or as knowledge of sources of human action and the ends of his desires. One of McKeon's basic tenets is that

> there are no objective facts or compelling truths in the lives and actions of men, except those which are recognized . . . , nor are there motives, however reasonable, or ends, however praiseworthy, other than those known and debated, followed, or rejected. (P. 246)

The good is viewed in any one of four senses, as utopian, circumstantial, constitutional, or operational and revolutionary;[12] and since they all can be justified both logically and persuasively, the difficulties of resolving their claims make not only for the clatter of discourse but also for strife in the activities of men and states (p. 247), even if Plato was justified in making his Socrates say that no man voluntarily chooses evil. It is bad enough when men choose goods inharmonious with each other, whose theoretic dimensions are equally discordant. Lacking the possibility of engaging all men of good will in a concerted, continuing analysis of society's aims, "simplified and atrophied" versions of each of the four methods might be tried, the utopian looking to conversion to a new revelation, the circumstantial attempting historical and factual studies to suggest courses of action, the constitutional cleaving to lobbying and power-politics, and the revolutionary to issuing threats or even using force. Each of these simplifications would be opposed. But on the other, more fortunate side, the resolution of political conflicts depends not upon attainment by all men of some sublime truth or scientific insight but rather upon their establishing devices for coming to agreement, devices adaptable to changing doctrines, circumstances, and aspirations. Each of the four analyses needs supplementation by all the others, but with careful thought such assistance can be given (pp. 260–61). On an intellectual level, the solutions may rightly be called philosophic, but if they "work" then they are practical as well (p. 261).

In a simpler essay, "Communication, Truth, and Society," [13] McKeon enlarges the scope of discussion, saying that "the problems of an age arise in what is said—in communications of the age—and they cannot be formulated accurately, intelligibly, or effectively[14] without taking into account how they arise and in what context they are stated" (p. 91; *FHOE,* p. 91). Now "communication" has become a kind of hall-closet word accommodating heterogeneous meanings earlier differentiated, so McKeon reseparates them, showing that they include discussion, disputation, and controversy; verbal behavior; technological devices for transmission of thought and speech; saying and hearing; interpretation; agreement and disagreement; self-expression; community; and more. Societies are systems of communication in a world of diverse cultures (p. 92; *FHOE,* p. 92). "Much communication," he goes on, "is ambiguous, disingenuous, deceptive, false, immoral, and fortunately, ineffective" (p. 93; *FHOE,* p. 93). (This sentence, McKeon later said, was meant to be ironic.) On the other hand, even when a society is rife with statements to which the average democratic man might impute any or all of the foregoing epithets, science and technology can still flourish (p. 95; *FHOE,* p. 96). In a freer society where truths are openly debated, the call to unanimity is not clear, but in either society truths do not come ticketed as such, and the way must be kept open for discussion and possible refutation.

The functions of communication are fourfold but inseparably bound together, each of them leading to problems every society must solve: truth, values, freedom, and the community as a whole. These are viewed differently by monolithic and pluralistic societies:

First, communication provides an instrument for discovering truth, but in an undifferentiated society this truth would be imposed upon everyone, and "a truth which is not subject to discussion is an impediment to the discovery of truth" (p. 94; *FHOE,* p. 95). Even so, truths, values, freedom, and agreement can sometimes be achieved in authoritarian societies; human beings often want to have the truth set out for them (pp. 94–95; *FHOE,* p. 95). Truth in a freer society does not dissolve into relativism and skepticism. Its basis in pluralistic societies is communication that facilitates discussion of differences and the clarification and utilizing of agreements (p. 95; *FHOE,* pp. 96–97). Yet—and this is important—for McKeon political and scientific truths are not eternal but subject to alteration in the course of history: they are "humanly stated," neither certain nor final (p. 95; *FHOE,* p. 97).

Second, if there were a unique system of values and ideals motivating mankind, deviations from it should be prohibited as "trivial, improper, obscene, or dangerous" (p. 96; *FHOE,* p. 97). But the aim of the artist is that of discovering the unexpressed values in his society and making them clear to other persons so that change may come about (p. 96; *FHOE,* p. 97).

Third, a single pattern for human behavior might well be forced upon everyone as a principle of free action, but here freedom must be felt. In any society, "restrictions and prohibitions are external constraints poorly suited to make men either free and responsible or wise and good" (p. 96; *FHOE,* p. 98).

Finally, if we knew the form of a perfect society, this too could well be imposed upon everyone, but that is a vain hope, for unity and diversity should jointly rule (p. 97; *FHOE,* pp. 98–99).

The bonding principle in these is communication between persons and between groups, otherwise society would depend exclusively upon genetic factors like those governing certain insects and other animals. Both the strengths of socially varied groups and their weaknesses too show that on many levels and through many means (from evanescent conversation to the long-lasting page that affects any reader), one person can be an agent for the choices and acts of another.

This theory evidently assumes that power should be in the hands of the intellectually or, rather, the philosophically elite, who have a place like that of the rich in the popular view justifying capitalism: if some persons are richer than others, their wealth will trickle down to the underprivileged. If philosophers initially misunderstanding each other can reach some accommodation, this capacity and habit would eventually be propagated and distributed to social groups where, prior to this, harmony or even common courtesy had never scored a notable success.

Even though McKeon's remedy seems unattainable, the world would be a happier place if dominated by twenty McKeons in positions of far-reaching power than it would be if twenty Nietzsches held those same posts or, for that matter, twenty Russells, let alone Santayanas. McKeon's whole enterprise requires a person of his gifts and balance if one is to dominate and at the same time provide an atmosphere where freedom of thought, speech, and action can flourish. Few citizens, no matter how good and true, are willing to undergo the burdensome disciplines needed to make them willing to place their own opinions in matrices according equal rank to views that stand in angular, hard opposition to them.

Ethics, A Note

Any reader would be struck by the relatively small number of entries in McKeon's bibliography dealing with moral habits, choices, and aims and concentrating upon the individual as he faces the exasperations, crises, and tragedies of a world partly ready to assuage his sorrows and partly arrayed against him. To be sure, there is an article on choice, but it is "The Choice of Socrates,"[15] and there are two essays with the word "ethics" in the title: one is a 1960 publication, "The Ethics of International Influence,"[16] and the other, of 1962, is "Ethics and Politics,"[17] to which I now draw attention. Plato was probably not the first, and Dewey certainly not the last, to insist that ethics cannot be separated from politics, and McKeon himself dealt with some of these traditions in his earlier writings, especially in his rewarding "Aristotle's Conception of Moral and Political Philosophy"[18] and in *The Philosophy of Spinoza: The Unity of His Thought*.[19] In the courses he offered in the 1930s he had much to say on ethical questions, for example in his fine presentation of Thomas Hobbes in the autumn of 1937. Throughout there was an emphasis strongly reminiscent of Dewey upon the inability to do full justice to *any* ethical problem without taking into account a moral being's human environment. In this sense, McKeon wrote dozens of papers on ethics.

John Dewey's early writings contained clearheaded notions of the close relations between the individual and society, and he never relinquished this persuasion. He said in effect that a desire, though it may commence by being a unit, ultimately must be fitted into the sphere of a man's entire being, yet he added that this realization of the full self immediately implies realization of a "community of persons" in which the single persons shares.[20] The converse also holds, making for an irremovable reciprocal relation between man and group.

This conviction, which McKeon supports, need not be arrived at exclusively by the dialectical method pursued by Dewey. No real goods of a man fail to be common goods as well; even the most private poetic or artistic inspiration has eventually to show its social bearings, according to McKeon's more nearly literal approach. But where Dewey saw a moral order for mankind, McKeon, with his eye almost continually upon what he calls the "diversity of cultures," sees a plurality, not to say a plethora, of moral orders, adjustments between which must be made if there is not to be a Hobbesian "warre . . . of every man against every man . . . , not in Battell only, or the act of fighting; but in a tract of time, wherein the Will to contend by Battell is sufficiently known."[21] In another point McKeon differs markedly from Hobbes, who sees passions, specifically competition, diffidence, and glory as the chief causes of war. For McKeon it is a matter of the words that go wrong.[22]

"Ethics and Politics" begins, as a public lecture no doubt should, with some quite ordinary observations but gathers momentum such that by the end there are so many interweavings and restructurings that their detailed exposition would, if taking them all into account, throw this chapter seriously out of proportion. In the beginning McKeon acknowledges our confidence in our knowledge of good and evil in assessing what has already been done but is dubious over our criteria of right and wrong in planning for the future (p. 564). "The problems of ethics and politics are in part problems of improving action in accordance with recognized criteria and in part problems of improving criteria in application to understand opportunities and dangers" (p. 565). So the problems are both old and new at the same time: persistent and emergent.

Unitary interpretations of right and wrong have recognized common values, and pluralistic ones have established different values prompting and different reasons justifying common courses of action. Modern life, however, has introduced paradoxes blurring differences between the two interpretations, thus weakening each one. McKeon now manipulates the original separation of the senses in which ethical problems are held to be ancient instead of being labeled as those pliant to distinctively modern methods of analysis. He first combines these with questions of tradition and innovation in finding standards, then with internal and external factors in seeking causes of action, and finally with real and apparent goods that create oppositions of values (p. 566). These four patterns of relations between ethics and politics (stemming from Plato, Aristotle, the Sophists, and Democritus—p. 567), influ-

Urphilosoph	Advances	Regressions
Plato	in mutual understanding and toleration	in undisguised prejudice and institutionalized discrimination
Democritus	in satisfaction of needs by technological and technical co-operation	in exclusivisms and multidimensional nationalisms
Sophists	in elaboration of rights and freedoms	in more systematic forms of suppression, slavery, and conformity
Aristotle	in provisions for self-government and rule of law	in dictatorships and suppressive controls (p. 573)

Figure 6.2   Four Types of Advance and Regression

ence both thought and action in the persistent problems (which history obscures) and the emergent problems (which history oversimplifies). Since the nineteenth century we have had to consider problems connected with freedom and democracy that neither ancient nor medieval thinkers needed to solve. Then too, the distinction of right from wrong is now complicated by our new powers of action and our enlarged responsibilities (pp. 567–69). At present the chief positions are expressed in programs reconciling old values with new ways of satisfying wants (p. 572). The changes in language in which democracy is discussed, together with the old vocabulary retained, breed confusions, and the literature analyzing relations of problems of the individual, governments, and whole peoples and nations is loaded with pessimism and pleas for instituting cures, many of them inadequate (pp. 572–73). The problems of ethics within communities have been viewed as problems of insight (harking back to Plato), of scientific knowledge (Democritus), of power (the Sophists), and of politics (Aristotle). McKeon lists typical advances and regressions of the twentieth century, which I present in tabular form in figure 6.2.

The rest of this essay (pp. 573–75) recombines in almost bewildering rapidity the classifications to give an enriched version of the benefits and ills of present-day society.

Freedom and Power

McKeon published several discussions of freedom, coupling the concept with and contrasting it to a number of others: history, power, being, nature, motion, democracy, and more. Because one important meaning of "history" places it among the arts, it is reserved for chapter 7, although a little book does ally it with freedom.

Freedom and History: The Semantics of Philosophical Controversies and Ideological Conflicts[23] is a book of scarcely a hundred pages in its original edition, and seems, as I have said, more like one of McKeon's longer essays than a volume in its own right. It is solid, making use of the threefold distinction between kinds of thinkers that he customarily made after World War II—the dialectical, the logistic, and the problematic—and replete with references to all manner of historians. A distinction carried further in his later work is given a preliminary hearing: philosophically, ideas may be viewed for their service in building up a whole system, a single doctrine, or a method, while semantically the concepts, principles, and methods in two diverging philosophies are compared with the ways they are related to problems and subject matters. (In 1966, "philosophy" became "inquiry.") In the first, principles determine concepts, while in the second the concepts guide the selection of principles (p. 23; *FHOE,* p. 175). Meanings accepted or imposed in early stages of constructing a philosophy may influence its assumptions and methods, while later on they are more narrowly defined or redefined consonant with the adopted method (p. 25; *FHOE,* p. 177). Obviously, the primary purpose of *Freedom and History* is to conduct a semantic rather than philosophic analysis, though the basis for such a choice is clearly made to rest upon philosophic principles.

That analysis uses a specific array, headed by the three familiar approaches. For the *dialectician,* freedom lies in the development of an all-embracing historical process, a power founded upon successful conformity to wisdom, spirit, or some other superior ordering principle. For the *logistician,* freedom is acting according to a thing's own nature, its own laws, which give the free person a kind of inner necessity; or else freedom is a probable outcome of the operation, or withholding, of external causes. Lastly, for the *problematic thinker,* freedom lies in setting up conditions in which actions not affecting the freedom of others to act are tolerated and protected by a sense of duty or the law. In this third view, freedom is purely an ethico-political matter, neither spiritual nor physical (pp. 38–39; *FHOE,* pp. 189–90).[24] Upon the problematic historian it is incumbent to reject the possible analogies of political states to kinship groups, voluntary associations, and economic institutions alike (p. 73; *FHOE,* p. 224); freedom becomes instead a function of the person and state, and is not some anthropological, mechanical, religious, or metaphysical concept.

Freedom and History is fleshed out with references to and passages expounding earlier philosophical views. A fairly appealing work, it could well serve as introduction to the middle phases of the author's thinking. It can be read either as a programmatic sketch or as a finished philosophic treatment of its twin concepts, for on one level it disregards the other interests of historians besides freedom, while on another it represents a commitment to freedom as the proper scope of history itself, the destiny and task of mankind. The other terms implied on that first level are, however, still crucial in discussions of men in states and relations between states.

Unusual in his general framework is that one of McKeon's most important contributions to the theory of human and other freedoms is found in the arduous, ardent metaphysical essay (1966) on semantics and inquiry (see chapter 5). Because metaphysics pervades all other sciences and arts as a reasoned account of their principles, what he offers there indirectly addresses aspects of ethico-political freedom, but directly treats the matter since freedom is carefully delineated. The essay's distinctions are fourfold almost throughout, adding, of course, the Sophistic-Operational approach to the three of *Freedom and History*, whose subject now takes up but a couple of highly condensed essay pages. The account of freedom uses headings of two kinds, the first being in terms of the types of questions asked, so that What is freedom? is split into three subordinate queries, the second of which is given in terms of the four approaches set forth elsewhere in the essay.

1. *What things are free?* is a question of fact or interpreted materials. (*a*) The entitative interpretation of Democritus would assert that freedom is unimpeded movement; all bodies lacking external impediments are free; thus inanimate nature is intimately bound to human nature (*FHOE*, p. 247). (*b*) The existentialist interpretation (the operationalist's) considers freedom to be spontaneous or otherwise undetermined activity. Animate bodies but not others are thus able to be free. Both of these interpretations say freedom is doing as one pleases, while the next two take freedom to be doing as one should (ibid.). (*c*) The essentialist theory (that of Aristotle) holds freedom to be action in accordance with deliberate choice; the blockade to this is either lack of or faulty deliber-

ation. Men, not all animate beings, are free (p. 248). (*d*) The ontological interpretation (Plato's) conceives freedom as autonomy of thought and action wherein the two obstacles, lack of wisdom and lack of will, are overcome. Men are not free unless they are wise, and this wisdom approximates the divine, the only truly free entity (ibid.).

2. *What property do free things share?* What is the freedom of the free? concerns thought, or method. (*a*) The dialectical method speaks of the hindrances to freedom as being (at least to some extent and in some persons) removable by education, whereas (*b*) the operational method sees freedom as achieved by acquisition of power. There is a bond here between (*a*) and (*b*), lying in this, that knowledge is by nature wisdom or power, however variously these may be conceived. (*c*) The logistic method restores freedom by some kind of therapy to those who have lost it, much as Spinoza thought of his examination of the weakness and strength of man to be a medicine of the soul, and Wittgenstein, a notch or two lower in his ambitions, undertook only to cure mental cramps. (*d*) The problematic method sees freedom as both the effect and precondition of democratic society. These two are again bound by the fact that knowledge is prudence (*phronēsis,* "practical wisdom") (pp. 248–49).

3. In respect of being or principles, one can properly ask, *What are the grounds of the possibility or the act of freedom?* What decisions, in other words, are wholly free? (*a*) The comprehensive principles (of Plato) establish a reflexive coincidence between what is, on the one hand, and what is intelligible, on the other. (*b*) The reflexive principles (of Aristotle) establish reflexive beginnings in separate inquiries, so freedom becomes self-rule in practical actions. Both (*a*) and (*b*), then, look to freedom as grounded in being, that of the cosmos and of man respectively. (*c*) Simple principles (Democritus) provide elements for constructing what is real—freedom operates in pursuit of pleasures and the establishment of preferences; for this view Jeremy Bentham is an excellent source. (*d*) Actional principles (operational) are quite arbitrary, set up to formulate the real and to advance pleasure for individuals or for the public. Both (*c*) and (*d*) take the actuality, not the mere possibility, of freedom as grounded in agreements or conventions; practical decisions are emotive and rest upon pleasure (p. 249).

One quickly notes how the order of presentation of the positions allows pairings for locating common points of view. The present exposition has been somewhat simplified and curtailed. Intricate though the original may be, it opens up new ways of thinking about what is without these distinctions both perplexing and momentous; detecting systematic differences in a welter of opinions is at least a long step in seeking to resolve them.

One hundred and fifty concepts were brought before a UNESCO task force, as I have said, and McKeon was asked to define "power." His results, in "Power and the Language of Power,"[25] an essay that also discusses several allied terms entering the thoughts and utterances of men, should be of help in determining individual behavior and structures of institutions. Early in the essay he looks at three other words associated with "power": "authority" (exercised by an agent regulating the power that is always the operation of something or someone); "force" (the external influence of one entity upon another); and "violence" (which destroys order and disrupts all purposes). These are ordinary practical definitions that collide with more metaphysical meanings of "power" (p. 104). Hobbes, Rousseau, and others seek to account for power as the principle of the state by relating it to "law of nature," "right," and "sovereignty," however much they depart in detail from each other. But these theories have to do with the relation of man to the state; pacific relations between one state and another could only be dealt with in terms of treaties and similar agreements. What is needed today, McKeon implies, is the exploration of common purposes, yet this must be freed from all suspicions of coercion to bring about subjection to common aims (p. 109). The important international problems—war and propaganda, economic development, and attachment to traditions—are problems of power.

Seventeenth- and eighteenth-century philosophers grounded their natural law, sovereignty, and last-resort right of revolution upon power, while nineteenth-century dialecticians transformed power into its own right because of its role in leading an ideal state in which—here is the paradox—power would disappear and the state would wither away. The official status of this latter philosophy in many countries compounds the difficulties in reaching international agreements. That the United Nations can do little more than discuss and make suggestions means that solutions reached are at a remove from those able to put them into effect (pp. 108–9). What men say in individual states or international bodies is generally opposed to what is the case, but this rigid opposition perversely denies that any statement of what is the case is still a sample of what men say. Turned about, the saying itself is a sample of what is the case. Both ways, the harmony of nations can be built up or broken down. Reason is better served when harmony is endangered, not by battling for principles but by protecting the conditions essential to the use of reason. Similarly, there is little point in seeking to remove all ambiguities; instead, "fruitful regions of ambiguity and tolerance" should be preserved (p. 112). Language in its practical use lies halfway between particular situations and emotions, and general principles and arguments. Truth and prejudice should be sharply distinguished, for discussion turns upon truth in relation to what men actually believe; it is the area to be explored. In men's relations to other men and to nature in general, the problems of right and truth are basically problems of power, whose effective form is knowledge, and communication, whose basis is understanding (p. 115).

Much of this theory is displayed in an essay, "Knowledge and World Organization." [26] I am not sure how much interest McKeon took in local, state, or national politics, for he said little concerning these at any time when I could have heard him, nor did his published writings often bear directly upon these matters. [27] The politics that did engage him, and for a long time, was that of world peace, and he had much to say about the structure and activities of an organization that was then at the forefront of the internationally sponsored efforts to find means to achieve harmony throughout all nations. The essay of which I speak is a report, chiefly, of UNESCO's efforts to settle upon and carry out tasks in pursuing this end. Its ten-item list (reproduced on p. 316 of his essay) is extremely ambitious but pertinent, and no doubt all the tasks it enumerates are essential. Its details, and whether any of the projected labors have ever been carried out successfully, is not germane here. McKeon stoutly affirms his pluralism, this time by advocating that even if an instance where men agree on a course of action exists, one should not expect that all their reasons for embarking on it will be the same or even cohere with one another (p. 289; cf. p. 322).

Knowledge—here McKeon agrees with Bacon and Hobbes—is power, but the offering of reasons and principles are likely causes of dissension; hence power may easily become misdirected. The problem is one of discovering connections between knowledge (possibly conceived originally as being for its own sake) and action, which is doubtless contaminated by irrational motives and conflicting needs and thwarted by a thousand external mischances. To diagnose some of the causes for philosophers' disagreements, McKeon introduces the four *Ursyteme* and then continues; "The sages, saints, and scientists, associated in speculation on truth and justice, have not always been scrupulous to respect the niceties of argument when they attack the sectaries of other theories" (p. 290). There are thus both analytical and rhetorical problems. The fact is, society is never benefited when politicians try to regulate science (as in Nazi Germany) or scientists are encouraged to determine social policy (as in the 1930s with the technocrats) or with other utopians such as Francis Bacon and Tommaso Campanella. The relaxation of tensions remaining after World War II is like that of all other times: discussion, which McKeon takes to be different from dialectic, logic, and scientific method, is what is needed (p. 329). It is a tested method, and more persons are prepared to engage in it than in those other three. Furthermore, its results are more immediately evident in the world of men and women whose lives have until now hung in the balance each day for four decades.

Responsibilities and Rights

McKeon offers a picture of the ethico-political realm, chiefly as if it were a sphere-shaped network of interlocking concepts, no one of them ever unrelated to all the others, regardless of how differently each one may be defined, its origins traced, or status determined in differently ordered systems. A paper delivered to the International Institute of Philosophy, "The Development and the Significance of the Concept of Responsibility,"[28] considers social aspects of a matter primarily ethical. The trend of late has been, says McKeon, to broaden the scope of problems concerning nations, but the methods intended to solve them are the subjects of controversy, so even mere communication is lacking (pp. 1–2; *FHOE*, pp. 62–63). Yet free discussion and with it the hope of solving problems is difficult when the state upholds but one philosophic system, and that system as a rule a narrow or even perverted one. A narrowed tradition usually becomes a way of unfavorably characterizing all opposed positions.

McKeon now considers responsibility in three ways: externally, in law and politics, where penalties are inflicted and governments held accountable for policies; internally, in moral analysis where an individual tallies up his choices and their consequences; and comprehensively, in social and cultural analyses ordering values in both individuals and civilization as a whole (p. 3; *FHOE*, p. 64). There follows an extended philosophic and philological discussion of the origin and usages of the word "responsibility" and associated words, "punishability," "account-ability," "immutability," and their French and German and (where applicable) Latin and Greek equivalents (pp. 3–20; *FHOE,* pp. 64–79), citing Lévi-Bruhl, Mill, Bain, Hume, Zeno the Stoic, St. Ambrose, Duns Scotus, the British empiricists, Pufendorf, Wolff, Reid, Bradley, as well as the staples, Plato and Aristotle.

The marked increase in contacts between nations and between cultures has increased the need for the recognition of responsibility toward persons. Of this there are three kinds. *Political* responsibility, the most important, requires that a government operate within the law and also in accord with the will of the people (p. 21). This latter, in turn, rests mainly on universal suffrage, which requires a reciprocal conferring and accepting of responsibility (pp. 21–23; *FHOE,* pp. 80–81). *Cultural* responsibilities encompass the religion, education, taste, ethnic derivation, economic status, and occupation, that form "communities" of which the individual finds himself a member and that are also responsible to him and to each other (p. 23). Responsibility of this kind both reflects and depends upon common rationality and action. The concept of responsibility formerly developed from accountability and imputation, both of them imposing limitations on freedom. Imputation is internalized when the person comes to understand the consequences of his own actions rather than relying on praise and blame from outside (pp. 24–26; *FHOE,* pp. 81–84). *Moral* responsibility evolved with the political and cultural types, making itself felt only when communities were formed and men became accountable, with actions being imputed to them; but it did not reach systematic statement before the advent of civil and divine law and especially when representative governments were formed (pp. 26–27; *FHOE,* pp. 84–85).

Accountability and imputation, when operating positively and internally, become freedom and rational choice helping to determine national policy; clear statements concerning them could contribute to resolving international tensions (p. 27; *FHOE,* p. 85). Means for solving the material needs have improved, but increasing sensibilities and reducing tensions have fared less well. Including citizens in governmental decision making has simultaneously restricted their thoughts and actions (pp. 28–29; *FHOE,* pp.86–87).

Our efforts to free men from pressures of material needs and to help them realize themselves have backfired—McKeon says "are reflexive"—

for we are ever more bound to material ends and despotic controls. A dilemma regarding the criteria for using responsibility is that tradition and innovation grow out of the need for a hierarchy of values that may either liberate process or stultify opposition. Another dilemma, of right and good, custom and duty, arises from a need for criteria of values expressed as antagonisms borrowed from the authority they should possess and the rationality they should embody. Can the analysis of responsibility increase the reliance on the kind of reason that could reestablish the relation between actual preferences and ideal values? (pp. 29–30; *FHOE,* p. 87).

This essay, like so many of the shorter Platonic dialogues and unlike almost all of McKeon's other writings, ends with this question mark and this challenge.

A paper of a later decade, "Philosophy and History in the Development of Human Rights,"[29] surveys rights in two different contexts: the formulation and dissemination of doctrines of such rights in the early and subsequent deliberations in UNESCO in and around 1950 and McKeon's own discussion of the theory, and it combines short historical notes with his own reflections on the way rights should be conceived. These two contexts, however, are not as different as might be supposed, for as already noted McKeon served as advisor to the American delegation in the early years of UNESCO, and some paragraphs that he quotes from the official documents are surprisingly similar to his own writings in style and content. The official side of his paper (pp. 300–310; *FHOE,* pp. 37–48) is chiefly a review of deliberations and declarations made in the organization between 1950 and 1970. To bring the account of human rights in action up to the time of his writing, McKeon points out that in the score of years since the Universal Declaration in 1950 there has been an educational impact upon the lives of men and communities all the way up to the community of mankind. A declaration, however, imposes no direct obligation upon states until a convention (or covenant) is signed—a ratification not always easy to secure, since many governments fear it will reduce their sovereignty (pp. 308–9; *FHOE,* pp. 46–47). The conventions confer no right to police upon any authority, only to report on whether guidelines are being followed.

The chief section of the paper (pp. 310–22; *FHOE,* pp. 48–61) is subdivided, the first part headed "Philosophy in the Development of Human Rights" (pp. 310–14; *FHOE,* pp. 48–53). These rights have a history neither necessary nor wholly fortuitous. The rights as achieved are particular for individual men, but as inborn they are universal. A universal declaration is also applicable universally, linked in essence to human nature (p. 310; *FHOE,* p.49). These rights must be developed in the midst of all the contingencies and calamities besetting nations and their citizens; and the addition of new rights that alter the conception if not the character of the old must be clearly recognized. Structured ideas, moreover, are of utmost significance in the highly paradoxical history of rights, as they embody all the paralogisms philosophers have constructed and detected: problems of whole and part (revealed in the Democritean approach), the universal and particular (Aristotelian), the internal and external (the Sophistic), and finally the apparent and real (the Platonic) (pp. 310–11; *FHOE,* p. 49).

Relations between rights, liberty, and democracy, McKeon goes on to say, depend on relations between the concepts of right and law, sovereignty being the power to make binding law and justice being what protects rights from the impositions of power likely to cancel them (p. 311–12; *FHOE,* p. 50). Where ruler and ruled are distinct, the question relates to the character of those who rule or should rule and of those who are ruled or should be; the differences are structured in forms of government. When the ruled are also the rulers, liberty and rights are found in the relations between individual and society. Instead of the natural law so prominent in theories regarding the first case, here the question is one of responsibility to self and to others. The danger is no longer the tyranny of the one ruler but rather that of the majority. If the ruled oppose the ruler, liberty and right are found in the inequities of current situations. The chief danger is neither created by the ruler nor by the majority but is fomented by the unrepresented minority (pp. 312–13; *FHOE,* pp. 50–52).

Part of the second subsection (pp. 314–22; *FHOE,* pp. 53–61) shows that philosophic difficulties over rights bring about paradoxes of using laws to secure rights, all of which in the end become the third kind of responsibility, cultural—though we reduce them through legislation to the second kind, civil. The ambiguities, however, are "productive" and result from the inherent situations (p. 317; *FHOE,* p. 56). Ambiguities cause changes. The next few pages deal with the constitution and the way it is preserved or overthrown by a governmental demonstration aimed at proving that a certain action exemplifies the enjoyment of a right, or by a group bent on civil disobedience. The play is for keeps. "Revolution" is another word designating first political, then economic and social change, violent or not, and now also referring to a cultural transformation to establish a group and group consciousness, much as the Jews became isolated and proclaimed themselves the chosen people and as can be seen in Gandhi and his movement for civil disobedience, the blacks in the United States, or students against the establishment. The clearest statements of their purposes are seen in what these movements are against and what can be done to repair the wrongs. Revolution is against neither reason nor nature, constitution nor law, for while words change the values are preserved.

In a postscript (pp. 321–22; *FHOE,* pp, 60–61), McKeon shows the independence of rights from *the* right. This right of the wise to be wise in fact, reality, statement, or action depends on the right of the foolish to be foolish in the same four respects. No antecedent rule defines wisdom; each man must be wise for himself. Plural philosophies (stemming from both study and life) parallel the many cultures fostering cultural rights. There are common experiences in these cultures, and there can be common ends, linked by diverse philosophies. The common problems should be discussed, not the common principles, which only divide parties. If methods, principles, and interpretations are shunted aside, criteria can be found in actions, not statements—certainly a pragmatic standpoint that McKeon adopts in a somewhat utopian vein, in his desire to confront new problems rather than ideologies.

Democracy

Considerably less attention is paid in these essays to differences between governmental types than one might expect,[30] for they were written when the world was shakily recovering from the clash between nations primarily democratic and those primarily fascist-totalitarian and then feeling new tensions between some of these same democracies and communistic-totalitarian states in rule and symbolism. From 1944 to 1964 inclusive, "democracy" appears but four times in the titles of eighty-three articles and chapters and the six books McKeon wrote or edited during those decades, when politics and related topics preponderated in his writings. "Should Communists be Allowed to Teach in Our Schools?" was a radio address and the only title that refers to an opposing system.[31] Most of his papers devote very few paragraphs to Soviet and other communist systems, and even these say little about structures in, advantages or disadvantages of, or conflicts fomented by those gov-

ernments. McKeon's principles for the most part cut across all governments, economies, legal enactments.

The chief exception is the long, elaborately documented essay composed in wartime, "Democracy, Scientific Method, and Action," [32] in
which McKeon takes up each of these three concepts, grounding his
survey in historical erudition that the ordinary scholar might require
some decades to master. He begins (p. 235) by noting that no matter
how they are defined, science and democracy have been in existence for
approximately the same length of time. One might suppose from this
that they are somehow conjoined or even identical, but there are
marked differences between technical questions and affairs of state (p.
236): hence there are no scientific tests for political judgment and truth-
telling and no popular votes to solve scientific problems, despite allegations by Dewey that because both science and democracy can be defined
as experimental agents of change, they are in effect the same (pp. 236–
37). McKeon proposes instead to deal with ways the community affects
science, then the latter's effects upon the former, and finally a balancing
of differences with possible samenesses. The effects of community upon
science are obvious, for scientific inquiry and truth are created not in a
vacuum but among social pressures and facilitations (p. 238). Science,
in turn, affects communities and their ends, modifying the means of
communication within associations and producing new material goods
for use. But, McKeon continues,

The influence of democratic institutions on the pursuit of science within the
framework of those institutions, and the influence of scientific and technological developments on the problems and forms of democracy, are not only distinct
from each other but they in no unique way predetermine the relation of the
methods of science and democracy, the use of scientific problems, or the use of
democratic processes in application to scientific problems. [33]

There follow two sections (pp. 241–55 and 255–68) citing respectively some of the chief approaches to the effects of community (and
more specifically, democracy), upon science and contrariwise, of science
upon community. McKeon finds in the latter four paralogisms, the first
being that although democracy has been subjected to scientific inquiry,
the supposition that the methods of the natural sciences can be the ones
so employed leads to unanticipated difficulties. The other three point to
the same double-edged weapon, science as an aid to society yet a danger
to it as well. In brief: "If science is certain, democracy is unscientific;

and if democracy sanctions the statement and defense of unverifiable opinions, science is undemocratic" (p. 289).

In his most succinct statement of the relation of the cognitive part of human nature to the structure of democratic society, McKeon says (perhaps following the lesson of the *Meno* that right opinion is the best we can hope for in the guidance of society):

> The formation of public opinion depends on prejudice, emotions, subconscious influences, factional interests, and expected benefits as well as occasional explicitly rational influences; and although these other factors are subject to analysis, and even to scientific inquiry, the employment of such scientific devices by agencies of government for the formation of opinion is dangerous to the ends of democracy and without justification on scientific grounds. This is the region of freedom, of free communication, free judgment, free belief. (P. 272)

Science, then, taken in its general sense, can aid democracy, but even unanimous agreement by experts is no necessary sign that what they say is true (p. 273). McKeon makes new use of an old distinction between science, dialectic, and rhetoric, the first of them having been shown inappropriate for the full exploration of democracy, while the second, the dialectical effort to come to terms with traditional assumptions, is more fruitful. Strict logic rarely holds in personal motives and social interchanges, but dialectic can penetrate and adjudicate the conflicts between firmly-held assumptions cropping up, especially in a democracy.[34] Dialectic conforms because of its suppleness to many of these debates, furnishing insights into their nature, though lacking the rigor of scientific demonstration. Rhetoric, which includes every sort of persuasion, is even more suited to political affairs, for it deals not with the consistency of arguments and their grounds in opinion but rather with the ways that opinions are related to particular events and revealed in utterances of individual persons (p. 275).

McKeon does not seek to define democracy or congratulate it for fostering the sciences as opposed to the ways totalitarian states treat them. Much is decided in a democracy, he says, by popular voting, and the better the populace is educated, the wiser the voting is likely to be. Votes, as McKeon says, "have the same weight whether based on fundamental knowledge, common belief, transient opinion, or reasonless whim" (p. 279).[35] The transition from the last back to the first of these four could justify the analogy between democracy and science, which begins in hunches and culminates in well-tested certitudes. But the two are not really similar and certainly not identical. Science cannot proceed by counting witnesses.

A companion analogy from scientific conclusion to political decision is equally distorting, since conclusions can and should be altered if new evidence upsets them, but decisions cannot be put aside for every new circumstance; precedent must be honored enough to allow for some predictability in public affairs (p. 282). Scientific principles and conclusions are attacked and defended with reference to the nature of things; differences of political creed are less solidly based and contain "seeds of heresy and schism" (pp. 283–84).

Of the four kinds of problems for which education in a democracy must provide help in reaching solutions, the foremost lies in this, that even if diverse organizations espouse mutually exclusive religious beliefs, moral systems, and political affiliations, still they must cooperate in reaching practical decisions in communities (pp. 285–86). The decisions are reached by voting, and education must prepare the public for this, though not, as a rule, by furnishing large amounts of technical information such as would be required in scientific investigations. Popular judgment, the moderately educated many as against the expert scientific few, can be trusted in national and international issues because the many "resists sophistries to which the learned are victims" (p. 286). I catch myself wondering whether this was not another piece of McKeon's irony.

Education

Followers of John Dewey would doubtless accompany a section on democracy with one on education. McKeon was ready to include educational theory in any account of what was needed, on any level, to ensure a better world. But where Dewey thought of all philosophy as treating of education, McKeon never concurred with this; and viewing his constant efforts to render his concepts precise, one realizes that agreeing with Dewey would have been inconsistent with McKeon's own philosophic method. For Dewey, the methodological reason for the universal scope of education can be discerned by noting some of his chief terms, such as *nature, life, organism, function, environment, adaptation, perception, experience, evolution, intelligence, communication, society, democracy, inquiry, valuation, education, art, creation,* and again *nature* . . . in a circle of concepts, each leading into the next, and although the concepts do not all mean the same in any flat, literal way, they can, through Dewey's own dialectic, be made to telescope into each other.[36] This was not McKeon's way of doing philosophy.

In an essay, "The Battle of the Books,"[37] McKeon raises a question that with his omnivorous reading he was brilliantly qualified to argue. He takes the battle to be a repetition in lesser compass of the passage from communication between writer and reader to the existence of an all-encompassing world community for which reading and teaching are preparations and then integrated as elements. He points out that the battle of the books waged by Sir William Temple and Jonathan Swift against a host of critics was but one of many waged throughout the ages between the ancients, the paleoterics, and moderns, or neoterics. The battlefields were belles lettres, logical theory, the sciences, rhetoric, encyclopedias, and more. McKeon contends that "the old and the new, the ancient and the modern, as their names suggest, have no fixed and absolute marks, but are defined by methods used and subjects treated" (p. 184). This is especially true in our century, when circumstances have radically altered conceptions of knowledge and its conduits. There are now four meanings of so-called general education that help determine its aims: first, as underlying *all knowledge*. The survey courses of the 1920s offered subject matters, but now they teach arts, methods. Second, as providing means of communication between *all men,* who become agents so that problems can be resolved by discussion. Third, as a way of organizing *all experiences* of individual men, this being an education for character, for ordering powers and actions. Last, as building on the values of *all cultures,* leading to "integrative interplay" throughout the world (pp. 188–89). Liberal education in separate fields taught by specialists is the aim of the paleoterics, while general education is defended by the neoterics in their advocacy of a plurality of disciplines dealing with common problems. Even the most radical courses offered just before World War II have needed bringing up to a new pitch. (Those courses in question at the University of Chicago were indeed quite experimental, far more so than the famous Contemporary Civilization and the Colloquium on Important Books in the Western Tradition at Columbia. I have said in an earlier chapter that McKeon himself was in good part responsible for the experimental undergraduate instruction at Chicago.)

After 1960, say, McKeon's papers often followed a pattern of starting with a limited problem and set of historical antecedents for its solution and then opening out like a river delta into a broader reach of world community. This was partly true of "The Battle of the Books," and in a measure it is also true of "Love and Wisdom: The Teaching of Philosophy,"[38] where his gift for finding common grounds linking concepts ordinarily thought far apart[39] is matched by his equally impressive ability to make distinctions between concepts seemingly one and the same.

Much as the history of philosophy is a branch of general history, so the teaching of philosophy is a proper part of education. "Love and Wisdom" obviously makes capital of the fact that "philosophy" means "the love *of* wisdom," but to an extent the essay separates these two conditions for the sake of examining their mutual relations. The paper has a triadic structure slightly reminiscent of Kant's thesis, antithesis, and synthesis,[40] except that the second member of the triad is not strictly treated as antithetical but merely as something different from the first. Although it uses a 3 × 2 array, there are no distinctions of approaches and no more than casual mention of the metaphysical concepts so liberally distributed in most of McKeon's other writings.

Love impels knowing, doing, and making. Education is defined as "the initiation of processes directed to ends by love" (p. 240) and must take account of the interests and motivations that the student already has but extends these to new ones. It places him in "amorous" associations with a teacher, other students, and the community, the writers and artists whose work he is exploring, and humanity at large. Education, furthermore, brings insight into ideals and values, operating by "charity," the harmony of different loves and desires, as contrasted to "concupiscence" or natural love, and "benevolence" or social love (p. 242).

Teaching in general inculcates wisdom and love, marking the dynamic tension between discipline and creativity in the individual learner, stability and progress in society at large, and knowledge and discovery in relaton to the state that knowledge has reached at the time (p. 243). The teaching of philosophy rests upon the study of philosophic problems and their proposed solutions. The learner should be made aware of "common structures" of thought and "basic themes or principles" (p. 244), but this teaching also takes values of the community into account. Here two devices are at work, the first being awareness of distinctions between the desired and the desirable and that between a posteriori cognizance of the conventional and a priori cognizance of the natural (p. 245). The second device is recognition of different characters of antecedents and consequences (p. 246). So much for the social aspects of this teaching. As for its relation to the state of knowledge, love of wisdom is both a passion, an action arising from communication mainly concerning the common good, and a synthesis of the forms external to the individual and his internal desires. Again there are two devices: the analysis of arguments, problems, and systems, and also intuitive perceptions, which the beginner may have in plenty even if lacking in exact formulations (pp. 246–47).

Finally, when love and wisdom are put together, "the teaching of philosophy should convey an orientation and develop a discipline" (p. 248). Individuals, societies, and the sciences all have two levels. In the concrete world of decisions, the loves of these individuals, societies, and scientific truths must be separate, while in the world that can be penetrated by insights, all three are interrelated parts of one question (p. 249). Actual cases, McKeon concludes, exist halfway between these two levels, and so does the teaching of philosophy, whose task is the showing of their connections.

Philosophy of World Politics

The word "practical" changes meaning as its application moves from one sphere to another, as indeed it must. First, a philosopher's own anfractuous reflective thoughts upon political and ethical matters are remote from action, his own or anyone else's, and these thoughts are scarcely distinguishable in kind from his theoretic investigatory wrestlings. But as formulated, written down later, and perhaps printed, these same thoughts take on a more relevant cast and now begin to have a bearing upon the actions of the philosopher himself or his readers or both together. In a more real sense practical philosophy has been created, for it is now an ordered sequence of ideas aimed at diagnosing and alleviating the world's evils or enhancing its goods. It is still somewhat remote, however, for these thoughts are merely represented by symbols on a page or entertained in a mind. When, thirdly, they are taken up and made operative as motives conjoined to other impulses such as ambition or the urge for self-preservation, they become more truly practical in the third and more proper sense. In a fourth sense they are put into action. In McKeon's person, practical philosophy ran the whole gamut of these stages.

In an essay published in a critical year of World War II, McKeon turned to what he called "The Philosophic Problem,"[41] that of finding and securing a decent peace, and distinguished three functions of philosophy when war has become unavoidable: the polemic, or theoretical

formulating of aims; the educational, or discovery of the means of persuading people to attach themselves to those ideals; and the irenic, the
practical task of interpreting other philosophies parallel to one's own
but not really the same (p. 202). Peace does not depend upon the ho-
mogenizing of all philosophies with our own, but unfortunately Americans have neglected the formulation of any philosophy usable in discussions seeking harmony though not complete agreement. As a nation we
have remained "inept, embarrassed, and belligerent," and our ideals
have deteriorated into slogans (p. 205). Some reference to utopian conditions of life and government is needed to establish and maintain
peace—Plato knew this, and the *Republic* was the result. On the other
hand, hope of universal peace lies neither with proclaiming philosophic
and scientific truth by decree nor with the pooling of private or national
interests while pretending that feelings are sound ideas. A path between
degraded power politics and degraded factionalism is possible only if
universal peace is conceived instead as a set of devices for discussing and
agreeing on principles and procedures (pp. 207–8).

In any discussion, attempts to reach agreements between participants, whether they be philosophers or not, may be hindered by tendencies to overgeneralize analogies and then to render them static and literal, treating the concepts by which a dialectician such as Plato isolated
the facts that interested him as if they were the facts themselves (p. 217).
Analogies are made under the delusion that the generality of phenomena indicates what is essential; the end is stressed as something fixed by
nature or something peculiarly adapted to present circumstances; peace
becomes a question of unchangeable order in the first instance or of
newly instituted structures in the second. A simplistic literal inquiry is
scarcely better, for it rests upon much more localized aims and circumstances (pp. 219–21). Rousseau, Bentham, Kant, and others thought a
constitution could settle conflicts and secure universal peace through
setting up an organization for future resolution of differences. There are
dangers even there, especially when an unexamined, dogmatic philosophy is adopted.

Because McKeon offered no courses before World War II bearing
directly on world problems, I cannot say how long before the war's
close the idea of a world community became extremely important to
him. Certainly by 1945 he was much engrossed with the concept of an
organization that could allay and possibly resolve the enormous number
of conflicts just making their appearance in new alignments.[42] The years

shortly after the war saw a number of his papers bearing upon this elusive, somewhat giddy topic;[43] I pick one to expound briefly, "World Community and the Relations of Cultures,"[44] in which he made clear that the organization he envisaged and for which in his own way he became a crusader, is not a superstate but a structure such as the United Nations, probably in "reinforced form," that could provide a basis for solving the common difficulties besetting so many nations. Improvements in transportation and communications technology as a result of the war effort everywhere have made it both possible and necessary to confront these exigencies (p. 802). Like Charles A. Beard, whose opinions McKeon cites with approval, he considers that the work needed to bring about some measure of understanding belongs to statesmen, not philosophers or men of science (p. 802). The interrelations of cultures in the world together constitute a world community in potentiality, since many of their values are common despite the specific cast that they manifest in each society (p. 806). Ideals must not be opposed by statesmen to facts, for ideals are facts in a cultural context, the use of tractors is a fact in farming or the number, speed, and maneuverability of warplanes is a fact of warfare. These values, however, are known only indirectly through their expressions in the arts, religions, science, and so forth, and it is impossible to secure unanimity in their interpretation (p. 807). To insist on the truth of any one doctrine would thus run counter to the overriding principle of freedom (p. 809). Yet the possibility of world community hinges upon the understanding of common values, although these may be expressed in many ways: cooperation in furthering these values is also required (p. 810). To achieve this there are, in addition to the inevitable political and economic tasks, four interrelated stages in the attaining of harmonious community: first, the defense of freedom, artistic creation, and expression; second, the education of the public in facts, methods, and values of all kinds; third, the understanding of common values underlying cultural diversities; and fourth, critical insight into ambiguities manipulated in conflicts of ideologies (p. 815).

I have the impression that McKeon was never aiming to write a complete philosophy of politics (as if anyone could!) so much as he hoped to firm up softer spots in existing theories, especially those lying between two established disciplines. All the topics, or nearly all, were ones already explored by others. His signal contribution, it seems, was to put together a very large number of these topics in a unique way, still addressing the problems one by one. By the aid of his arrays and with his ever-present but oft-concealed immense learning, he could examine a single concept in relation to countless others, of which I have offered but some samples. He thereby avoided any temptation to "freeze the dialectic" and make war exclusively a matter of economic motivations, power a matter of oppression directed against those below, honor a matter of what other men say or think about oneself, and so on for a host of formulas not without some foundation but easily perverted into doctrines all-embracing and dogmatic.

In "The Battle of the Books" McKeon stresses a shade more forcibly than elsewhere that he is on the side of change, of meeting new conditions of life, much, I suppose, as Herbert Spencer defined it as "the definite combination of heterogeneous changes, both simultaneous and successive, in correspondence with external co-existences and sequences," or, more simply, as "the continuous adjustment of internal relations to external relations."[45] McKeon says plainly, "I have always been a neoteric" (p. 191), and in light of his ceaseless work for reforms in higher education, for a new and hitherto little tried expert tolerance for plural philosophies, even those decidedly monolithic, and because of his work to secure international accord to bear fruit some day in world peace, one must acknowledge the eminent truth of his remark. Somehow I am reminded of an episode (one that led to controversy, as it happened) in the history of the University of Chicago, when during or not long after World War II Chancellor Hutchins proposed dropping the traditional University motto, "Crescat Scientia Vita Excolatur," on the ground that "excolatur," "will be enriched," was too suggestive of money and material success to fit the notion that this should come about through the growth of knowledge. I leave aside the question whether this motto should have been discarded (it was not) but do wish to say that Hutchins proposed in its stead a line from Walt Whitman: "Solitary, singing in the West, I strike up for a new world." Whether this would be suited to the University as a whole I leave aside as well; but I have often wondered whether it could not at least serve as an epitaph for Richard McKeon.

7

The Arts: Principles and Methods

Prefatory

One may well ask whether the elaborations of philosophic types that seemed clear enough for logic, metaphysics, and the natural sciences can be made equally suitable for the traditionally less rigorous subject matters relating to what the Greeks called the productive sciences or arts. Action of any sort rarely fits neatly with concepts, and it is especially discouraging to attach to classificatory thought and language to action that the Greeks termed making and we call creative. Art is notoriously slippery. Not only are relevant concepts harder to define than in geometry or meteorology, but their application in criticism to individual works or historically united groups of works seems to depend upon instinctive feelings. These merge with intellectual insights in combinations that only with greatest difficulty are installed in well-measured rubrics. Often the mood of a genius is the last step toward the divine madness and amentia that Plato affirmed of poets.[1] Such a thoroughly trained performer as Beethoven said that he hated to have to think of a "confounded violin" when the spirit spoke to him. An imaginative painter I once knew spoke of working in his studio "like a mad bull." Can such a creature be corralled into a matrix?

Richard McKeon would answer, of course, that such cries for freedom are relevant to art theory only if you wish to make them so, that one can deal with the object created as having its own character apart from any human activity, or that one can take up the audience and its responses regardless of whether they have the same intensity as those of the poet.[2] But these broad approaches at the very least can be put into arrays. McKeon's own detailed labor on the arts can be partly defined by steps he did *not* take in his published work, steps long deemed essential in art theory: (*a*) a definition, universally applicable, of art itself: (*b*)

125

a definition of beauty or pleasure or some other human feeling to which art must subscribe, as Santayana would insist; (*c*) a theory of perception applicable to arts, as in writers from Baumgarten through D. W. Prall and Arnheim; (*d*) a hierarchy of the arts, as with Hegel, or a classification of them such as Paul Weiss offers; (*e*) an examination of any particular art as prototypical for the others, as with Eduard Hanslick; or (*f*) a set of prescriptions for creating a work of art, as in the writings of Joseph Schillinger. I would have added a seventh category, the examination of some particular work of art, but there is one essay by McKeon, "*Pride and Prejudice:* Thought, Character, Argument, and Plot,"[3] that would be a counterinstance, as well as classroom teaching, and an address on Thomas Mann to be reviewed later. It might be thought from this list of neglected topics that McKeon had little to say, but in truth he reached manifold insightful conclusions regarding art in general, its kinds and purposes. After giving a brief account of the liberal and humanistic arts as he perceived them, I shall turn to four of the arts to which he gave much attention. To forestall disappointment, however, I remind the reader that McKeon as philosopher paid this attention to the ideas of artists, not their brushwork, much as his writings about sciences clarified theories, not laboratory verifications and failures.

Arts, Liberal and Humanizing

"The Future of the Liberal Arts"[4] is a short piece using an array of what can be called an extended trivium, all four of the arts put forward there employing what McKeon calls a principle of indifference: (1) the art of rhetoric conceived as innovative, not repetitive, must be used to adjust facts (idolized in our time) to the student's consciousness; (2) grammar, restored to its early function as an art of interpretation, must heal schisms between interpretation of facts and values; (3) logic, restored to its function of examining consequences in the flow both of nature and of discourse, will relate the unique experience of particulars to the regularities of knowledge; (4) dialectic should bring a sense of system into thought, using the principle of indifference, which might also be called that of the tolerant adjusting of conditions apparently in collision and of statements apparently incompatible. In dialectic, indifference is used to combine literalness with the stimulation of ambiguity, but as used with all four, it liberates men with respect to other men, to the world, to the achievements of men, and to one's own potentialities.

Two new tendencies in McKeon's thinking become prominent: the first is radically to extend the range of the liberal arts and the second, more surprising than the first, is to accord greater scope to rhetoric. One of the later essays summarizes McKeon's attempts to penetrate the proper subject matters, general characteristics of methods, practitioners, and purposes of the liberal arts. "The Liberating Arts and the Humanizing Arts in Education,"[5] a thoughtful, learned study tracing certain convictions about arts in society to antiquity, closes by offering suggestions for a thorough revision of important modern educational practices and with it the artistic aspects of our entire culture.

There are four liberal arts (replacing the well-known seven of the Dark and early Middle Ages), but a necessary prelude to these are the humanistic fields (pp. 176–78):[6] *invention* (discovery, creativity), traditionally contrasted, as by Whewell and Mill, with proof. Discovery extends not only to words but to things, arts, and sciences; *recovery* includes what has already been thought and presented. This is also a means for discovery and moves from documents to objects, processes, to action, values, and finally to ideas themselves; *presentation* is determined partly by the subject matter and partly by the presenter and his audience. The devices of reason move back and forth among rhetorical, psychological, and calculative expedients, ultimately to determine the character of the subject matter; the *arts of common action and thought* transcend ordinary tolerance, which is mere indifference to what other people do, and should include some interest in the values of other persons. These arts should transcend the ordinary desegregation of social entities usually separated and should develop freedom and responsibility. They should also transcend the ordinary one-world hypothesis to become a closely reasoned understanding of interrelated interests and opportunities in order to facilitate a community of values. All four of these must be cultivated as they are first applied to verbal devices of all sorts to reach at length to objective realities.

On the other hand, the four liberal arts, in modern dress, are the disciplines of humanistic education and are analogous to the four fields: *canonics* would set forth the simplest, most significant forms of general expression; this falls under the head of communication and is essential for any discovery. In this art, tradition would be related to its contrary, innovation (pp. 178–79); *hermeneutics* would and should be broadened from the interpretation of texts to that of facts and values, bridging the gap between what is and what is desirable (p. 179); *homiletics* (this is McKeon's own coinage, I believe, with but a very casual connection, if

any, to homiletics) would relate to each other those arts explaining sequences of discourse and those explaining consequences of occurrences
in things. The relevant contraries are particulars and universals. Here
determining the true depends on facts and principles, but truth is also a
value, and the determining of plural truths, like that of facts and principles, depends on circumstances. Determining the good depends on
preferences and prudence, but determining individual goods must itself
be a truth depending on its proper facts and principles. We come to no
unshakable certainties in either process—note the implied skepticism—
but homilectics will at least provide needed guidance in pursuit of the
true and the good (p. 179); *systematics,* finally, would help provide insight into the coherence of experience, value, and knowledge, relating
parts and wholes within each self-contained whole or among many
wholes such as man, states, or cosmic worlds (p. 180).

The X matrix, (see chapters 4 and 5) can serve as basis of the list of
humanizing fields and (indirectly) of the liberal arts; the fourth item in
each is the summating principle of the other three, separately and collec-
tively taken. The Y matrix deals with methods, and surely the liberal arts
reflect this emphasis upon orderly making. From another standpoint,
the fields echo Aristotle's four causes, since discovery deals with the impetus for finding new connections and distinctions, expressing the efficient cause; recovery relates to already-established combinations of facts
and represents the material cause; presentation gives the form in which
facts, principles, and values are related in intelligible combinations;
lastly, the final outcome is a summating whole.

History and Its Kinds

Clio is one of the Nine stationed on Mount Helicon, so I shall include
most of McKeon's treatment of history with his examination of the arts.
In many essays, but chiefly in the political, he divided into phases, some
but not all of them chronological, the kinds of activities or institutions
under discussion. Thus he looked at the beginning points of any social
change, then at its career as it is affected by exterior causes as well as
those inherent in it. Results can best be understood this way, whether
they comport with the original purposes or not and bring temporary or
more permanent advantages. The analysis is not strictly genetic, for it
never presumes that there must be either linear (or cyclical) development or a single set of necessary causes. There is room for chance; historical changes are grasped only after much weighing of groups of data

almost never the same in kind and in degree of influence. The causes of one war cannot be assumed to match those of another, except by coincidence. The varieties of evidence, starting with simple, named data set into propositions to convey integrated facts rarely suggest that historical events are uniform. The result of this analysis, basically problematic in kind, is a history containing few generalizations beside the one that there can be few generalizations.

The triune concept of freedom expounded in the little book, *Freedom and History: The Semantics of Philosophical Controversies and Ideological Conflicts,*[7] has been noted in chapter 6. Expectations that the three linked concepts are matched with three similarly related ideas of history will not be disappointed. *Dialectical history* assumes that processes operating in historical evolution and processes of proof in discourse are at bottom identical: the basis for rationality is the same as that for the historical process in concrete reality, for they are both resolutions of contraries leading to larger and larger absorbing phases. This is epochal history, revealing traits characterizing organic wholes of all sorts, wholes found in all activities of the group or epoch (p. 30). *Logistic history* is based upon events and their relations, originally recorded in annals and chronicles of limited areas or times and leading to more complex units for which causes must be found in social sciences. It is not a universal but a causal history, seeking limited truths (pp. 31–32). *Problematic history,* based on some evolution in the recognizing and stating of problems, in the solutions found for them, and in the human activities made possible by successive solutions, consists of accounts of specific human achievements and is dubbed disciplinary history (pp. 32–33).

These three methods, like the three corresponding philosophic methods, are, despite differences, equivalent in scientific precision, explanatory power, and inclusiveness (p. 33). Here McKeon is talking; historians of any of the three sorts could hardly be called upon to be so generous to their rivals. Be that as it may, McKeon's own method in his actual writing of history—chiefly intellectual history—finds its problems in individual situations, rarely seeking to solve them by straight-line causal sequences or an appeal to cycles inevitable and all-embracing. At a gathering one evening, I think in 1937, McKeon said that Spengler's famous simile of plant life in the four seasons and his uniform separation of cultures from civilizations, a turning point always occurring (barring interference from outside) four hundred years after a culture had been established—this system was a method for avoiding rather than facing problems. This condemnation does not really fly in the face of the assertion that the three historical approaches have equal merit when practiced in their purity. Spengler was not a dialectician in the full sense; he made rigid one simple likeness, losing the fluidity essential to dialectic that never gives up searching for new meanings, never takes a structure as finally established. (Lovers of Hegel or Marx will have something to say to this, but Plato would have something to say to them.)

Similarly, there is a passage, almost unique in McKeon's writings, in which he enters into an extended account and emphatic rejection of Wilhelm Dilthey's historical and semantical conceptions of *Geisteswissenschaft* (that almost untranslatable word!). It is in one of his longest and best essays, "Imitation and Poetry,"[8] and is one of the few places where another author is subjected to a regular drubbing (pp. 201–13). With all of McKeon's almost limitless opportunities to bring up his artillery against his predecessors, both philosophers and historians, it is noteworthy that he made so little of these occasions. Dilthey, the ornament of German intellectual circles shortly before the turn of this century and one of the few thinkers to have possessed the same sort of wide-ranging mastery as did McKeon, is buffeted repeatedly, in terms partly reminiscent of what McKeon had said of Spengler so many years before.

Firmly persuaded of the need for a comprehensive reading of the literary and other remains of an epoch, Dilthey treated texts as his facts, but like McKeon his primary concern was with an integrated culture. Objections to him could not have rested on his taking all disciplines to be components of a much larger whole that would perish unless merged into a living machine (Dilthey's expression), a unity absorbing all constituents. (Hegel had made the *Idea* the architectonic notion, and culture one aspect of it, while Dilthey reversed this, taking culture as the pinnacle and ideas as the chief steps of his dialectic.) For Dilthey the subject matter of philosophy is properly man, not as definable in some formula but rather as a living creature with some independence, some individuality in his hopes, fears, and conceptions of life. This is hardly McKeon's starting point; instead it is the philosophic discourse so rife with ambiguities that only a recognition of its division into incommensurable kinds and divisiveness into potentially irreconcilable factions can aid in dispelling it. Dilthey's effort to find an overall *Weltanschauung* characteristic of an age, a whole view that comprehends the philosophic systems of the time, the music, visual arts, and so forth, would be to McKeon a matter of adding apples to oranges, even when the philosophic systems are considered by themselves, unrelated to other arts and sciences.

For Dilthey, experience, his starting point, can stimulate many cultural responses, and these take shape as law, economics, art, religion, philosophy, and the other pursuits playing such a role in German philosophy, Kant and Herder to Weber and Cassirer. These pursuits in turn are gathered into a new unity, the cultural *Geist* to be penetrated by *Geisteswissenschaft*. An octahedron, its axis vertical, would be the most suitable figure for diagramming his three-stage philosophy. But what, then, is so inimical to McKeon's approach, especially in view of his oft-stated tolerance for plural constructions of truth and truths?

During the mid-1930s at the University of Chicago there was much talk by McKeon and among his students about intellectual rigidity, and a good way of squelching anyone was to assert that he was freezing the dialectic, that having made analogies to entities or qualities within or outside the ordinary range of a subject's connections, he was keeping this structure invariably to those farther connections, closing off open explorations bearing different meanings and relationships of the concepts. It is Dilthey's tendency to make "rigid and dogmatic" (p. 212) his semantics and history that McKeon objects to most of all. Dilthey's method forces him to say, for instance, that the Romantic movement killed the last remaining adherence to a theory of imitation in poetics, so that a wholly new concept could take its place.

McKeon does not actually refute Dilthey by commencing with one of the latter's basic propositions and then showing that with it his theory runs into contradiction. Instead, McKeon puts forward his own type of history as "problematic and disciplinary" and offers a number of names of those coming after the time of Goethe and Schiller to demonstrate that "imitation" is by no means a dead expression (pp. 205, 212). Where Dilthey sees in a cultural epoch little but agreement on propositions thought to be characteristic of that epoch but now discarded, McKeon sees earlier disagreements as to meanings, methods, and principles, but now eventuating in a sense of common problems solved differently in every age but never going away. Whether the introduction of counterinstances is ever a real refutation of a theory of culture in general is a perplexing question in light of McKeon's insistence that alleged refutations of one approach by another cannot be decisive, complete, and permanent.

In sum, then, it is not that McKeon thinks Dilthey has used an analogical method with an epochal cast but that he has misused it, that he has made his net at once so broad as to catch every sea creature but has tied the reticulations so tight that none can escape; there can be no distinctions between meanings if the leading terms appear in a set of texts stated to be the same. All authors and artists of the time are caught in the same net without exception—until the fateful day when suddenly the net, fully extended, is found no longer able to prove itself wide enough to ensnare the schools lying beyond it.

The pivotal essay of 1966, "Philosophic Semantics and Philosophic Inquiry," says virtually nothing about history, though it is crucial to the conception McKeon was to develop in subsequent papers. Besides adding the Sophistic-Operational approach to the canonical three McKeon greatly refined the accounts of each of the four and all their intermixtures. This also clarified what he sometimes called the gobbling up of one philosophy by another. The metaphysical emphasis in this essay is carried forward in a condensed paper, "Has History a Direction? Philosophical Principles and Objective Interpretations," which he did not read but handed out to an assembly of scholars meeting in Paris. Together with remarks by several of these scholars and McKeon's rather full responses, the work is a source for the fourfold scheme of history. A student of mine once brought forth this polished gem on an examination: "Plato's thoughts eventually became complex and finally acute." The same, with a few editorial improvements, could, I suppose, be said of McKeon. The schematic character of "Has History a Direction?" is an aid to composing and reading thoughts both complex and acute. Rather than burdening my reader with prose that will doubtless seem repetitious, I present the outline of the whole as McKeon must have conceived it in an array closed horizontally—there are but four kinds of history—though not vertically, for rows were appended in his responses to the comments of Jean Wahl and others in the meeting (see fig. 7.1).

Some almost unavoidable ambiguities intermingle in a vocabulary employed in McKeon's own approach as a whole and also used to delineate the characteristics he attributes to the four types of historical approach. He thus speaks of raw data in general as "simples" but also of logistic as "simple" principles. There is a resemblance, to be sure, but this scarcely makes McKeon a logistic thinker, even in regard to principles. His own simples of history are named but not analyzed and not related; they are events, persons, or the like, and must be put into statements in order to become facts; they are not joined as Lucretius would join atoms with hooks, obviously, or as Hume would join ideas by an associative force, or as Russell (in his earlier phases) would join the primitive propositions *p* and *q*.

Another such term is "inquiry," which for McKeon both describes Aristotle's method and also refers to half of the entire enterprise of philosophy. Reasons for this dual meaning are not farfetched: the vocabulary available to philosophers is not the complete dictionary, since the number of words conveying just the right shades of meaning are relatively few. If "inquiry" is right then "quest" would probably not be right in the same contexts. Then too, McKeon quoted with approval William of Ockham's distinction between the broad sense of a word, the strict sense, and the "very strict" (*strictissima*) sense and felt empowered to make use of this distinction from time to time.

The History of Philosophy

One kind of history deals with culture; to the problematic historian this is chiefly a history of sciences and arts, their pursuit and dissemination. In turn a special kind of cultural history is that of philosophy, which can be taken in many ways. Problematically, it is viewed as a succession of philosophers each contributing some solutions to common problems. Mostly these solutions are useful for erecting a system more complete, precise, and of more immediate concern to the world at large, although such appropriating of ideas almost invariably implies their distortion, except in McKeon's own pluralistic approach. I turn now to various aspects of this treatment of philosophic history, which he extracted from both the facts of that history and the ways it has been written in tradition running from Plato and Aristotle in their historiographic moods[9] all the way to moderns as flamboyant as Will Durant and as assiduous as Frederick Copleston.

1. McKeon once told a friend of mine commencing his studies in philosophy that the two best ways of starting to learn its history were to pick a major philosopher and read his books beginning to end or else to select a topic, such as justice or substance or the like and then work minutely through the treatments offered by successive thinkers. Each method I suppose has its advantages and if one cares to look for them,

	EPOCHAL HISTORY (Plato)	CAUSAL HISTORY (Democritus)	DISCIPLINARY HISTORY (Aristotle)	EXEMPLARY HISTORY (Sophists-Operationalists)
BACKGROUND FOR ACTIONS AND SOCIAL OCCURRENCES	transcendent intelligibility, giving an organic unity	underlying material structures—physical nature, human nature, "natural law," economic production	conditioning circumstances, biological, political, social, cultural, giving circumstantial particularity	impulsions and repulsions, giving an operational schema
PROCESSES AND CONNECTIONS	treating objects and processes providing material and nature of cosmic myths and ages of man	processes in causal sequences taken from physics, biology, psychology, politics, economics, military strategy; depending on uniform human nature	facts and their connections brought about by problems faced; experience, art, and science, customs all supplementing human nature in solving problems	regarding acts; their connections providing forces in determining others, or models for others; great men as examples
ANALOGIES	seasons, birth and death, or the being of the City of God	power, economically interpreted	—	—
DIRECTION	degradation, advancement, cycles, emergence	random or progressive	fanlike, the solution of a problem providing no end of historical process	random interplays of external forces until coordinated by a great man or his followers

HISTORY OF PHILOSOPHY	synthesis by later ages of previous philosophers—cumulative nature of historical sequence	philosophy: once whole of knowledge; subsequent splitting off of sciences seen in history; philosophy now a remnant of problems	sequences of problems and hypotheses set forth, falsity or utility of solutions learned	how problems were posed by great men seen in careers and achievements of great philosophers
TASKS OF PHILOSOPHY AND HISTORY	fundamentally the same	not the same, not relevant to each other; an account of how problems ceased to be philosophic	—	—
FACTS AND DIRECTIONS	evolution of treatment of time from scholastic to baroque	treatments of problems for their utility to sciences	past treatments of problems of time, verification, etc., their adequacies and inadequacies	how great philosophers faced like problems that are faced today
EXPONENTS	some classical and medieval writers; Hegel, Marx	Thucydides, Lucretius, Buckle, J. H. Robinson	Aristotle, Polybius, Fustel de Coulanges, Maitland	(Plato's) Protagoras, Rousseau, Sartre

Figure 7.1   The Four Types of History

its disadvantages. Both are genuinely historical; the advice was *not* moderated by an exhortation to my friend to "think things out for yourself; you will not need books, and you will be a philosopher sooner or later." But when someone complained to McKeon about the commentaries then (1938) existing on Aristotle's *Physics*, he replied, "Write your own" in a tone neither encouraging, discouraging, nor sarcastic. It was not independence in studying the history of philosophy that McKeon deplored, but undisciplined independence.

2. History in one sense encompassed the whole of philosophy, for as McKeon once affirmed at an association meeting, as soon as they are uttered the words of a thinker become part of history, even before he has left the room. There was an accumulation of the data of history and patterns could be traced in it, once these data had been properly assembled. It does not contradict what has been said about differences between epochal and problematic history to point out that McKeon himself discerned swings in the course of centuries that included a limited cycle, with philosophers concentrating first on things, later on ideas, and then on language, presaging a subsequent return to things. There is no attempt to link this other cultural change or to demonstrate causation from economic or other external conditions.

3. Apart from the book on Spinoza,[10] McKeon never published a detailed analysis of any philosopher that followed his works in their original order, chronological or conceptual. Instead, McKeon picked the author's chief distinctions on a theme and then kept to their order in his own exposition, even had the philosopher himself not invariably done so. He grouped together subordinate sets of terms having immediate bearings on the main set and would locate the chief problems suggested by the philosopher and pursue these in sequences dictated by the innate rationale of the system. Never, so far as I know, did he print an unanalyzed list of citations that all happened to contain the same term or terms, giving a topical but informal, unmethodical grouping.[11] Books that lodge together bundles of remarks culled from Plato's dialogues without taking pains to find their dialectical relations to each other distort their meanings and lose the hairline distinctions that Plato evidently wished his readers to catch. No real sense can be made of a philosopher, McKeon often pointed out, unless one uncovers his reasons for having made his statements; and these must come from the parts of the proposition in question, its total sense, and its relations, semantic and syntactic, to its neighbor propositions.

4. Many have been the attempts to relate history to philosophy, and nearly always one or other of those disciplines has suffered, either by invidious comparison or by being swallowed up or by having done the swallowing. McKeon tried to give something like equal weight to both disciplines but—to borrow from Orwell—philosophy emerged a little more equal than history. As for what he himself principally derived from the history of philosophy, I have sometimes thought it was the groups of concepts he appropriated and reshaped so freely (see chapter 2). Because these were not terms having to do either with chronology or political ideologies (the two chief headings customarily used for classifying epochs and trends), they were of a general character that did not prejudice the analysis before the first step was taken. Arrays and matrices could thus be found to dominate those studies that relied very heavily on historical data, but they seemed to fit rather effortlessly, though they were based on philosophic principles.

5. McKeon selects not only for his historical studies but for his analytical ones as well the four basic types of philosophy that he chooses. But why? I can only suggest, with some misgivings, two answers. First, the history of the discipline seems to show the clearest divisions between Plato, Aristotle, Democritus, and the Sophists; using these is an easier way to read the others than is, say, the quartet Husserl, Heidegger, Jaspers, and Sartre, or, again, Carnap, Neurath, Schlick, and Wittgenstein, or even figures more remote from each other such as James, Russell, Quine, and Santayana. The Greeks—this is my second point—possess the advantage not only of having been probable originators of their respective approaches but also of having had considerable influences on later thinkers, bumpy and uncertain as the paths obviously were from them to their successors. If these two reasons do not suffice, perhaps the purity of their approaches, including Method, Principles, Interpretation, and Selection in each case, serve as a better explanation. This happens to be a matter so complicated that a separate study would be required.

6. Although three great thinkers and a collection of itinerant teachers-for-hire are made prototypes for subsequent philosophizing, they in no way actually determine what later philosophers must or can say. Aristotle falls on one diagonal of the matrix, Plato on another, but the ticket for those same berths does not require anyone to copy or mimic or even agree in all respects with Aristotle or Plato; the matrix is a way of keeping interpretations clear and distinct, and since the study

of prototypes is so extensive and so careful, the use of the word "Platonic" must be hedged with cautions when it is applied to other men, such as Schopenhauer or Whitehead, who might fit the same line. Still, using the writings of a single man as a base, it is far easier to be clear about affinities than to speak of "the realist position" or "the positivist outlook," when it is notorious that realists in any age are a heterogeneous lot, as are positivists, and this is scarcely less true when one talks specifically of the New Realists or Critical Realists, or of the Logical Positivists, who stretched their Vienna Circle out of shape time after time with heterodoxies and squabbles.

7. The matrices and arrays are schemata both for clarifying likenesses and differences and for reducing the chattering and bickering of philosophers, bickering that usually becomes more raucous in later stages of major epochs. The later thirteenth and the fourteenth centuries were prone to this, and our century has been a rowdy one. McKeon's advice would be against thinking one's own philosophy unique—others long dead have occupied the same matrix line, even if their vocabulary was different—or to think it invincible, able to stifle even the stupidly stubborn adversaries. Since the refutations are born of quite diverging approaches, they are of but incidental relevance to what is deemed to have been refuted. Although refutations may encourage making precise formulations, they also narrow the scope of philosophizing, taking up valuable time and generating querulous and what Kant would call stepmotherly natures.

8. McKeon's insights into individual philosophies, especially in his classroom expositions, resulted partly from his bringing out the connections and contrasts implied but never quite stated in a text. If concepts A and B are claimed to be contraries, and B and C are similarly contraries, then what about A and C, regarding which an author happens to be silent? Syllogism cannot give the answer, which can only be found by attending to usages in other connections. If, again, "nature" and "art" are linked at one point, and "art" and "purpose" are linked at another, can we tease Euclid's first common notion, that things equal to the same thing are equal to each other, into a shape permitting us to identify "nature" with "purpose"? The answer turns upon whether a consistent method requires that words retain or change their meanings in the several contexts in which the first two propositions have been included. In these searches and juxtapositions McKeon brought himself and his hearers closer to the real center of a philosopher's thought; and most

other kinds of exposition, no matter how elaborately documented, would by comparison seem outside rather than inside the system being examined.

The reason for laboring these points is that any defensible history of philosophy rests upon the interpretation of texts, and if you say that social or political history or psychological peculiarities bear a heavy weight in that history, the answer can only be that the knowledge of them, too, with very few exceptions, must depend on the study of texts. Distinctions between philosophers qua philosophers are inevitably of a philosophical type and highly varied. Once the reading of Plato and Aristotle is straightened out there is no reason to believe that the rest of philosophic history will be easy to grasp, though it may be marked by a few signposts. Those two men are, however, good object lessons, despite the fact that a philosopher can use a different submethod (to put it thus) in different parts of his system, as when Kant employed an analytic instead of a synthetic method, though both were parts of his overall critical method. If, again, you object that this has little to do with what a philosopher really *says,* that it all lacks relevance to his statements, the response can only be that statements without a way of generating and connecting them will at best yield supposition and belief, not knowledge.

Poetics

For some of the Greeks, poetry was the subject of a productive *science,* poetics, which for them included more than our modern "poetry" would allow. The topic of "The Philosophic Bases of Art and Criticism,"[12] a distinguished essay from his middle period and perhaps one of the half dozen best among McKeon's published writings, is not so much art as it is theories of art, and not so-called practical criticism of individual works but explanations of what the critics of those works were trying to do. Philosophers have frequently thought their writings on beauty and art are the very foundation that critics should build upon, and critics have propounded their own principles, virtually indistinguishable from philosophic ones. On both sides these are touted as unassailable fortresses from which their authors will conduct sorties into works of art. The drawback is, of course, that unanimity in choosing the principles is lacking: the more appeals made, the more targets are set up for enemies to tilt against.

Statements of such writers on art, says McKeon, may be treated first in relation to subjects to which the principles make them relevant; second, to other forms of judgment such as the sciences, history, the rest of philosophy, and art itself; third, to various terms in which they are stated. The essay is organized with these three relations dictating the topics, but the main distinction throughout is between the analogical and the literal use of terms.

In the first section,[13] the subject matter of statements about art is shown to be determined as much by the principles selected as by the topics discussed. Similarities, apparent or real, in modern discussions originate in part from the appearance of leading pairs of terms, such as "form" and "matter," "expression" and "content," and so forth. Other likenesses are suggested by the common use of terms such as "processes," "symbols," "effects," and the like; but upon closer scrutiny most of the resemblances melt away, since the analyses can be conducted in light of a Platonic dialectic of being and becoming or a logic of cause and effect derived from Aristotle. Either analysis gives unique results. In the first, a poem may be likened to other art objects or to living things, including human beings. In the second, poetry is differentiated by its qualities as a thing, by the kind of judgment appropriate to it, or by its effects. Fundamental to the theory may be the poem, the poet, or the impact upon the audience. The analogical method applies the same terms to all three but links them by proportions. In any of these, the emphasis may be upon things natural or artificial or both (using likenesses), upon mental faculties such as visions or other special powers; upon (again using likenesses) the sameness of the efforts of poets, scientists, moralists, or indeed all mankind; upon processes, in which case operational or semantic principles are determined by symbols or effects of art as distinct from those of science or ordinary human affairs; or upon discovering all knowledge and action in terms of symbols. Plato explores the poem as a thing, by means of a series of proportions; Aristotle uses a subject genus divided into species each with its defining characteristics. Kant, for all his separation of faculties, treats the judgment of the beauty of art as analogous to that of nature, while Bacon makes Aristotelian separations between the faculties yet follows Plato in considering aesthetic and moral judgments to be identical. Tolstoy's operational theory makes art an activity for bringing all mankind together and thus resembles Plato in uniting art and morality so far as judgment is concerned. His counterpart, Horace, sets up the "art of poetry" as precepts for poets wishing to please audiences.

In the second section,[14] McKeon shows the artist, critic, and philosopher as possibly being a single source of judgments or else plural and dissimilar sources. If, for instance, the act of criticism is creative, then critic and poet are the same. Artists (Horace, Pope, Dryden, Coleridge, Emerson) have often written outstanding criticism and may or may not have identified their enterprise with philosophy in so doing. Rivalries, however, between poetry and philosophy have also sprung up, as shown in the banishment of Homer and his clan from Plato's *Republic,* even though the dialogue form is conceived by Plato himself as a poem, the state as a work of art, and the cosmos as a thing of beauty made by the demiurge, a craftsman. Hobbes, again, treats nature as a work of art, but the artist is God. In the literal tradition rivalry between philosophy and poetry tends to disappear, each of these arts having its own principles and functions. Plato views the poem as an imitation of some exemplar, the latter being more perfect, more real, than the former, while Aristotle distinguishes between natural objects having an internal principle of motion and artificial objects requiring exterior causes: the plan and handiwork of a craftsman. Again, "criticism" for Plato is a very general term applied to all processes of judgment between better and worse, just and unjust, kinds of lives and kinds of pleasures, true and false. As one may expect, Aristotle limits the word not to art objects but to moral matters, that is, to practical as opposed to productive questions.[15] Writers in the literal tradition who seek (although not in quite the same way as Aristotle) to limit criticism to one kind of operation are Longinus, who transforms judgments regarding great authors into a quasi-science that has for its summit the sublime, and Bacon, who divided criticism applicable to all writing and interpretation from that pertaining to mythic poetry only.

If, however, the art work itself is being considered, the points of evaluation are words as related to things, style to content, and we look to such men as Horace and Cicero, who no doubt are more influenced by Aristotle's *Rhetoric* than his *Poetics* when they are judging poetry and writing criticism.

The third section[16] deals, as already indicated, with relations that statements made by philosophers and critics bear to the various terms used. These terms also derive their meanings from the ends and criteria of criticism. Just as the terms are not ticketed to show unambiguous meanings, except possibly in limited contexts in a particular man's discourse, so the subject matter is no rigidly bounded mass to be fully and exclusively explored, however differently, by all who call themselves critics. The only way that exact meanings can be imposed and discerned is through the eternal vigilance and tolerance of writer and reader alike. First, McKeon considers once again the possible ways the scheme is determined by statements in relation to their components and then, in a finale of unusual interest, the half-dozen ways in which these components shift meanings, owing mainly to kinds of intermixtures of the analogical and literal methods used to establish them. Two of the six are old friends. "Dialectical" (McKeon's quotation marks) criticism is the broadest, most amorphous type of all; there are innumerable variants from Plato's version. The other five are more nearly literal, though not always as "literal" as that of Aristotle, the founder of the second type,[17] accompanied by Edgar Allan Poe and T. S. Eliot, who alter Aristotle's preoccupation with kinds of things into a concern for kinds of thoughts. The "poetic," the third, begins with taking passages from great authors, as did Longinus, and ends with the conviction that the critic must be able to arouse poetic excitement in his reader much as does the poet himself. The fourth is "scholarly" criticism, represented by John Dover Wilson, who reconstructs, where possible, the peculiar character of the author from his work. Far from the universality ascribed to poets by the "poetic" mode, this one stresses their particularity to explain the effectiveness of their works. For the fifth there is the "technical," which erects precepts about what is pleasing to audiences, as we find in Boileau. Lastly, there is "formal" criticism, which, reversing the "technical," commences with the art work (as did I. A. Richards) rather than with the audience; the work is broken up into parts to decide how effective they are in relation to their assigned purposes. It is no surprise that judgments made in these six modes and couched in the same language are found to be quite different in meaning or else in agreement when superficially they seem opposed. The dialectical mode often makes forays into physiology, psychology, sociology, economics, or elsewhere to explain an art or an art form or a particular work, and the danger lies then in pinning faith upon some dogmatically proposed "truth" (by which to render all one's subsequent statements perspicuous and true. The five relatively literal modes, on the other hand, deal with art as nothing but art, and then there is the danger not of misplaced dogmatism but of an isolation from other concerns that might be exploited. Hence solidity of adherence to one mode or another is by no means always a virtue, as an intelligent combination of two or more may well avoid the faults peculiar to each one pursued separately.

This elaborate and penetrating essay is composed in the dialectical mode, its author says, but plays fair with the literal ones, seeking to show their virtues and limitations and with them to open up to synoptic view the enormous variety of concepts available in the discipline of art criticism. McKeon's aim was to reduce the fantastic tangles of ideas not to one single strand but to an ordered network. The critic who asserts that McKeon did not succeed is invited to do better.

The 1954 essay, "Imitation and Poetry,"[18] one of the longest of McKeon's published works, could with little trouble have been printed as a separate volume. To my mind, it represents one of his best attempts to show that history, as Dionysius of Halicarnassus long ago said, is philosophy teaching by examples.

The introductory pages (pp. 102–8) set the stage by showing that relations between philosophy and poetry have been manifold, with no single tradition that either separates or fuses them once for all, and that practices of both philosophers and poets have varied along with theories. In much the same way, the question of what poetry is prompts many disputes—whether it is imitation (and if so, of what) or an act of creation and thus of imagination, or of expression and thus of communication.

Both theoretic and practical criticism can be fitted into one of the schematized approaches that McKeon outlined in the early 1950s. Perhaps the simplest way of conceiving his essay structure is to take as fundamental methods the dialectical, problematic, logistic, and operational (one of the first times he set up four types), putting them in a long horizontal array. All essay sections could be written on some transparent material, each section occupying a separate fold, so that by the end the entries were superimposed many times and could be read through all the layers, top to bottom. The four types are made first to operate upon three terms, "imitation," "imagination," and "expression," taken in their immediate, original contexts and meanings and then as each of these can view both of the others, one at a time. The situation is complicated historically by the fact that a theory of imitation, as the first arrival (with Plato and Aristotle), is the one least cluttered with traces of the others, which by the time of the cardinal appearances in the literature, when they dominated critical discussion (the eighteenth and nineteenth centuries respectively, give or take a decade or two), must face a long succession of differing opinions, inharmonious with them.

Application of the methods is widened, moreover, when attached not only to the art work as independently existing but to that work as an act or object of thought or set of linguistic symbols. But a principle of indifference does not entirely hold: as a rule, "imitation" remains central primarily when a poem is taken as an objective thing; when it becomes an act of thought or its object, then "creation" and "imagination" occupy this favored position, and with a further shift to constructions of language as the essence of poetic art forms, "expression" and "communication" regularly become the chief terms (pp. 119–20).

So much for the general outline, now filled in with multitudes of references to specific writings from all periods. The essay, not counting the introduction, is divided into six sections, in which McKeon employs analogies and a method of involution to bring various trends into line with his three sets of basic terms: (*a*) the four methods; (*b*) things, thoughts, words; (*c*) imitation, imagination, expression; and subsidiary to these and introduced intermittently, (*d*) theory, practice, production; (*e*) dialectic, rhetoric, poetic; (*f*) philosophy, poetic, criticism, history. The variations are almost endless, virtually all kinds of joinings making some sense if properly interpreted. Moreover, they relate back to very early doctrines, with the proviso that intermediate links can also be traced and schematized. Thus a thing can be taken not as an object of knowledge with a name merely attached but as a symbol itself (smoke for fire, a cross for Christianity), a word can be the generative cause of all things, a thought can be treated as a thing independently existing or as something that receives its nature and delimitation only from a linguistic symbol.

The first numbered section (pp. 108–18)[19] discusses imitation as a full-fledged concept developed and applied using various methods. The dialectical method makes imitation a term of universal application so that, for example, the cosmos imitates eternal forms; the problematic method narrowly defines imitation to be appropriate to certain kinds of arts; the logistic method preserves the Platonic terms but shifts from forms to atoms and clusters of atoms and from intellectual cognition to sensation; and finally, the operational method makes imitation primarily a relation of followers to other artists taken as models. For Plato "nature" and "art" are virtually the same, since the cosmos is a beautiful artifact made by the art of God, the Demiurge, and all natural processes within it imitate in whole or part the motions of this cosmos as the most nearly real thing—or the motions of *its* imitations—and accordingly have imperfections. For Aristotle, nature is a source of motion inside,

	FRANCIS BACON	HOBBES	DESCARTES	MALEBRANCHE
METHOD	problematic	operational	logistic	dialectical
CONCEPTS	operational	problematic	dialectical	logistic

Figure 7.2   Seventeenth-Century Combinations of Methods

art a source outside, the substance; art contributes something to that object that it would not naturally possess. Moral habits are in turn distinct from both. For Democritus, nature is simply the motion of atoms in a void, combining or separating them; art is the same, but is restricted to human activities. Because for the Sophists man is the measure of all things, the sciences and moral virtues are legitimately products of his arts and teaching and persuasion.

The second section (pp. 118–31) commences with a broader review of Plato's treatment of imitation, which because it is dialectical is well adapted to reinterpretations. In the dialogues, "imitation" is always placed in a proportion to a reality superior to it. This conception plays host to later traditions reflecting the same split between better and worse aspects of existing things: in writings where the paradigm is not Plato's cosmic entity but the Roman state (Cicero), or the universe as created by God (St. Augustine, St. Bonaventura), or the world as seen by seventeenth-century men of science. In each tradition, other methods are admixed, so that problematic, logistic, and operational intrude in greater and greater measure until only traces of the dialectical remain. In what Whitehead called the Century of Genius, McKeon locates an interesting set of agreements and oppositions in art theory (see fig. 7.2).

In the third section (pp. 141–55), attention is turned to theories finding their metaphysical basis in the movements and halts of thought in the soul. McKeon's old hypothesis is revived, that cycles institute change to another approach when the first has been fully exploited, and they later change to another still. Where thought is the subject matter, the conditions of knowledge itself must be settled upon before discussing its objects and whether they have in fact any nature independent of being known. The Platonic dialectic, with its analogies to subjects of every kind, is well suited to this shift, as is the sophistical operational tradition emphasizing rhetorical devices. Aristotle and Democritus are more unbending in this respect. At any rate, every important figure of this new psychologizing inquiry reduces imitation to an issue subsidiary to some mental faculty, as with the Epicureans and Academics and their successors. The rhetorical tradition bent "imitation" to mean simply playing Stevenson's sedulous ape to great artists of the past. Longinus expects an especially eloquent passage to induce a kind of thrill in the reader. For Baumgarten the theory of the arts, which he like most critics after him called aesthetics, was rooted not in imagination but "sensitive cognition." Hume chose the emotions for this role, their basis being pleasure and pain. Yet another kind of subjective faculty here is the intellect, and its exponents are German literary and philosophical writers: Novalis, Schlegel, Hegel, Schelling (McKeon's order).

The fourth section (pp. 155–73) treats another "dimension" of art: the symbol or act of the artist himself, which is not easily separated from what has immediately preceded, though there is a distinction. In the third section McKeon was considering individual artistic faculties revealed in the works of art or involved in judging them whereas the fourth discusses the word or deed itself, not the agent. The difference is one of emphasis, the chief metaphysical context of the fourth section being no longer the mind as knowing the thing constructed but rather the words in which a work is couched or the deeds by which it is made or of which it is, so to speak, the benchmark. A further distinction characteristic of McKeon is that he finds in Plato or Aristotle doctrines of expression as well as imitation and things, however much these aspects seem to belong solely to the linguistic mode. On the other hand, scores of philosophers have scant use for Aristotle's object-oriented system, and they replace "imitation" with "expression" yet somehow manage to find a subordinate role, for "imitation," treating it as ambiguous or of trifling import. An open but frequently recurring list of terms is found throughout history, terms exchanging their positions of prominence and subsidence, like corks rising and falling on the waves, but according to patterns.[20]

A double involution arises when Platonic dialectic is reinterpreted as taking imagination for the principle that unlocks the most arcane aspects of art, but viewing this dialectic in turn as saying something about expression. Such a man was Coleridge, who speaks of "the best part of language . . . formed by a voluntary appropriation of fixed symbols to internal acts. . . ." Croce and Dewey are among those committed to language and actions as representatives of dialectical and problematic methods, respectively. The positivists and logical empiricists, led by Charles W. Morris, developed a three-pronged semiosis for the study of language: semantics, syntactics, and pragmatics, the acts of expression and the psychological grounds of pleasure and pain. Santayana, too, pursued a logistic course, conceiving beauty as their objectification of pleasure. For him, associations produce "hushed reverberations" that confer upon objects their complete expression.

The fifth section (pp. 173–92) considers meanings of "imitation," which instead of forcing differences upon philosophers or critics "focus upon four different aspects of poetry" (p. 173) in hopes of framing a unified theory: as mirroring or embodying values (dialectical); as an object made by a poet's art, be it productive, imaginative, or linguistic (problematic); as a means for conveying emotion (operational); or as a state of mind (logistic). All of these can be viewed from the standpoint of any one of them; hence, agreement might be reached through them. Even so, history shows that each becomes a position from which the errors of other critics and philosophers can be pointed out. Compromise in the sense of a mixture does not heal cleavages between doctrines; instead, seemingly opposing doctrines can be stated clearly and convincingly, and then tolerated. Tolerance, which allows one to restate a doctrine other than one's own in more congenial terms, thus differs from compromise. McKeon, not surprisingly, runs through all four of these aspects from the standpoint of the four *Urmethode*. His examples range from minor thinkers, many almost unknown today, to several very prominent ones, Rousseau to Russell. After this new involution, McKeon has still another string to his bow.

In the sixth section (pp. 192–221), the four aspects of art, when rendered not as imitation or imagination but as expression, take on new forms: dialectical, as the expression of values; operational, of content; logistic, of objectification of pleasure; and problematic, of organic unity. In each, a danger exists that the art object will somehow dissolve into clouds of mystery—of which again there are four kinds.

The main purpose of this section is to show that "imitation" is still a most useful concept in analyzing the arts, although in the latter half of the twentieth century it is frequently so conceived that "expression" is still dominant in the same theory. There is a further involution: expression is still looked upon as if we were back in the eighteenth century with Hume's association of ideas and Kant's forms of cognition, so that the concepts of imitation and expression are to this extent distorted, being seen through two glasses, each clouding the issues. To clarify them, two disciplines have been resorted to in the past, history and semantics, but unfortunately in forms "superannuated and inapplicable" (p. 197–98).

At one point in a fine old motion picture, *An American Romance,* the hero, an immigrant laborer, comes to a schoolmistress bearing a lump of iron ore in one hand and a steel spike in the other. "I want to know," he says, "how dis become *dis.*" I have never thought of Plato or Aristotle as being crude ore, and certainly modern critics are something sharper than a railroad spike, but the truth is that McKeon in this essay gives one of the best examples of his power to trace the changes in structures of ideas through an extended time so that the shapes and textures become altered almost to unrecognizability, even when the underlying material evidently remains much the same.

The remainder of this intricate, profound essay (pp. 213–21) comments on the tasks of philosophy in connection with both knowledge and values, problems forced upon it respectively by advances in science and in communication.

Sciences of all sorts can be called in to explain various aspects of its own accomplishments, but the question *why* people say what they say is largely unanswered. Similarly, our own values are clear enough, but values different from our own (in different times or cultures) are thought absurd, useless, or devoid of any interest. With respect to knowledge, philosophy must contribute to the advance of sciences by preserving rational dialogue, while with respect to values it should install criteria of action and judgment.

For the first, our concepts and methods must be flexible and allow for other possibilities. To assume that Aristotle's theory of imitation, for instance, could not include the poet or audience because of its concentration upon the work of art, is false. The poet, says Aristotle, is a maker of plots, and furthermore the effect of a tragedy upon the audience is that of catharsis. But theories of imaginative creation also take into account what is represented (the object of imitation in the older theory) and also the values making the work effective (to an audience). Theories of expression include the matter reproduced in content together with the form that is perceived. Studying the structures of problems, themes, and techniques is essential for achieving the flexibility and clarity much needed for the enriched enjoyment and understanding of poems. Differences in philosophies of art should lead not to the formation of schools but to the better grasp of principles.

Imitation and imagination are "dead and unpromising as basic themes" (p. 218) of criticism, yet they should serve those who would develop a theory of expression—who would do well to look at the acts uncovered by the other two theories.

For the second, imitation is useful not only as a propaedeutic to a theory of expression but also in the discussion of the emergence of values, for these have "objective contracts" (p. 219). Imitation as a core of a theory of poetry brings to mind the values in a poem (the dialectical interest), the nature of the poem (the problematic), the form of expression employed (the operational), and the sensibilities that are affected, especially the feeling of pleasure (the logistic). Whether or not imitation has a place in any of these, they can all benefit from close attention to the facts that it has made prominent.

One of McKeon's two or three published exercises in practical criticism was occasioned by a ceremonial dinner (June 1945) honoring Thomas Mann's seventieth birthday, when McKeon was invited to speak. His address[21] is one of his most graceful, gracious writings, for despite his own prefatory recognition of the irony in choosing him, a representative of philosophy with all its old antipathies toward poetry, still he attributes an insight to the hosts of the dinner in looking to a higher level where truth encompasses mysteries and poetic beauty expresses truths (p. 223). This same irony and insight is found, says McKeon, in Mann's writings as well, for he follows in the Platonic tradition of tending toward a merger of poetry and philosophy despite their occasional discomfort with one another. Mann's novels, McKeon adds, transformed the literary form into one of philosophic depth, seeking to discover the foundation for human relations and for the sequences of the thoughts entertained by human beings:

When Mann wrote *Buddenbrooks,* the novel was passing, as an art form, from a structure adapted primarily to plot and narration to a structure in which the development of the character of men, of families, and of times assumed primacy. He completed and published the *Magic Mountain*[22] at a time when novelists built a new structure for the novel on the intellectual content which animates the associations of men and the flow of their thoughts and feelings, and he revolutionized the mime by putting it to philosophic use. The change in the form of the novel no less than the change of its content removed the antithesis between art and philosophy. (Pp. 224–25)

Plato, says McKeon, is a poet who becomes a philosopher as one who knows; Mann is a philosopher who transcends common rationality and thus becomes a poet. In the efforts of Socrates in the *Symposium* and of Hans Castorp in *The Magic Mountain* to realize the full essence of love, music exerts a force on the human spirit to ground and inform the more indirect influences of refined argument (pp. 225–26). Mann's dialectic—for that is what it is—of the artist and art is based upon yet breaks away from bourgeois normality and displays form as a resolution of analyses, health as based upon the experience of disease, and innovation as rooted in tradition; it is a dialectic that repudiates naive, static oppositions. It is a dialectic, furthermore, recognizing that facts and history are not all that we can trust; the myth, exemplified in the Joseph novels, is true because it has happened so often that it must be told and retold fully to explore its varied latent truths. The poet is the maker, and here McKeon quotes the isolated and to outward appearances forlorn Tonio Kröger, who could in turn be reading the hidden thoughts of Plato's Demiurge in the *Timaeus*: "I am looking into a world unborn and formless, that needs to be ordered and shaped." This brief essay strikes me as one of McKeon's best short studies, written by a man who also published a paper extending the Pell equation in theory of numbers,[23] one on medicine and philosophy in the eleventh and twelfth centuries,[24] and several detailed reports and deliberations in UNESCO.[25]

There cannot be pluralism among the objects of artistic production such as there is in philosophy. If St. Thomas and St. Bonaventura are in effect opposite to each other or alternative, two sides of the same coin, well and good; but the novels of Dickens are not contradicted point for point by the novels of Rolland or Conrad or D. H. Lawrence. If one can select particular concepts from the novels of these four and examine them in terms of the statements they embody regarding time, death, justice, love, this is enlightening, but it requires turning the novels into repositories of philosophic propositions, which enriches philosophy, no doubt, but removes those books for the time being from the list of narratives of human actions; nor could the results have met the hopes and purposes and challenges of the original novelist.

I pass to what seems a real turn in McKeon's thought in the last two decades of his life, one that might in the end prove the most controversial part of his career.

Rhetoric in History

Plato had several kinds of opponents, to most of whom he gave explicit attention. Of these one was Isocrates, who did not so much entertain a set of doctrines contrary to Plato's as he belittled the whole study of philosophy, ranking the art of persuasion higher than the dialectic that Plato had considered the art of arriving at truth. Plato speaks of this rhetorician but once (unless *Epistle 13* is genuine, which it probably is not), voicing his hopes that Isocrates will turn to philosophy.[26] Because this rival, like his Roman followers Cicero and Quintilian, looks upon the good rhetor as the completely educated man, morally and intellectually alert, technically trained and well-disposed toward audiences, he could never accept Plato's suggestion (implied in the *Phaedrus*)[27] that good rhetoric is really the same as dialectic. If anything, for Isocrates, the rhetor is ready to gobble up philosophy.

In a sense, McKeon himself adopted something of this viewpoint and so was forced to revise parts of his own topics earlier explored. He had done this before in his structures when he expanded his basic distinctions from dichotomies to trichotomies and then to a fourfold division of philosophy, all of which required all sorts of new differentiations and pairings. In the late 1960s and 1970s he turned his attention more and more to the uses of rhetoric, which he now called an architectonic art. This may have been owing to his realization that one must use all available means of persuasion if one hopes to win hostile persons or states over to a search for common understanding, peace, and world unity. Not that McKeon grew disillusioned with philosophy; he merely approached it from another side.[28]

Much material for these later studies reapplied the historical accounts written in his earlier days. I list the historical pieces in an order of the first persons mentioned and expounded in each essay:

1. "Criticism and the Liberal Arts: The Chicago School of Criticism"[29]—begins with Democritus
2. "The Methods of Rhetoric and Philosophy: Invention and Judgment"[30]—begins with Gorgias
3. "The Funeral Oration of Pericles"[31]
4. "Symposia"[32]—begins with Plato
5. "Aristotle's Conception of Language and the Arts of Language"[33]
6. "Rhetoric and Poetic in the Philosophy of Aristotle"[34]
7. "Introduction to the Philosophy of Cicero"[35]
8. "Creativity and the Commonplace"[35]—begins with Cicero
9. "Rhetoric in the Middle Ages"[37]
10. "Poetry and Philosophy in the Twelfth Century: The Renaissance of Rhetoric"[38]
11. "Renaissance and Method in Philosophy"[39]—begins with Peter Abailard
12. "The Transformation of the Liberal Arts in the Renaissance"[40]

Some of these papers deal at least in passing with the future of rhetoric. Although there is occasional overlapping in the later papers, even so there is much to distinguish each one. McKeon was in his seventies when he was most concerned with that rhetoric, refurbished, improved, its techniques disseminated to a wider group of speakers and reevaluated, might accomplish in human life. The late essays prove that his manner of thinking had lost neither its sharpness of focus nor its panoramic range, though he did lean to what can be called programmatic writing in these essays.

For Aristotle, demonstration always begins, for the theoretical sciences, with one's own best-known, prior, and perfectly true principles; but dialectic employs syllogistic structures identical with those of demonstration yet is content with principles stemming from the pronouncements of others, whether all or most men or the experts.[41] These pronouncements could be upon any subject matter, and because of the relatively informal character and the lack of strictest logical control over them, this knowledge, in changing hands, becomes opinion, for its embodying propositions no longer come from the amassing of one's own evidence and arguments but through the medium of discourse, no matter how exactly framed. The truth of opinion, however, can be tested, and Aristotle's *Topics* is a highly detailed list of prescriptions for conducting these tests on the proposed statement by another, in order to discover whether its predicate has been properly asserted as a definition of the subject or is a property of it, or a genus, or an accident (the first of these being hardest to prove, easiest to disprove). Pursuing a science requires specialized empirical information (in the case of physics) and the most accurate classification by the scientist, but the successful dialectician has to amass a stock of general information, the bigger the better, and all this can be done through discourse with others.

Rhetoric, for Aristotle, is the counterpart (the *antistrophē,* the answering reverse movement in a choral dance or procession) of dialectic.[42] For syllogisms it has its own correspondent enthymemes, looser and more easily adjusted to the emotions of audiences; and for the inductions necessary for arriving at scientific principles (though their final grasp must be intuitive), rhetoric has its corresponding examples, better able to incorporate individual persons and events in a speech. Like dialectic, rhetoric has its commonplaces, some of them suitable for all types of speech, others for the three kinds differentiated first of all by their audiences: political, for the councils of government; forensic, for the courts; and epideictic or display, for casual audiences. The first has to do with deliberations over advantageous and disadvantageous actions that may take place in the future, the second with the accusation and defense of past actions, the third with the honorable and dishonorable, fixed with respect to the present. The political and forensic are limited in scope, dealing as they do with matters of public policy and with criminal and civil cases, but the display oratory ranges much more widely— a writing or speech, to use Plato's instance in the *Symposium,* could be about salt as it could about the god of love (177a–c). Whether this would permit one to say that rhetoric is for Aristotle a universal or architectonic art is another question. Certainly it is for him an instrument of the political sciences (they include ethics) just as logic is an instrument of the theoretic sciences principally and of the others in a looser sense.

Aristotle's remark that rhetoric is the counterpart of dialectic was taken by Cicero to mean that rhetoric is broader, being concerned with the flow of continuous speech, whereas dialectic deals with disputation only. Cicero reviews the concepts engrafted on this distinction, most of them simplifications of the Aristotelian treatises. Cicero's method aims at probabilities about things, for on the one hand he did not consider himself one to investigate disagreements about words and ideas, and on the other he himself was no Aristotle, setting standards of utmost logical rigor and certainty where it was essential that they apply. Like Aristotle, however, Cicero distinguishes three elements essential for rhetorical mastery, defining them quite differently despite fairly similar labels: the orator's character, which has chiefly to do with the commonplaces that he "collects" in order to be ready in oration and debate and that advance him in his powers of invention, arrangement (disposition), diction (elocution), memory, and delivery (pronunciation); these might serve as basis for a 5 x n array. Then there is the speech itself, consisting of exordium, narration, confirmation, refutation, and peroration; finally, those elements arising from questions with the speech, and here Cicero separates the indeterminate (i.e., whether theoretical or practical) from the determinate (i.e., epideictic, deliberative rhetoric, which replaces Aristotle's old category, political and the judicial, which replaces the forensic).

The Middle Ages played numerous variations on these themes, and the Renaissance adapted them further in the interest of the fine arts, chiefly poetry, rather than the theology and jurisprudence that had dominated the previous period. In his "Rhetoric in the Middle Ages" McKeon reviews the history of the distinctions and interrelations between and the reciprocal absorptions of grammar, rhetoric, and dialectic and other parts of logic. Aristotle's *Rhetoric* was one of his last major authentic works to be translated into Latin, and it was less influential than the writings of Cicero. In philosophic history, after the elaboration of theories, their branches, and attendant subtleties such as one finds in Aristotle, there is usually a gradual falling off in the exactness of the distinctions, stringency of the requirements for principles, and flexibility and scope of the applications of the language arts; and we find this in the early medieval period where rather soon the twists and turns of Aristotle's thought, which to some extent Cicero had preserved, were smoothed away until one or other of his disciplines could be ignored entirely, or else put in a weakened form into another art. The thirteenth and fourteenth centuries built up parts of Aristotle's disciplines again, so that the *summae* and *summulae* became ever more complicated, while the fifteenth and sixteenth centuries were to simplify again, generally in the name of some master art that could safely be applied to all subjects. The Renaissance, one might say, bypassed the Middle Ages in its return to a remoter past now mantled by a romantic glow cast over the sources.

In Rome, Lucretius and Cicero had between them taught philosophy to speak good Latin, and for various reasons, chiefly the preponderant interest of the Romans in law and politics, Cicero had the greater effect upon writers of the Empire. Because his subject matters were better adapted to homiletics and even theology, he was again, after the employment of Greek had dwindled, the useful source for pre-Christian philosophers and Christian fathers to follow. From St. Augustine the ideas were transmitted in altered condition to the succession of ecclesiastics. Many if not most elegancies of the Roman style were played down or tacitly ignored in the thirteenth and fourteenth centuries, and the beginning of Renaissance humanism initiated the rediscovery and adoption not only of the general principles of Cicero's rhetoric but his practices, his style so well suited to a sensitive ear.

In a short paper, "Creativity and the Commonplace,"[43] McKeon displays, with a not unusual mixture of proficiency and devilish innocence, his ability to extract from a relatively neglected corner of the history of philosophy a whole program for that discipline and, if carried a step or two farther, a philosophy itself. He commences, innocuously enough, with the observation that even the concept "creativity" becomes a commonplace, that is, a broad and quite ambiguous word serving as a place from which another statement or argument may commence.[44] Memory and invention are thus both activities and commonplaces, and creativity can be plausibly ranged on the side of either one. All these terms tend to vary in their successive contexts. The basic point, which Aristotle hints at but does not state emphatically, though Cicero picks it up as significant, is that as soon as one creates a new combination of words or ideas of any sort—be it a sprightly metaphor, a serious insight in politics or logic, or a new mathematical proof—this may take its place among the common assumptions and orthodoxies of the day, becoming thereby an additional commonplace. The liveliest ideas of today become the bromides of tomorrow simply because they *are* appreciated, accepted, and then repeated.

McKeon runs through "invention" and "memory" as contraries and relates them briefly to two commonplaces that divide into sets of four: things, thoughts, actions, and words on the one hand, and term, statement, argument, and system on the other, as ways to clarify the original pair. Any expansion of rhetoric's functions, any attempt to make it an architectonic art, necessarily comes not from a revision of the educational program of the orator but from a radical revision of all the substantive categories of being and method connected with the art; as a result, it would not be a universal art of words but a universally traveled path for inquiring into, demonstrating, and disseminating truths to be reached in no other way. It would assume roughly the function of Plato's dialectic, the all-embracing technique of inquiry, the capability that first sought to reform rhetoric and then united with it to turn common opinion into real knowledge and to turn narrow and prejudiced men into independent-minded, wise ones.

To this widened, deepened conception of rhetoric we now turn.

Architectonic Rhetoric

In the later decades of McKeon's life he gave increasing attention to world problems, and when he sought to improve individual disciplines it was for the sake of placing them at the disposal of mankind at large. Refurbishing rhetoric was for the sake of outlining the needs for, antecedents of, tasks imposed upon, and general character and affiliations of this universal art that could both solve problems and communicate the solutions of people everywhere. It was not a way of reducing all problems to a few kinds, nor would it condense all solutions into one that could resist every opposing faction, nor could it assume a homogeneity of rulers or populace in order to promulgate and accept the solutions offered. Ambiguous but common problems and precise but plural solutions were still the order.

In a manner resembling McKeon's characterizing of the later medieval period as an attempt to fit Aristotle's philosophy into the triune division of knowledge (by St. Bonaventura and others) as subordinate to God, McKeon's own late work on rhetoric was an effort to accommodate its new extension into the framework whose perfection had been approximated but, he thought, not fulfilled, in "Philosophic Semantics and Philosophic Inquiry." Thus the slightly modified four questions of Aristotle are there, also the four types of modes of inquiry as well as their subtypes. In some respects the use of these to order rhetoric is difficult in view of the fact that this art of words is protean, much more slippery than demonstrative syllogistic logic or dialectical logic, not to mention mathematics or physics. Yet for that very reason rhetoric can be adjusted to fit all the more easily, given the proper rubrics to which it should be fitted.

Such a unified source is not what one finds in the early essays at all; they approach their own topics from the standpoint of different structures, although one finds little contradiction in them because of their heterogeneity of subject matter. The political writings of the middle years approach what comes to be a common topic from the standpoint of a small number of diverse conceptual structures, and there is a much stronger feeling of integration than in the earlier pieces. The late works on rhetoric treat of somewhat varied aspects of the same subject matter, it is true, but their springing from a common source makes it easier to pick the salient passages from these essays without tracing the arguments of each. The links among these papers shows the firmness of purpose in their writing; it was no aberrant tar-water enthusiasm.

The papers of the late date dealing almost exclusively with rhetoric are as follows:

(*a*) "The Methods of Rhetoric and Philosophy: Invention and Judgement"[45]
(*b*) "Discourse, Demonstration, Verification, and Justification"[46]
(*c*) "Philosophy of Communications and the Arts"[47]
(*d*) "The Uses of Rhetoric in a Technological Age: Architectonic Productive Arts"[48]
(*e*) "Creativity and the Commonplace" (last half)

I shall not draw on these in the chronological order, for the essay setting the stage for the discussion was printed last in time, and to its second half I now return. In these pages, creativity, which had been contrasted with rhetorical commonplaces and attached to communication, is thus removed from the confines of an art practiced by the supposedly gifted few—the poets and artists—and transferred to discourse of every kind and between virtually every member of the human race. The transfer need not be interpreted as a contradiction in McKeon's thinking, but it does represent a change in its priorities. Even if "communication" is a term less suitable for analyzing abiding problems of poetic inspiration, it is more useful for the crises of the present age.

This change in tone is marked as well by a great—one might almost say infinite—expansion of rhetoric in every respect. This art that served earlier as the handmaiden, scorned stepchild, and straw boss of philosophy should now, if McKeon is correct, be elevated to a position far higher. The last few pages of "Creativity and the Commonplace" (pp. 27–36) outline two "paths" for relating the two concepts of the title. First there is the traditional way, the doctrinal, and here McKeon tersely sketches the fate suffered by commonplaces over the centuries, when they were increased in number but frequently diminished in significance as means to inventive novelty under the hardworking hands of Boethius, Lully, Nizolius, and others. The seventeenth century was inclined to transfer some of the commonplaces of rhetoric into the logic of science: Bacon, Descartes, Leibniz, and (in the following century) Vico all hoped to found a universal art that would solve the resistant puzzles offered by nature and man. In their hands Cicero's five commonplaces were all transformed into a discipline of wider import, but in the process they moved further away from generally applicable verbal practices and closer to scientific discovery and presentation.

So much for doctrine. "The present exposition of creativity and the commonplace," says McKeon, "is not designed to uncover and state truths about creativity but to explore the commonplaces which determine the varieties of ways in which it functions in exploring the old and constructing the new" (pp. 34–35). Unfortunately, most of the history of commonplaces reveals how they have been altered from springboards of the innovative into cabinets for the remembered, the unoriginal, the safe and sure. Much as Kant lamented the condition of metaphysics in his time, McKeon laments what has been done with the essential concepts of rhetoric in our century, in an attempt to make language over in such a way that the concepts can speed growth of knowledge. "The commonplace of commonplaces," he says, "is the place in which the certainties of the familiar are brought into contact with the transformations of innovation" (p. 35). Contemporary philosophers seem not often to have recognized the need for this. By such a means the commonplace of "creativity" is expanded to become yet another commonplace, the "known and unknown." This notion cries out for elaboration and a careful accounting, which the brief essay does not supply. McKeon had already furnished several more ambitious pieces to fill this need.

The essay, "The Uses of Rhetoric in a Technological Age: Architectonic Productive Arts," which gave most of the general structure of the new theory, was published in the year "Philosophic Semantics and Philosophic Inquiry" was written. Perhaps McKeon thought at the time that in the piece on semantics he was summarizing all that needed to be said about the foundations of philosophic thinking and he now should outline something by its nature freer, less amenable to division into categories and subcategories. The peculiarity of this new treatment is that in the hands of a master dialectician who wrote and spoke with almost none of the blandishments of oral showmen or literary stylists, we have a vision of rhetoric that far outdistances any other responsible versions coming from earlier exponents of the art. The rhetoric that has burst its former bounds as a mere counterpart of dialectic is no longer concerned with the restrictions of the three originally proposed types literally taken as what used to persuade political and legal bodies and casual audiences.

In "The Uses of Rhetoric" McKeon adopts the Latin names for the three Aristotelian types, namely, deliberative for political, judicial for forensic, and demonstrative for epidictic, and then greatly extend *their* meanings to cover all scientific, logical, moral, and other sorts of inquiry into truth. Second, he makes rhetoric an art, not an instrument, and a productive art at that. This can only be done, he says, when rhetoric and philosophy are rejoined, so that eloquence and wisdom are made one and can then become an art of producing both things and other arts rather than mere words and arguments. The road to this in our time would be to relate all things by means of science and experience (pp. 12–13).

In a section of this paper entitled "The Fields and Problems of Rhetoric" (pp. 18–24), McKeon outlines the functions-to-be of the three kinds of the new art to make a quartet of terms now grown familiar:

1. Where the old verbal demonstrative rhetoric merely sought to praise or blame events and things in the present, the new architectonic rhetoric is to produce action; its scope extends well into the whole of human activity and knowledge. Its statements, being related to the present, are all assertoric and concern the data of existence (pp. 18–20).

2. Judicial rhetoric formerly dealt with accusation and defense in courts but is now recruited for verifying and falsifying not past actions but any facts and values needing determination and laws needing establishment. Judgment will slough off its old legal connotations, taking on the somewhat Kantian task of relating facts and values to experience (p. 21).

3. Replacing the old deliberative rhetoric with its connections to choices or decisions is an expanded version that includes "all discursive sequences—inference, narrative, plot, lyric, history, aphorism, paradox—with related forms and methods" (p. 22).

4. To complete the list, dialectic is now introduced *under* (instead of alongside) rhetoric as a kind of summating principle of the new art,[49] that becomes dialectical rhetoric, on a footing with the others, except for its even greater universality. With the extension of community eventually to include the entire world and with the enormous advances in the technology of communication that bring a universal audience that is mankind, rhetoric must extend the boundaries of its functions as well as of its audiences. What McKeon does to his predecessors in rhetoric is much the same as what Cicero did to Aristotle when he enlarged the old art of language into a "universal productive art, an *ars disserendi,* and applied it to resolve what he conceived to be the basic problem of Roman culture, the separation of wisdom and eloquence, of philosophy and rhetoric" (p. 5).

One can pass rapidly over "The Methods of Rhetoric and Philosophy: Invention and Judgment," which argues this very point again, now in terms of the commonplaces of dialectic and rhetoric and the proper places of the special sciences, and in terms of what happens to Aristotle's four scientific questions, Whether it is? and What it is? (questions of fact) and Of what sort it is? and Why it is? (questions of cause), and what happens to these in the hands of Cicero and Quintilian, who try to merge the philosophy and rhetoric that Aristotle had so carefully distinguished (pp. 61–62). McKeon moves quickly to the modern scene, arguing for a uniting of the two because philosophy and rhetoric have already greatly influenced each other and because modern philosophic problems are especially suited to the methods of rhetoric, although he confesses that the discussion of these problems is "betrayed into verbal, abstract, and fantastic formulations" (p. 64).

In "Discourse, Demonstration, Verification, and Justification," another tightly packed essay, McKeon distinguishes the arts of discourse into those of words and those of things, reflected early in the trivium and quadrivium respectively. Demonstration, verification, and justification each have four definitions, accepted and acceptable, answering to the four chief approaches to philosophy (McKeon does not claim this, but his sternly compressed paragraph is, I think, intended to be read in this way). The central part of this essay (pp. 42–45), which is of all those on rhetoric the most obviously connected to "Philosophic Semantics and Philosophic Inquiry" and (I may be forgiven if I sigh in making this judgment) most closely resembles it in style, can be conveniently rendered in tabular form to illustrate what happens when rhetoric is "universalized," that is, when the old barriers between rhetoric as an art and the sciences with their own separate methods, principles, and subject matters are removed (see fig. 7.3).

The rest of the essay (pp. 46–55) is an equally concentrated account of what happens to the old commonplaces when rhetoric has undergone its transformation, and what happens to the perspectives in which common questions become particular when theses are used as principles. In regard to the first, McKeon runs through the employment of commonplaces in the three old types of rhetoric and, with an eye on the material cause, says that the realm of discourse is no longer the merely possible but the omni-possible. In distinguishing the purposes of discourse, the commonplaces are directed to the omni-desirable (the final cause). When facts are universalized, commonplaces are turned toward the omni-present (the efficient cause, as stimulus for knowledge). When discourse has supplanted metaphysics as the architectonic method, facts of existence become indubitable truths, and their marks and tests are used within a totality, the omni-existent, exemplifying the formal cause.

The account of perspectives revives a secondary distinction from "Philosophic Semantics and Philosophic Inquiry" between knowledge, the known, the knowable, and the knower; these are filled out more than this brief summary can convey. The last pages of the essay surely constitute some of the most compactly presented of all McKeon's writings, none of which is ever sparse in ideas or wasting of words.

This is McKeon's project in outline, omitting most of the conceptual details of these essays, much as McKeon himself omitted all the partic-

TYPES AND FUNCTIONS

	Political Rhetoric future: expedient and inexpedient	Forensic Rhetoric past: just and unjust	Epidictic Rhetoric present: honorable and disgraceful	Dialectic
ARISTOTLE Commonplaces				
CICERO	Deliberative	Judicial	Demonstrative	Dialectic
MCKEON Universalized Contexts	Justification decision making choice and decision	Verification judgment definition and opposition	Demonstration exhibition inquiry and presentation	Discourse summation af all three rhetorics
Topics	means *and* ends	the accepted *and* acceptable	what is praised *and* praiseworthy	Common facts and hypotheses, problems and themes, assumptions and theses
Subject matters	planned actions, and predicted outcomes	*any* statement (proposition)	*all* subject matters	every possible subject

Figure 7.3   The Expansion of Types of Rhetoric and Dialectic

ulars of technology, scientific discovery, cultural values, and public policy to which he repeatedly drew generalized attention. I feel an air of optimism here, despite the extreme rigor, that the objectivity of so much of his earlier writing did not purvey. The essays on rhetoric are in a sense a correction of his political writings, which most often left the impression that if one could come face to face with an opponent—*any* opponent—and make clear enough semantic distinctions, harmony could be assured. Rhetoric, which now deals with every conceivable subject, would presumably reach every conceivable human being on this planet, and this would afford the basis for peace and understanding.

This presentation of McKeon's view of rhetoric requires, however, a reattachment of another discipline, of more strictly theoretical import, one that has been left behind in an earlier chapter.

Metaphysics Renewed

No simple documentation could show it, though the later writings suggest a gradual shift in McKeon's thinking from a firm belief in apodeicitic necessity to a willingness to accept probablistic results in the sciences and in philosophy. He was as aware of the need for pluralistic attitudes in reading all philosophers at the beginning of his career as he was at the end, but pluralism carries a twofold interpretation: that with so many ways to chose from, each statement with its accompanying context that offers its defense is a little more secure than its rivals; and that all properly formulated and defended statements are correct as they stand and that one can attain certainty wherever there is sound philosophizing of any sort. The second interpretation is generally associated with a firm attachment to metaphysics or logic, or both, while the first often has its base in psychology or theories of society, or both. One who comes to McKeon's writings for the first time and reads hastily would conclude that he eventually decided that certainty would best be secured by general agreement. But this would imply a homogenized world society, one that McKeon vigorously rejected.

His reading of the history of philosophy, that what seem to be contradictions are ordinarily not that at all when the texts are carefully read, implies that anyone can oppose Hobbes or Kant or Husserl and still be as correct as they are—provided that the opposition is as workmanlike as they. It is for reasons other than mere wrongness that a philosopher should be rejected, if he is to be rejected at all. But what is acceptance? It can be "Let us stick with the best that we have" or even "with the best

METAPHYSICS	KANT	McKEON
ACTUAL	metaphysics is not actual (in 1781)	metaphysics is actual today
IMPOSSIBLE	as speculative knowledge	as apodeictic science of connections
NECESSARY	in order to distinguish truth from illusion	to provide ordering principles
CONTINGENT	on completion of a critique of reason	on circumstantial developments of culture
POSSIBLE	to show how to extend the categories beyond experience	to show interacting communications and interrelated communities

Figure 7.4   Modalities of Metaphysics in Kant and McKeon

that we can hope ever to find." McKeon's optimism about the future of rhetoric and philosophy did not take rise from the linguistic philosophers of the twentieth century; they had not built a bridge adequate for passing from the turns of language to the nature of things. This may explain some minor triads to be heard in the midst of McKeon's tutti orchestral passages, and the crowning of rhetoric as a master art.

There is perhaps a better analogy drawn from musical literature than the shift from major to minor key. Richard Strauss's *Also Sprach Zarathustra,* regardless of its much overplayed opening bars, is brought to an equivocal conclusion that is in two harmonically unrelated keys— both major, incidentally—thus indicating that the bold, strident confidence of the first sunrise is at last answered by eternal doubt. Now is this really suited to McKeon's philosophy? When his hope for a greater rhetoric was well established and he had already completed several articles expressing this hope, he also published a paper, "The Future of Metaphysics."[50] Read in one way, it seems to presage a split in the thinking of the last twenty years of its author's life.

It opens with a stated contrast (pp. 292–93) between his own views regarding the solidity of metaphysics and those of Immanuel Kant; this may be put in the form of a table giving the modalities that McKeon draws from the *Critique of Pure Reason* and the *Prolegomena to Any Future Metaphysic* (see fig. 7.4). Kant listed three kinds of metaphysics that he deemed futile: skepticism, empiricism, and self-arrogating reason, all of which he criticized and rejected. He sought to replace them with his own, critical approach, which McKeon holds to be equally actual contingently but necessarily impossible.[51]

Philosophy has traditionally sought to model itself upon science, but the latter has now become "a greater variety of operations and formulations" and is in effect so like a technology relating laws to concrete operations that their relations are a topic of controversy (p. 294). The upshot is that metaphysics had best seek its principles independently of scientific findings and scientific method. But if it is not connected with science, then with what is it connected?

The truth is that McKeon effected a rapport between rhetoric and metaphysics that he probably did not take to be either a brief tempestuous liaison or a marriage of convenience. Instead, it was to be a permanent partnership, though never a merging to a point of identity. Its basis was the fact that a metaphysics of culture is possible, and this must be a perduring total reliance upon communication. Such a metaphysics must have its focus on the diversity of cultures, and because of this there could never be a separate metaphysics beyond the reach of political, economic, and artistic institutions and the changes they undergo.

I cannot take my reader through all the complexities of this brief essay, which, had explanations been offered in it, condensations expanded, and much-needed examples supplied, would have been four or five times longer. Suffice it to say that McKeon's four approaches, no longer directly drawn from the familiar Greek quartet of thinkers, now stem from Kant's three mistaken types, the skeptical, empirical, and idealistic (that generated the paralogisms, antimonies, and ideals of reason), and one that is left over, the circumstantial (pp. 291–96). The skeptical holds that nothing exists save existence and experience, the empirical that what happens and what is done acquire meaning from what underlies experience and existence, and the idealistic (which McKeon now calls the transcendental), that experience and existence gain intelligibility from what transcends experience. Obviously the last, to which McKeon gives credence, derives from the circumstances and problems encountered by man (p. 296).

In the future, metaphysics will continue to be pluralistic yet it will be singular by its relating of many approaches to the continuing inquiry that results from continuing communication. This, McKeon says, with a nod to Niels Bohr, is true even in physics, where an experiment is said to be a communication (p. 298). The new metaphysics is one that in effect transforms and universalizes the old method of deliberative rhetoric, taking it out of the confines of the legislative assembly and putting it to work on all manner of problems. It will not be limited to discussing means but will propose new ends. "The sequences of action and statements are not modeled to observed consequences of thoughts but are built from [linguistic] ratios, relations, proportions, rhythms, and analogies" (p. 307).

This, then, is the future of metaphysics, bound up as it is with the future of rhetoric. An unusual proposal, one might think, coming from a pluralist whose power of apprehending distinctions is so great. Common sense and rhetoric, he is suggesting, may lead both to metaphysics of rational faith about the nature of things, thoughts, linguistic usages, and actions, and to a metaphysics of scientific inquiry, though not copying so-called scientific methods. This has some basis in the dialectic of Plato, who took the opinions of ordinary men, and of others far from ordinary, and showed how, by turning them upside down and redressing them in the new meanings, those opinions could imply, at least, firm knowledge of the highest realities. One also recalls a sentence in McKeon's own brief but invaluable introduction to his selection from the *Oxford Commentary* of John Duns Scotus, the incredibly subtle master metaphysician: "It is not safe to state the project of his philosophy in any single form, but it might be ventured that he was concerned to discover the necessary truths in the philosophical discussions he encountered in the writings and debates of his times."[52]

There seemed to be no way to make sense of McKeon's later writings except to uproot this account of the late metaphysical teaching from its proper place in a chapter on that branch of philosophy. I believe that in earlier days he leaned toward a metaphysics of substance and essence using the self-reflexive principles that he espoused, whereas in the late publications it becomes a philosophy of changing opinions and circumstances, and metaphysics is therefore no longer secure, like mathematics, but takes on the character of moral science or one of the arts: disciplines that perforce alter even as one is formulating their principles.

For McKeon the apparent retreat from certainty by metaphysics and the apparent advance toward certainty by rhetoric suggest that they could indeed meet somewhere in the middle, not quite merging, and somehow pursuing the same course. In that case, one might have to concede that reference to the two-keyed ending of the enigmatic tone poem of Richard Strauss was less improbable than might at first be suspected.

8

Theses and Distortions

In expounding any philosopher it is risky to try a reduction to a small, manageable handful of theses, for the methodic connections between such theses are perforce lost, and an air of dogmatism overwhelms any flexibility that the original system might have conveyed. An author, moreover, tends to change in degree of complexity as he moves from earlier to later stages in his career—becoming simpler if he is a David Hume, more complicated if he is a Plato or Immanuel Kant. Indeed, the early essays and lectures by Richard McKeon are in some respects supplanted or at least corrected by and absorbed into the more inclusive statements appearing in his work later on. Such disadvantages to easy summary militate against successfully condensing a varied texture of ideas into a small number of flat propositions. On the other hand, Kant, Hegel, Schopenhauer, and even John Dewey have attempted such reductions of their own writings or have at least written textbook simplifications.[1] McKeon himself frequently required a pupil to compress salient elements and prominent methods of a treatise into a limited compass.

The emphasis in the twelve theses I am presenting will traverse a path across his principal teachings, as I see them, as they relate to the nature and history of philosophy. It is somewhat more applicable to his earlier and middle career than to the later period, though I do not believe that he repudiated outright any of the propositions late in life, however much the details of their application came to be altered when he took up again and again the myriad exasperating details of philosophy's history or the urgencies of the new world that he envisioned. His main effort was first to divide and then, having conquered in this way, to integrate what he had separated in a new way to make a fresh whole. This, more than any special topic, was the heart of his most important contribution, the fullest expression of his gifts, and although he worked tirelessly on educational administration and reform, the dissemination of knowledge, and the accommodations between different cultures, as well as the theoretic foundations of world peace, these others depended for their formulation and their stimulus upon his conception of philosophy itself. I have said that McKeon was a practical man; his solutions were not simply laments ("If only men could act reasonably. . . ." "If there were a more equable distribution of wealth. . . .") or expressions of cynicism ("If all the earthworms were destroyed, life on land would virtually cease; if, as is more likely, mankind were destroyed, this would benefit all other species, land and sea"), or outlandish demands ("The old make the wars; let them go out and do the fighting").

Each of the dozen theses to follow has a precedent in McKeon's writings or the oral teachings. They seem so representative of his thinking that to remove or modify any of them would adversely affect his provocative system of ideas. But despite the fact that McKeon repeated the contentions of these twelve (and other) theses many times, there have been dishearteningly many misrepresentations of each of them, both by his antagonists and by some of his would-be defenders—nearly always those who had had only the one-drachma course, not the fifty-drachma course.[2] If my own condensations are a little misleading, certainly the misrepresentations I offer to accompany them are more so.

It has been said that we have three kinds of contemporary architecture with us, the modern, the modernistic, and the modernesque. So I shall distinguish between the McKeonian constructions of his thought, which are as close as possible to the original, and the McKeonistic, and the McKeonesque.[3] The McKeonistic doctrines seem fairly consistent with each other in small selected groups, though taken all together they collide. In addition, they are only clumsily applicable to the history of philosophy, being too literal and restricted, too rigid. But the McKeonesque revisions meet with difficulties at every turn, for they err by widening the original terms to extreme limits. It is these distorting versions, too taut or too flaccid, that are often set up by opponents of McKeon as objects of refutation or polite scorn. Students taking McKeon's courses for the first time or individuals hearing his addresses or comments at professional meetings have been the unintentional originators. Some of the distortions are not mistakes but merely hypothetical questions raised in fairly well-informed discussions. It is impossible at this remove to document them all. McKeon himself said to me that the two dozen errors were virtually those that he had "run into many times."[4]

Thesis I: It is unnecessary to disentangle oneself from the history of philosophy, for both the statements of one's predecessors and one's own share in its general forms of statement and accumulated vocabulary discourage any radical separation of the two. This is not, of course, because of any simple identity between McKeon's methods and any one of the traditional philosophies or any obvious conflation of them all, though one expects that many terms and some doctrines are borrowed from the past but altered vigorously to conform to new conceptions. Nor is it, to be precise, any infusion of McKeon's doctrine by some "spirit of history." Instead, this relation is like that between participants in a running conversation—two, three, four, or a host of participants with McKeon himself occupying an advantageous position and having the dominant word; it is he who speaks last and who can therefore summarize and transmute without being summarized and transmuted. Every philosopher is of course beholden to his predecessors; and certainly McKeon's studies of Aristotle, Aquinas, Spinoza, and the others would encourage us to think they bear much the same relations to their forebears as McKeon does to his.

The *McKeonistic version* of thesis I contains a hardened notion of *sameness,* making the word literal; thus it assumes that the whole of McKeon's doctrine is identical with what can be picked up, piece by piece, from the work of predecessors. The *McKeonesque* is a still poorer rendering of the original, which contends that all new philosophy is entirely assimilated to past systems and that no fresh combination can be made. This latter version stretches "history" so that it is metaphorical and includes not only what has been said earlier in time but what is implied by or dialectically related to what has been said.

Thesis II: Because the good selected existing systems are roughly equivalent in their self-consistency, we can, when planning to adopt one, choose between them on the basis of our own needs. The *McKeonistic version* is that the adoption of a system is idiosyncratically motivated—a version that takes rise from a sharp, fixed-for-all-time separation between the knower and the knowable. The *McKeonesque version,* stemming from the turning of McKeon's own tight analogies into loose metaphors with the broadest of meanings, is that all philosophic discourse is simply a reflex of psychological impulses at bottom unrelated to rationality or the nature of things.

Thesis III: Philosophy is connected to, enriches, and is enriched by no one other discipline but all others.[5] A first point is a general reflection on the history of philosophy, that the best system builders did not try to write all their disciplines in terms of one discipline, say mathematics or biology or politics, but either they refrained from such analogies or else they varied them so carefully that the system does not suffer from the imprint of any one image of an intellectual process. A second point is perhaps as important: the reader coming to McKeon and the matrices with a grasp of the algebra of determinants might evince undue temptation to read those matrices and with them philosophy in terms of his specialty, producing a tidy set of likenesses between metaphysics and his expert knowledge but forcing the metaphysics to lean in one direction and with it all other disciplines that use the principles justified by metaphysics. A third conviction is linked to a dramatic difference between McKeon himself and those who merely profess to adhere to his teaching. I have heard it said of a certain master's essay that it was "pure McKeon." The remark was intended as praise. But the real purity lies not in the holding of some doctrine, no matter how "correct," but in the totality of the enterprise; and to try to run through the bare schemata without at least serious consideration of McKeon's own incredible historical and philological learning is to risk falling into formalism and dogmatism. This holds for the knowledge of allied arts and sciences; one cannot be unequipped in the history of mathematics, physics, law, and the humanities and still travel McKeon's same path, even if but a short way.

The *McKeonistic version* of thesis III supposes that any dividing line between philosophy and other disciplines, in order to be meaningful, would be quite fixed; and this being in disaccord with what McKeon used to say, the version decries any such demarcation as being meaningless. The *McKeonesque version* is that philosophy disappears into the other disciplines, and as a corollary, what is left of a distinguishable philosophy is McKeon's own enterprise, a kind of metaphilosophy stubbornly resisting assimilation to the arts and sciences both of languages and of things.[6]

Thesis IV: Psychological and social reasons are the last resort in trying to account for apparent inconsistencies—or consistencies—in a philosopher's work.[7] So much of twentieth-century Platonic scholarship, for instance, has been devoted to explaining the apparent shifts in doctrine in the dialogues as the results of elementary changes of mind or mere reflexes of historical episodes or trends that it is refreshing to find in McKeon one who reads the dialogues as really significant precisely because they possess dialectical shifts of meaning justified at every juncture by reference to a total pattern of terms. Doubtless Plato did possess quirks, perhaps a flock of them, and doubtless he was acutely conscious of what was said and transacted in Athens and other cities. But McKeon has resolutely avoided appealing to idiosyncrasies as substitutes for the hard thinking required to make out the simple compendencies of the dialogues. This fourth thesis should not be confused with the first, which admits that McKeon's own philosophy is embedded in its history or with the third, that philosophy has affinities with all other disciplines. Thesis IV moves to its relations with matters of action, belief, and institutional arrangement.

Distorted in a *McKeonistic rendering,* the same thesis would read: We must study philosophy so as to find consistencies regardless of all sociological and psychological explanations. This of course turns the interpreter into a special pleader who must justify every alleged dialectical connection regardless of its tenuousness. Worse still is the *McKeonesque version,* that all circumstances and attitudes are irrelevant for the interpretation of what philosophy is in general—a statement directly contradictory to many of McKeon's own published views.

Thesis V: We must look not to willful misinterpretations but to patterns of terms to explain varied readings of earlier philosophers by later ones, but some new patterns of terms are far better than others for laying against the old.[8] Superficially, it would appear strange that McKeon should press for very precise interpretations of texts, requiring that methods as well as concepts be repeatedly brought into focus, and at the same time be lenient toward other interpreters who have patently neither employed his means nor reached anything like comparable conclusions. But the rigorous application of his criteria for deciphering a philosophic system is not essentially different from its application to someone else's interpretation. (One finds a method, principles, and the rest in each.) It is not leniency but a recognition that the errors and successes of each reader are the consequence of deploying his terms. There are perhaps infinitely many interpretations of Plato, and a few of these are illuminating and important, even if they do not fully recover the one very large set of meanings that Plato evidently intended and might be elicited from the stringent use of McKeon's own exegetic procedures.

This idea entailed a divided set of attitudes in McKeon's published remarks and his private asides, for he felt that each commentator and historian had a right to his own schemata for explaining original texts, but even so, their errors resulted from their having taken insufficient pains to visualize the structures of those texts.

In saying that he wished to represent every system with minimal distortion, McKeon created a difficulty, for it involved presenting every one in a favorable light, if at all possible, thus making it necessary to find a neutral ground on which to spread the contrasting doctrines. This implied disruptions in the order of presenting at least one of the original philosophers—an order that McKeon said was highly significant for the understanding of their works.

Even the most neutral terms used for interpreting the thought of others are still terms, and these must be chosen with extreme care. Wherever possible, McKeon chose them from the constructions in which they appeared in the original writings; obviously, to use the term "judgment" in explicating Ockham's propositional logic would be unfair. Such terms as "realism" are not ordinarily embedded in the substance of a man's system, and McKeon dismissed them as shibboleths unless the debate happened to be on "realism" and *its* meanings. The terms, in other words, should refer to the most fundamental aspects of the system under scrutiny, the terms used to raise and solve its chief problems. "Tender-minded" and "tough-minded," for instance, are characterizations that necessarily lie outside the systems of philosophy to which James applies them.

The *McKeonistic version of thesis V* is that distortions of other philosophies are difficult to make because each interpreter has his own pattern, and tolerance is an obligation without exceptions. The *McKeonesque version* is, of course, more extreme, and would have it that whatever is said about other philosophers is true.

Thesis VI: A philosophy can best be studied when one relates it to others, but its statement should be reduced to a small number of generic headings under which individual variations can be subsumed. There can be alternatives to each of these topics in equal numbers. The result is either a square or an oblong array or a matrix in which every mode is labeled first generically with some terms serving as principle, then specifically, with suitable modifiers, and finally with the individual choices made by the given philosopher. McKeon started with a very few such philosophies, enabling him to show opposed pairs of terms or methods and then if necessary, to show the terms and applications of the methods leading their respective exponents into subordinate and usually self-consistent doctrines within a discipline or group of disciplines. He could accomplish this with groups of philosophers as well as with individuals.[9]

Some dilapidated rectangles must also be mentioned. The *Mc-Keonistic* quadrilateral is hard to distinguish from the original; the square or oblong is reduced to a simple classification, the rows and columns fixed so that each term has a limited set of connections. Alternative rectangles are not permitted for the same system being analysed, and so the same method must be used each time in progressing from one term to the next. A McKeonistic array tends to become oblong by opening the lower end so that the result is a couple or trio of lists that lose their systematic value together with their flexibility.

The *McKeonesque version* is less specific. Here, despite the apparent fixity of places, the terms are stretched in meaning so that each one of them can do service for every other one, thus for them all. The reasoning behind this is that if a category reflects truth, it should reflect all truth, and moreover any category related to it dialectically should reflect the same truth. In effect we have a matrix or array collapsing into one all-inclusive, deplorably vague term.

Thesis VII: The enterprise should obtrude no philosophic assumptions of priority or excellence to begin with, either for determining which single line of an array or matrix should be occupied or for determining precisely how a given line of nodes ought to be occupied, even though subsequent study will reveal successful and unsuccessful types of occupancy. The *McKeonistic version,* arising from literal identification of all philosophic history with positions on the matrix, holds that the more assumptions of one's own made about the history of philosophy, the more bias is bound to creep in. Evaluative judgments of philosophy disappear into an account of the historical succession of systems. The *McKeonesque variant,* which, by the way, I heard from a visiting scholar at Chicago, was that real philosophizing involves no assumptions of preference at any time.

Thesis VIII: We can introduce broader and broader contexts of inquiry and semantics, in which previous contexts (provided by previous small arrays) show up as subsections of the larger. This introduction is not owing to whim, and I doubt that even a Norman Kemp Smith or a Werner Jaeger could show definitively that McKeon changed his mind at any time on the basic approach, however much the details might have been altered.[10] With the larger arrays more prototypic philosophies can be winnowed out, but there are also more identifying marks for each system. Regardless of these technical points, however, the triple assertion is still true: that there is a small finite number of original and wholly self-consistent types of philosophy, that there can be no more, and further, that the great variety of systems flooding history owes itself to the mathematically possible permutations and combinations implicit in the arrays and in the matrices but also to the many ways that philosophers can occupy any given set of nodes, simply by varying the terms or inverting the order of postulation and deduction.

The *McKeonistic version* of the thesis requires that we exaggerate the notion of change, making it predominate rather than be balanced against stability: There is no fixed, let alone final, interpretation of a system. McKeon repeatedly inveighed against dogmatic interpretations of a text as well as against dogmatism in constructing original systems. Yet he insisted upon trying to find an interpretation that would give maximum clarity and compendency to the propositions using the working assumption, not an absolute rule, that the text is philosophically sound.[11] The *McKeonesque version* of this tolerance regarding shifting contexts is even more mistaken, and is, I think, the work of persons perhaps dangerous to themselves but probably not to society: The All is Everything.[12]

Thesis IX: There are cycles, so complex as to seem informal or even chaotic, in the history of thought; philosophers return eventually to the same linear sets of nodes on the matrix, and are opposed as before by thinkers using similar sets on different lines. What is changed is in the details of formulation. The clear apprehension of these details requires a nice sense of discrimination, for admittedly the mere employment of the common term "idea" by no means serves to put two employers of it onto the same node, nor did the first appearance of the word "existential" usher in the earliest existentialist philosophies.

The *McKeonistic version* makes too fixed the main lines of all systems: only in detail can a philosopher ever pose any problem or offer any new doctrine. The *McKeonesque travesty*, based upon stretching the notion of "return" to its limits, says that there is nothing really new under the sun. Clearly this would put a halt to all inquiry and curtail philosophic semantics itself.[13]

Thesis X: Philosophic questions are simple because they are common, but have simple, one-sided answers only in single contexts; yet one such context is never sufficient finally to solve a problem. This makes it possible to trace complex applications of what may be called synergic methods, each simple component of which sets up a separate context wherein a given proposition is made dialectically legitimate and hence true. Regardless of a philosopher's express advertising of his "synthetic" or "critical" or "empirical" method, inspection reveals that he uses more than one such type and varies the combinations.

The *McKeonistic construction:* No question has a simple, one-sided answer, for there is never a simple context in philosophy; plural contexts only confuse matters further. The *McKeonesque distortion:* We may say *yes* or we may say *no* to everything indifferently.[14]

Thesis XI: We must permit only the most precise interpretation of a given statement in its original context—the most precise, that is, justifiable by the particular devices that the philosopher furnishes to guide our interpretation.[15] Again I should emphasize the inherent difficulty in reading a philosopher, for not only are his means of assisting us to see his meaning different from those of his rivals, but also his expectations of the kind and firmness of truths are quite different from those of any other system.

The *McKeonistic variant* on this also requires that we seek the most literal meaning for each expression found in any system. The *McKeonesque version* is not so much a doctrine as a practice: a kind of Talmudic pilpul, with trifling distinctions that become the center of what should be philosophic analysis, with scarcely a sense of what is important to the whole and what is not.[16]

Thesis XII: Since major philosophers are roughly equivalent in the truths they expound, the worth of a philosopher depends not so much upon his choice of a series of nodes in a matrix as it does upon his capacity to make a new and strong case for the philosophy he has selected. There are thus good neo-Aristotelians and also tepid occupiers of his matrix line, and though their doctrines may have fairly close resemblances to the Master of Them That Know, there is a vast gulf between their relative merits. This does not contradict thesis VII, really, for the issue is that each thinker comes to another's texts with a different system of ideas and we must be tolerant of this fact and not of the way he has made his case.

The *McKeonistic version* errs in removing the distinction between the originality of a philosophy and the way it occupies the matrix and holds that any philosophy is good without further ado if it occupies an acceptable line. The matrix then becomes the sole principle of interpretation of a philosophy, as well as the sole ground of its composition. The *McKeonesque exaggeration* is to the effect that all philosophy is a vast tetralemma, or rather polylemma, of equivalent choices without regard to any fixing of distinctions or assertions or proofs, and without any need for locating the problems of existence. It becomes a game played with terms instead of counters or with Hilbert's mathematical symbols, all of which lack fundamental meaning.

A cursory glance at these twelve assertions (in any of their redactions) will show that we cannot learn from them alone whether being is prior to becoming, whether substance is really separable from property, whether truth is the whole or is in individual minds or propositions. Indeed, we learn no strictly metaphysical doctrine apart from the fact that any proposition cutting across the disciplines and referring to their possible truth or falsity—all twelve thesis do this—is a metaphysical statement, even if it seemed couched in logico-dialectical terms. True, an assertion identifying and describing the matrix as a whole cannot at the same time be a part of the matrix, although the parts of the statement are of course subjects for entries. It would also be a mistake to exclude this effort to grasp philosophies from the purview of philosophy itself. Nor need it be done, since there is nothing in the matrices that sets boundaries to the total number of philosophic propositions that can be framed. Even if the aim of McKeon's enterprise were to examine doctrines this would not, by reason of some ad hoc theory of types expressly invented for the occasion, make this a metadoctrine, a metaphilosophy. William of Ockham long ago asserted—as did many others—that logic deals not with things but with terms that are about things, yet this does not disintegrate logic into metamathematics, metabotany, metaethics, and meta-everything else. It remains simply another segment of the multiplex of disciplines in the sweep of human inquiry.

These twelve theses were, in McKeon's mind, to be adopted and applied together, but since they urged tolerance and breadth of approach upon the user, they could not be termed dogmatic except in the lone sense that one should be firm in their adoption. Failure to make use of them *would* result in a dogmatic approach. As for their wholeness, they resembled the notes C, D, E . . . as together constituting a major diatonic scale, although it is true that the notes, to make such a scale, would have to be sounded separately.

I have no way of knowing whether all twelve theses came into McKeon's mind at roughly the same time—perhaps something in the *Nachlass* would throw light on that question—or, as seems much more likely, they were conceived separately or in small groups.[17] An interesting puzzle, though not a philosophic one.

9

Concessions, Queries, Objections, Refutations

To undertake to disagree with Richard McKeon betokens what has been called in another connection stark insensibility or, more simply, foolhardiness. In life, McKeon was a formidable debater, not because of any asperity—although there were some exceptions to this—but because he knew the texts, knew the problems, knew how to frame a relentless logical sequence, and could argue endlessly for any opinion in his storehouse. Second, his papers were carefully written, and though their appearance as papers made his philosophy seem a trifle diffuse to new readers, at least they could form series of their own. Yet it is difficult to argue with these papers, for any new one was more than likely to fill older gaps, to forestall further misapprehensions, and generally to strengthen what the earlier essays had said. Third, McKeon's philosophy was in its very essence protean; it was not a system in any ordinary sense, for much of it was about the systems, where words, thoughts, things, and even actions meet and are put through their paces. Fourth, and perhaps not least, he has many second- and third-generation followers who will rise up to defend him. One who raises objections to him will doubtless soon be reminded of Peer Gynt's desperation when fighting the trolls: "The old one was bad but the young ones are worse."

The way from outright concessions in face of what another philosopher has said on some topic to full-scale refutations in which no tree is left standing is marked off by degrees of positive and negative response. Someone coming at a philosophy with a mere query is, personalities aside, a less threatening opponent than one giving voice to an objection. The query asks for a slightly different vocabulary or slightly different reason to clarify the original, while an objection contains, if only implicitly, a premise forming the basis for a conclusion contrary to the one reached by the original. Statements containing explicit premises capable

176

of establishing a proposition contradictory to the original doctrine form a refutation. (Dr. Johnson's kick, heard around the philosophic world, was at most an objection; he did not refute Berkeley.) Since both members of a pair of contraries may be false, this is less dangerous than a contradictory, which if established—and it is much easier to establish a partial rather than a total proposition—leaves no hope for the truth of the original.

In some of his late writings, McKeon used four related terms to separate aspects of cognition,[1] and I retain these to classify the twelve theses: numbers I and II have chiefly to do with the knowable, III through V deal with the knower, VI through IX take up knowledge, while X through XII are directed to what is known.

Negative arguments are of two sorts, exploratory and confirmatory. Neither kind lies far away. In the *Republic,* Book I, for example, the queries, objections, and refutations are exploratory (as they are in Book I of Bradley's *Appearance and Reality*), but these give way in later books, especially Book IX, after Socrates has shown the superiority of his peculiar plan for educational and social reform, to confirmatory refutations. Queries belong, of course, chiefly among exploratory examinations; without a stated, proven theory at one's disposal as reinforcement, one can easily ask questions but cannot without difficulty state opposed premises. The possible refutative power of querying is mainly evinced not in a single query but in a carefully planned succession that jointly can turn into an objection or even a refutation. In strict two-valued propositional logic there can be but two responses; one either accepts a proposition or one does not. But acceptance with modifications, provisional acceptance with a query or two regarding its meaning or application, is different from blanket acceptance without quibbling.

The Knowable

Thesis I says roughly that we are enmeshed in the history of philosophy, and that if that history were markedly different, then McKeon's matrices, being both general and neutral, would remain unchanged, or if the matrix were changed in detail, it would still be a matrix with the same intent. (This also holds for arrays, but in a different fashion.)

I. Query 1. Even if later philosophic statements do turn out to be chiefly recombinations, summaries, expansions, or analogizing paraphrases of earlier formulations—and this is not by any means universally true—still the history of philosophic literature grows ever richer, for any latecomer can now call up more topics upon which to cogitate. This is exemplified as well for those periods when the philosophic problems and possible systems into which their solutions can be organized have been sparser and contracted in scope. Must not the latest philosopher, despite the potential richness of the tradition, actually make use of the less available sources of his time since he remains its creature?

I. Query 2. The reader will have noticed long since that in addition to offering classifications of previous systems (whether two-, three-, or fourfold), McKeon furnishes a great deal of material, ordinarily appearing late in his essays, that contains his own solutions. It is almost as if the divided philosophies appearing in history constituted the problem, not that they had explicitly stated it. These solutions, which do not merely adopt some one of the horns of the polylemma earlier recounted, still use the key terms presented in them as ordering principles for the last pages. The result is a tie to the earlier without being a duplication, inasmuch as the new employment of the terms is analogical. Does this then split them between what history supplies and what McKeon upholds for himself, and does this splitting, if it exists, permit a unity within these writings?

I. Objection 1. There is reciprocity of agent and patient in philosophical interpretations. Throughout the centuries, whether engaged in broadening or narrowing their discipline, philosophers have accepted their predecessors as furnishing object-lessons in what to do or not to do.[2] Even when one is paraphrasing or otherwise expounding another man's work one becomes tinged with something new. Like the motley Russian speaking of Mr. Kurtz, he must say, "This man has enlarged my mind." In turn he tinges what he has been paraphrasing. In his twenties McKeon said that the retelling of a man's philosophy must express still another philosophy—even though this second philosophy might be both minimal and somewhat inchoate. But it is easy to see what happens when A's philosophy is retold by B who does his utmost to repudiate the system he is retelling. But supposing it is A's system that by anticipation, as it were, casts a most unfavorable light upon future retellings of one sort or another, including that by B? I fear that if this happened with McKeon's historical procedures it would be damaging to them. The effect would be exacerbated by the construction of an array that aids in justifying a number of philosophies, each of which would deplore in its own way this array and seek to undermine the procedure.

I. Objection 2. Nearly all the writings of McKeon's first period had to do with antiquity or the Middle Ages, and it was not until after World War II that the great majority of them took up difficulties to which the twentieth century was especially subject. One notices, furthermore, on reading the later essays, a far greater concern for the rapid changes taking place in our century—political revolutions, economic waverings, improvements in communications, the technology of the arts, and changes in values, to say nothing of the staggering scientific achievements of the past six or seven decades. Philosophy, even metaphysics, would have to change, said McKeon, to remain in tune with the cultural transformations going forward on every side. But this raises the question: How does one remain rooted with the four *Ursysteme* whose bases have not changed in two thousand years? Granted that McKeon's listing of these was augmented from two to three to four, and granted that his descriptions of even the first two, Plato's and Aristotle's, were more closely specified; granted also that the allowances for mixtures of methods and the rest were much more liberal partly because of the mathematics of permutations and combinations. This question could be put aside were the *Urphilosophen* used only for historical analysis, to trace lines of influence throughout the various epochs, but Mc-Keon used them also for the construction of solutions to problems to which he addressed himself, especially in political matters and theory of discourse. Different kinds of explications are intelligible, different phrasings of points relating to them reflect understandably different emphases, but there is still a theoretical question, Why is this quaternity so fixed in a changing world that in turn changes the limits of relevance of metaphysical science?

Thesis II says in effect that we are free to choose between systems, because of the equilibrium in their worth, according to our personal comfort with one of them.

II. Query 1. A *tu quoque* paradox (an old trick!) might well be interjected: What superior claim does McKeon's own self-consistent system of philosophy, that is, his theory of arrays and matrices containing the *Ursysteme* as its proper parts, possess such that he should choose it, and such that we ourselves should choose it above some other of equal value? Will we feel more comfortable with it, and, of course, is comfort the criterion for choice when so much is at stake?

Thesis II commences where thesis I leaves off: McKeon's own theory, so runs this modified version, is self-consistent in a sea of systems, and his special claim is one of extra completeness, not of unique validity and truth. In the latter respect, there is no hold upon its being a necessary improvement over the previous or contemporary systems. Indeed, if it is to live up to its own recommendation for pluralism, can his theory claim any radical superiority?

II. Query 2. There are great differences in the efforts McKeon made in expounding the four approaches to philosophy. In a sense, of course, in the papers specifically using the *Urphilosophen* all four are given equal space, as in "Philosophic Semantics and Philosophic Inquiry"; but outside of those papers, Aristotle has the commanding lead (see chapter 2, note 28). But then, why did McKeon do so much to vitalize the interpretation of Aristotle as self-consistent yet in the end treat him as but one of the four, a mere alternative? I ask this not because of a wish to see Aristotle somehow restored to a place of special power and distinction but because the philosophy, as McKeon has reconstructed it, appears to be such a flexible yet precise one, minute yet wide-ranging and above all based upon a theory of truth combining elements of correspondence, coherence, pragmatic utility, and subjective involvement, and thus no doubt preeminent by McKeon's own standards.

II. Query 3. McKeon's theory, if not really an improvement over others regarding comparative value and the possibility of accommodation between systems, then loses much of its uniqueness and with that its purpose, becoming an object chiefly of aesthetic interest. But philosophic convictions are not mere verbal obstacles, such as ambiguities, in the way of complete understanding. The dialectic of philosophy is not a diversion of old men, despite Plato's remark in *Laws* III (820c–d). Anyone disbelieving the practical effects of such convictions should go back to the lives of such sixteenth-century thinkers as Peter Ramus, Juan Luis Vives, Giordano Bruno, and Tommaso Campanella. The difficulty is that this side of philosophy, the pistic aspect (as McKeon so often termed it), and the strictly analytic cannot be separated yet are often at war one with another. Cannot logic lead thinkers into adopting positions that they will shortly feel obliged to adopt, even though to this point their own premises had not led them to consider, much less accept, such conclusions?

II. Query 4. The aim of pluralism is not to achieve monolithic identity but diversity with mutual tolerance; but the tolerance should not be one of indifference, since that usually implies serious potential subterranean disagreement. A closed system, so tightly constructed that accepting one part would require accepting every other, would also be against the spirit of McKeon's theory, for this would enforce a kind of total rather than partial agreement. Indeed, he was far more likely to discover distinctions where others had not bothered to look and thus detect disagreements where none had been suspected. Nor did he ever say that there were just four philosophies, or four types of philosophy, but instead that different principles, concepts, subject genera, and methods could be assorted so that the possible combinations would come to a far larger number, that even these delineated no more than general types, the particulars of a system being again multiplied.

The question is, then: What is the real difference between philosophies that have, so to speak, made peace by having the ambiguities lying between them resolved and a truly unitary system (such as Hegel's), of which the warring philosophies would become proper parts? Is not pluralism lost in either case?

II. Query 5. On the one hand, there is the pluralism required by the theory, which to put it briefly is that any good representative of one approach has done as well as any good representative of another, even though one or both may have adopted a mixed rather than a pure approach. On the other hand, to uphold this there must be a view that pluralism is a better doctrine than any other, and this is encouraged by the evenhandedness with which McKeon applied his prodigious learning to support the claim—an illustration more convincing than the flat statement and also more convincing than any attendant proof by logic that might be forthcoming. Does this mean, then, that since the theory refers chiefly to four approaches to philosophy, together with combinations of aspects of them, and says furthermore that the four are all we need to count and that no theory is above them, McKeon's theory must be given hospitality by all four, becoming one of the proper parts in each system?

II. Objection. McKeon used to say that a well-made system stands alone, answers the objections brought against it, and does not require to be translated into the terms of any other system in order to be justified. I would counter first, however, that any philosopher, no matter how able, seems to have left gaps or irrelevancies and superfluities when reviewed in terms of the system itself (so far as this is possible) or blatant mistakes in terms of any other system. That other system then presumes to "take care" of the first, but this time in the sense of impeding it through objections and perhaps defeating it through refutations. Thus the system formulated later in time (assuming reasonable parity in the talents of the respective authors) is at a distinct advantage, and the possible equality of worth is destroyed.

The Knower

Thesis III implies that we can know the arts and sciences as philosophers might know them, that is, as understanding the principles but lacking the talent or practical experience necessary to bring about proficiency in them. The philosopher would be able to establish a *logos* for the sciences and arts, but no practice, no making need take place.[3]

III. Query I. This thesis should extend, as it does, to the sciences closest to metaphysics—pure mathematics, astronomy, general physics, theoretical chemistry. Yet I do not concede that the arts are "knowable" in any primary and proper sense in this way.

If philosophizing primarily and most properly is the constructing or active understanding of a system, then this demands the making or understanding of metaphysics, together with all that it most brightly illuminates, including sciences such as those just named, and with what it lights less brightly because it contains a smaller proportion of the principles couched in terms that are the same as or immediately derived from the leading terms of metaphysical science.[4] Insofar, however, as the philosopher has an understanding of principles of all disciplines, even the most lowly, his knowledge of metaphysics will enable him to state any intelligently formulated questions or propositions—questions, chiefly—pertaining to the sciences and arts, their methods, aims, and relations to generic subject matters.

This does work the other way, though, so that a grasp of the arts and sciences, including their details, invariably raises issues that the systematic philosopher should be glad to consider.[5] For certainly the philosopher who betrays little expert information in at least one of the sciences, who has a tin ear and might as well be colorblind for all his sensitivity to painting, architecture, or weaving, will be all the poorer, all the more remote, in forming a comprehensive system of ideas promoting clearer understanding. New developments need not change the problems of metaphysics—indeed they should not—but they do revive old questions. The cybernetic basis of computing machines revives such problems by reducing organic operations to separate units and kinds of motion in inorganic and organic bodies. Each is broken into discrete pathways and bits of information are routed along them. No argument by an engineer or neurologist, qua engineer or neurologist respectively, can prove one side or the other to be correct here, for this is solely a metaphysical dilemma to be met with principles, including definitions, not pulses in a wire or nerve. Obviously the facts are discovered by the special sciences, but the claims are adjudicated from a more general standpoint. This example is from the twentieth century, but the form of the problem became apparent when likenesses and differences between living and dead bones were first noticed.

The question, then, is whether or not a reciprocal relation exists between the sciences (and arts) and philosophy and not whether philosophy merely needs to be "enriched by all the sciences."

III. Query 2. Despite the close ties and mutual supports enjoyed by metaphysics and the special disciplines, a caution against the undue influence of any one science upon metaphysics should be registered. To view all being as evolutionary, for example, makes it unlikely for the stable essences of mathematical objects ever to be accounted for; to view all being as a creative act, similar to writing a poem, would hinder explanations both of stellar changes and of accidents befalling terrestrial bodies. Extending the same set of analogies over all the sciences, or all parts of the same science, would impoverish the distinctions such as McKeon worked to preserve.

The question is, How many and what sciences and arts should one know for the purposes mentioned? Many of the philosophers of past centuries had extraordinarily wide interests, some making important contributions to a number of sciences or arts other than the standard philosophical subject matters. Can, then, a philosopher survive without an adequate grasp of mathematics as was enjoyed by Plato, Aristotle, Descartes, Leibniz, Kant, Russell, Whitehead, and others? Yes, because the marks of philosophy were upon St. Augustine, St. Anselm, St. Thomas, Duns Scotus, Francis Bacon, Hobbes, Locke, Hume, Kierkegaard, Nietzsche, who either had little to say or made glaring mistakes in that science. If so, what about poetry? Clearly, again, Plato, Aristotle, Augustine, Hobbes, Schopenhauer, Nietzsche were thoroughly conversant, and some of them were skilled in writing it. But there is little evidence that Roger Bacon, William of Ockham, or most moderns had more than a passing interest in the art.

Thesis IV is pragmatic, like its immediate predecessor. McKeon did not altogether reject psychological and sociological reasons as fully intelligible aids in explaining the intricacies of philosophical formulations—he invoked a few, to take one instance, in his 1937 course on

Hobbes—but he thought of them as being a last resort, after all the more appropriate analytical means had been tested. Circumstances surrounding philosophic speculations must in some way enter into such speculations, but precisely how is not always determined by what is going forward in the outside world; the knower is in a degree independent of that world, and his philosophy is what he chooses to fashion, often in disregard of the way the world is. To this I partly concede, but not more.

IV. Objection I. There is no doubt that although textual analysis is from the reader's standpoint the first and best method of divining the intent and drift of any writing, external circumstances could easily dominate the author. Influences differ from case to case. One might suppose all ethico-political texts are written out of experience and conflicts between man and man, man and government, or between governments, and that less personal matters might be discussed in relative freedom from those circumstances. This generalization is a half-truth, for the aftermath of Plato's Syracusan failure, or the imprisonment of Boethius, the gruesome deprivation of Abailard, the cannonading of Hegel's Jena, and the imprisonment of Bertrand Russell—each of these had a very different effect upon the authorship of the books whose dates of composition tally with these circumstances.

A good philosopher seeks among other things to condense life experience, whether it be the events and trials he undergoes or what he merely conceives and imagines; he does not obliterate the experience altogether, for if he is at the moment writing a book on mathematical philosophy he can later turn his sufferings in prison to good account in his ethical and political writings.

Exactly what constitutes the personal differs too. The use of "I" by no means implies in every instance the inclusion of a living self, for this pronoun can be used for such a self or for a transcendental ego, or for Wittgenstein's "extensionless point" as well.[6] Again, individual cases must be decided. The only rule that seems to hold generally is that such a bloodless, perceptionless self could not be the one at the center of hard moral choices, nor could a coterie of such selves ever form a political faction or trade union local or gaggle of tourists. The pragmatic connections of the self to the world demand that such a self be full-bodied, bound to touch and interact with that world. I never saw any of McKeon's arrays attempting to deal with this distinction; if there are none this is, I think, a lacuna that might well have been filled.

IV. Objection 2. The solidity of the self bears upon solving philosophical differences, which are mainly generated not because of abstract calculations, as if this were an offshoot of the remote logic of the Polish School. All metaphysical propositions are, if not drawn directly out of personal natures, at least defended in accordance with a feeling of proprietorship that is well-nigh universal among thinking persons. It is unlikely that philosophers enunciate their doctrines, then wait patiently while these are slowly assimilated, argued, altered, reassimilated, or rejected. Presumably, certain kinds of philosophers, who happen not to be controversialists, approach this ideal as closely as any group of creative thinkers on earth, but these choice spirits, as Spinoza might call them, conduct their debates altogether differently from a fist-shaking Iranian on a Teheran street, a Chinese peasant whose land has been plundered, or a black prisoner held on dubious grounds on death row. The solid self includes emotional elements beyond the control of their faint powers of reason, but these are still persons who entertain propositions, defend them, cast them aside. Disagreements between persons such as these count, and they are no more games than are those of their intellectual superiors. It is unlikely, therefore, that seeking to resolve their differences by a dialectic of semantic adjustments will moderate, much less fully placate them. The three kinds of persons mentioned wield very little power, but highly charged emotion is not limited to individuals in such groups, and when men whose offices enable them to control others become aroused the repercussions for those others may increase to the point of total calamity.

IV. Objection 3. Verbal communication and actions frequently take quite different directions. Not only terrorists but politicians, lawyers, building contractors, and others see themselves as forced by circumstances to undergo conflicting emotions resulting in wide discrepancies between what they say and what they do. This compounds the frustrations of trying to resolve the differences between persons that underlie the political havocs of a distraught world.

Thesis V implies that McKeon aimed at a pattern giving rise to a minimum of distortion that was to be fitted to the philosophers of the past, thus forcing their texts as little as possible. Here I would offer a couple of demurrers.

V. Objection 1. When a new system if fitted into a classification, then either the headings of this classification are so broad that they bear little relation to the specificity of the topics to be placed in them, or else narrower headings must be interpreted analogically so that the fresh system will not be narrowed and distorted. If "building" and "painting" were to be placed successively on a node labeled "visual art object," this generic label is vague; and if the label be the narrower term "construction" then this epithet fits architecture in a way quite different from easel painting, where Naum Gabo, Picasso, and a few others developed a style termed Constructivism and executed works they called constructions. The word then fits painting only if it is a term much contracted, and this does not comport with its far broader signification in the building arts.

V. Objection 2. Some philosophies fit easily into a matrix, while others must fit more loosely, and only by either making the terms highly analogical or else by reconstructing weak sources (as in the records of the Milesians, Heraclitus, the Sophists, and more), in a way making them amenable to being placed on the matrix to suit one's purposes. In truth I have found it difficult to use the X matrix or its companions, for in changing the emphasis only slightly in reading a text, one almost invariably changes the selection of nodes. This is so even if we possess enough writings from a philosopher so that serious gaps do not remain in the texts. A good case can be made for most of the mappings on a matrix, but arguments almost as strong support many alternative mappings—not in all instances but in enough to warrant uneasiness. If this is so, the matrices are more educative as peirastic devices than as scientific certainties, for they encourage—require—the reader to look closely at every detail of a text in order to settle on a defensible selection of nodes.

V. Query. Are there not certain affiliations between items in separate columns of the semantic array, and in those of the array of inquiry too, that militate against (I do not say make altogether impossible) a perfectly free set of permutations? The broadest hint is, of course, the fact that the four *Ursysteme* are characterized by flat lines on the simplified array (see chapter 5). There are others where a mild repulsion tends to separate kinds of choices. Thus I think it next to unreasonable to expect a logistic Method and a verbal Selection that describes a reading of texts to be joined in a single philosophy, for I do not see how the derivation of complexes as theorems from simples could make much sense if the starting point were what is written in books. A slightly lesser stretching would follow attempts to use a problematic method with the same materials.

The Knowledge

As for *Thesis VI,* it says in effect that to rid itself of dogmatism any philosophy must permit alternatives carefully provided for by the methods adopted within the system itself; this is in order to avoid indecisiveness and require all acceptances and rejections of those alternatives to have their origin inside the system rather than arising adventitiously.

I would add that the matrices are accordingly useful, but up to a point: first, they make clearer differences in doctrine and in methodology, where the reader might be inclined to gloss over these; second, they make possible prediction of further differences consistent with the former set; third, where there are agreements (as when two lines cross at a node or occupy the same two end nodes), the matrices can ensure that this is not happenstance but is again a sign of consistency in each of the two systems.

VI. Query 1. On the other hand, do the matrices indicate the relative distance between two doctrines? For example, a proposition containing "part of painting considered as craftsmanship" and again, "steady attention given to the need for control over the medium" are closer together than either expression is to "Painting is the embodiment of geometric relations."

VI. Objection 1. The matrices, once they have shown differences between doctrines, go but a little way toward making any resolution between them. That little consists of clearing the air and showing that the differences really exist and are justifiable, but this merely leaves the doctrines "pinned and wriggling" on nearby nodes. What would resolution mean in terms of the matrix? Similar doctrines can only mean that two men occupy the same nodes, and this would imply that one of the two thinkers disagreeing would have to be wrenched from his position and moved to the other's node, for there is no such thing as pitching on the space between—this would be not compromise but total inarticulateness. I am not saying that the employment of matrices actually bars progress toward resolution of conflicts, but only that the help it offers cannot reach the end result so ardently desired.

VI. Objection 2. We return to the point that there are a small finite number of pure systems and these are of approximately equal value when seen whole, although each may excel a little here and there in its parts.[7] I believe, on the contrary, that alternatives outside that are not lifted out of their rightful historical contexts are perfectly permissible, but they are not of the same quality and rank. If, for example, a distinction between nature and art has been worked out carefully within one system that supplies definitions, properties, and applications all in good order and is supplemented by statements of what art and nature have in common, then I cannot believe that a doctrine that they are essentially and always identical ever will be as effective in dealing with whatever problems arise that are relevant to this distinction or identity.

VI. Objection 3. To the degree that philosophy allows alternatives from outside as if fully justified, it become self-cancelling. The problem would never arise were we to deny initially that all lines of the matrix are equal, or nearly equal, in value. Alternatives within an outside-generated argument are possible, but only if one allows differences in excellence between the diagonals of a matrix, with the best line necessarily the one positioning the methodology whereby the matrix is obtained and vindicated. If a matrix containing alternatives in equilibrium is but an alternative in some other classification whose terms are in a similar equilibrium, it is hard to see how any positive statement of truth or of the commitment to truth can be found.

But this raises a ticklish question in logic. For simplicity's sake I shall reduce the number of coequal doctrines on some topic to two instead of four. The logic most applicable here requires that the pair of doctrines be so arranged that they (*a*) speak alike in order to be thus grouped, (*b*) differ considerably in what they say and, even so, (*c*) apparently contradict each other, or (*d*) make really contrary statements, or (*e*) differ so markedly that there seems no common ground between them, and (*f*) they can ultimately be reconciled by first recognizing the real, not verbal differences, and then by finding a way to restate the doctrines to show a new, hitherto unrecognized harmony falling short of unity.

McKeon never denied the existence of truth in general and of determinate truth belonging to some given statement though it could not exhaust the truth. Consequently, the question arises whether there can really be truth in a proposition *p or q,* for when we open up such a chrysalis proposition to look inside, we find several interpretations possible. We can take *p* and *q* as discrepant propositions symbolizing respectively the Epicurean *The end of moral action is pleasure* and the Kantian *The end of moral action is performance of duty.* (I leave aside the historical question, whether each party did or did not add riders, so that the Epicureans ended by saying that the greatest pleasure lay in doing as one ought, or the Kantians that doing one's duty turned out to be fun after all; the italicized propositions must be considered here in isolation and as if bearing fixed meanings.) The propositions can be symbolized, when we look at the subjects and predicates inside *p* and *q*, as *A is b* and *A is c*, respectively. (F. H. Bradley, no lover of symbolic logic, analyzed relations between these two generalized propositions, and I follow his very simple representation.)[8] The question is, what is their real relation? Truth tables, again of the simplest sort, can be used in a first approximation to discover the answer, but they are limited to reducing all truth and all falsity to dead levels. If John is wearing a green coat, is there no difference between "John is wearing a blue coat" and "John never wears a coat"? Logistic tables would label both with the letter F, but surely this ignores an important distinction of degree.

(1) The desired relation might be read as a conjunction of implication and counterimplication, *p implies q and q implies p,* thereby making *p* and *q* equivalent in every way, as in "He was reading his usual newspaper or journal, as he called it frequently," and a fortiori the predicates *b* and *c*, or rather, the assertions that the propositions connecting them to A are equivalent. The truth-profile here is TFFT, assuming that the truth-possibilities of *p* are TTFF and of *q* TFTF. In one sense TFFT is weaker than an alternative, TTTF, for it requires more conditions to be met before it can be called true, while in another (and more popular) sense it is stronger, asserting a much closer connection: *p* and *q* stand or fall together, and the double proposition is a roundabout way of saying that pleasure and duty have not only the same status and inhere in their common substrate in the same way but they coexist, even if they are not identical in nature. But this in fact is debatable: if there is indeed any equivalence, this must be provided with an interpretation distinguishing kinds of ends, such as proximate and remote, or desired and necessitated, or perhaps humanly and divinely ordained.

(2) *If A is b then A is also c* (material implication, TFTT) can be rejected as a way of connecting the two propositions, for although it holds, it says nothing about what happens when one begins with *A is c,* as did the previous formulation, where one can start at either end. Nothing requires that we begin with the Epicureans.

(3) *A is b and A is c* (conjunction, TFFF) is more promising and fits McKeon's repeated assertions that both the Epicureans and the Kantians can be right and in fact are right. There is no hypothetical attitude of withholding assent here; the statement demands immediate acquies-

cence. The truth table will have to be discarded, however, for it is as applicable to *Justice is red and Justice is green,* and this hints of contrariety—and is nonsense as well. Actually the two propositions about moral action can be asserted together provided their predicates are not exact contraries; having been aired by diverging methods and thus related to other concepts not only different in precise meanings but in their natures as concepts as well, the two are rather like plums and turnips. This leads us to conclude that *b* and *c* are merely discrepant from each other, not contradictory or contrary, and as a double affirmation they can be asserted. To McKeon this would be no problem, but a solution. Or would it? Suppose the opposition were between *The end of man is performance of duty* and *The end of man is to win at handball.* The two could not be paired in a meaningful way.

(4) *A is b or else A is c* is the usual interpretation of disjunction offered by historians when confronted with a pair of propositions differing so widely in effect as the examples offered here. This relation is much favored by Bradley, and its truth-profile is FTTF. One can call it an amalgam of more than one proposition: *A is b or c* together with *A is not both b and c.* This can be dismissed as rendering McKeon's view if one takes it to mean that merely because Hume is right then Kant is wrong. If, however, one thinks of it in terms of what Hume or Kant believed, seeing it as a piece of history, then McKeon would have to countenance this interpretation of sharp opposition. One might call this a pre-McKeonian view of the raw materials of the texts. Disjunction is slightly less dogmatic than bare assertion, *A is b,* but the latter is so remote from any McKeonian reading of philosophic history that it need not be considered.

(5) *A is b or c, or both* (inclusive alternation, TTTF) has a much better chance, from a strictly formal standpoint, of being true than *A is b* or again *A is c.* This is undoubtedly the best of the interpretations of McKeon's thesis, for it does not require that the truth of any proposition be the reason for falsifying another of different import, nor does it insist, as does *A is b and c,* that both propositions are in fact true. That philosophers have made sense is a generalization of McKeon's, subject also to exceptions of obvious mistakes of fact or logic. Inclusion in effect removes any connection between *b* and *c,* except the minimal one that both cannot be false.

But the question is not simple. If McKeon was right in his contention regarding alternants, both of which are or can be true, then his being right depends not upon the truth of the constituents *A is b* and *A is c;* instead, *they* become dependent upon the truth of his overall thesis, which says not that they cannot be false but simply that they need not both be false and that one of them need not be false merely because the other is true.[9] The primary question then shifts to the truth of McKeon's contention, while the subsidiary one has to do with the actual moral aims of mankind. But it is even more complicated than that, for the debate over whether pleasure or duty is the proper end of choice must be regarded as resting also upon the premises with which the respective authors commenced their arguments. Otherwise—if no argument has been offered, or if one or both arguments were slipshod— then to say that they could both be true conclusions would remove McKeon from his seat as spectator, so to speak, assessing rival proofs, and would convert him into a chooser and even a proponent of one side or the other, or an inventor of a new solution. His role as adjudicator and peacemaker would then be gone, or, as he used to say, referring back to the thirteenth and fourteenth centuries, he would no longer be dealing with terms of second rather than of first intention.

VI. Objection 4. We have already considered the truth or falsity of each proposition in the pair; now we consider the factual situation, peculiar in that it is interpretable in two such different ways. This is no contest over whether the needle is not really sharp or the grass is wilted, but over something more nebulous yet describable in precise terms. The propositions containing "pleasure" and "performance of duty" are treatable as if they were contraries in the pre-matrix analysis, but they do not differ by reason of affirmation and negation. Hence they do not violate the principle of contradiction, and in that sense both can be true when placement on the matrix is accomplished. The factual situation, however, is different, for unless one can show that this is like the four blind men giving their varied reports of an elephant, which to them was an animal only as a substrate for the tusks, trunk, flank, and tail, it will seem odd that the end of man can be so diversely described. McKeon would have said, I think, that in important respects this situation does resemble the elephant; mankind is a substrate, and pleasure and duty have as little likeness to each other as do tusks and tail. After all, different methods were used at the outset to arrive at these differing conclusions, and this difference underlies the incommensurability of the two statements in their original setting. If the aim of philosophers seeking to grasp the Selection known as things is to grasp the unintelligible through the intelligible, and of philosophers looking to the nature of thought is to grasp the unconditioned through the conditioned (Kant said it was), that of McKeon was to render the incommensurable commensurable.

For my part, I am less certain of this approach to disparate doctrines purportedly dealing with a single topic. Though plainly human nature must undergird what is sought here, pleasure or duty must attach to *it* rather than be merely two entities attaching to different parts of man's nature; further, these two terms qualify only the end of mankind. The upshot is that the two statements are not on the same footing; they are not equally true and do not resemble the honest, essentially truthful reports of the blind men—bar, pipe, wall, and rope.

If, then, both pleasure and duty are true ends of moral action, one of these must be more definitively true, the other less so. It might be that McKeon would have acceded to this, adding that the reason they are on different levels, one subordinate to the other though not deducible from it, is again that they were arrived at by different methods, so that "the end of moral action" must change from one inquiry to the other accordingly. To which I would tentatively respond—although not *very* tentatively—that each philosopher had grasped a partial truth, and it was now an opportunity for a third to place the two answers in their proper order in an even fuller statement of a complex hierarchy, though not one patterned after a mechanically-derived Hegelian synthesis.

Thesis VII allows no assumptions of superiority to the prototypical systems with respect to each other.

VII. Objection 1. From the assumption of equivalence of value of the four *Ursystemen* two possibilities arise:

(1) that the assumption itself is superior to the individual systems that it is supposedly judging to be equal in value; thus it belies the letter of its own content; (2) the assumption is not superior to the individual systems; then it is but one of a possible pair: (*a*) the assumption is equal to the others in value; (*b*) the assumption is lower than the systems it judges. In case of either (*a*) or (*b*), the assumption is not strong enough to assure that it would hold of four disparate systems.

Some remarks on the content, not the nature, of the assumption are in order. For McKeon, the interchangeability of systems would lead to their horizontal disposition—all systems would be on much the same footing. This implies that the nature of things is so indeterminate that it could fit *any* method and consistent set of concepts. The real world then becomes not a shadow or a mere "basis"—Stephan Körner's word—but it loses any determinacy because it is now indifferently approachable in any consistent way.

The question is, how can it be possible for four quite different systems to be *equally* valuable, not only as exercises in consistency, breadth, and precision of statement but also in truth to the way things are? It is always possible for two men to be treating of things marginally different and thus not be in conflict, but if one philosopher says that matter is infinitely divisible and the other denies this, the possibility that meanings are univocal as entertained in common is at least conceivably a violation of the principle of contradiction.

In some respects, one's own philosophy is in a privileged position, for even though I know that my thinking is nebulous, inexact, and incurably incomplete, it still remains *my* thinking. Although the labors of Richard McKeon have gone a long way to elevating the study of systems to the level of operations of Aristotle's active intellect, which is always and everywhere the same,[10] nevertheless what is personal, without being idiosyncratic and possibly evanescent, will always thrust itself into philosophic deliberations. *I* have a new insight into being, or have rejected another one, and in much the same way *I* have a new friend or mourn an old one. This is implicit in human existence, and philosophy is incurably human, though not exclusively so.

In the comparison of systems we must begin—it cannot be helped—from the point of our own, if that is fairly well articulated, or from some minimal commitment of ours, a commitment to a simple distinction, whatever it may be. What is involved in comparing other systems F and G is always *some* philosophic idea of our own system, O, and we are immediately caught up in the contrasting of statements in a fashion more elaborate and more uneven than might at first be supposed.[11] The barest statement of someone else's position is itself a statement, and the only evidence needed that a philosopher F or G said something is in the texts. One should locate not only the individual statement but also the means whereby multiple statements are related by the method. To make a logical comparison between F and G, one must keep their terms neatly distinguished, then decide in a heuristic, provisional way upon the relative truth or falsity of the respective propositions, balancing their truth-degrees by referring to the common facts to which our own reference can now be made. It is then time to decide upon the epistemic validity of the statements as supported by arguments; this goes beyond formal logic in which the real truth-values need not be determined beforehand by investigation but are arbitrarily imposed upon the constituent propositions.

The final issue of comparison is not that of putting estimates of relative worth upon systems other than O, but of simply trying to set forth their tenets in a common language selected from one's own convictions. System O is still the basis for comparing F and G, since to expound G in terms of F would place G at an extreme disadvantage with respect to both F and O. Of course, the intrusion of O-terms can be just as risky, for one never finds terms sufficiently neutral that the formulations of both F and G can be translated into O without distortion of some kind. It is, however, a risk that cannot possibly be avoided.

Thesis VIII defends the expansion, not the contraction, of a matrix or an array used for interpretations, and justifying this expansion from within the array is permitted.

VIII. Objection 1. This makes my statement of relative superiority something adventitious with regard to the matrix, and the latter becomes further and further divorced from any assumption of uniqueness or definite advantage. I do not expect the matrix to deal with all questions whatever regarding systems, but I do think that one of the first obligations is to answer the question arising for all the sciences and arts, How true is it? regardless of whether or not the answers to this question must be stated in terms of some ideal that can only be approximated, not fully attained.

VIII. Objection 2. One wider context for many terms in McKeon's analysis is the extension of rhetoric (see chapter 7), turning it from its earlier confines into a kind of informal logic of discovery that permeates and serves all sciences and arts. An eminently practical art, rhetoric is open to practical questions about it, for the mere addition to the old lists of topics (commonplaces) does little more than suggest that rhetoric could in fact be used for numbers of new intellectual ventures. But by whom? How? Under what circumstances? Politicians, generals, researchers in medicine, physics, anthropology, and the rest, as well as the common man—would it be of importance to any of them that the limitations of discourse had been widened and with this the means for persuasion of a universal audience cutting across the cultural boundaries? I cannot see easily how the new directions for rhetoric would change any of its actual uses—politicians would still speak in time-honored ways of whatever enhanced their popularity, the general of whatever made his troops courageous, and so on. Although philosophers as long ago as

Plato and Aristotle, and doubtless Empedocles and Gorgias before them, spoke of rhetoric as a universal art, the fact that it is unattached to any scientific subject genus or method does not imply that it can reach out to huge audiences on every topic imaginable. No doubt in time virtually worldwide audiences will become a matter of technological routine, but they will still be addressed, I think, in ways limited by their understanding, by circumstances, and by the precise intentions of the speakers.

Thesis IX states that there are cycles in the history of philosophy, with the same espousals and oppositions returning many times.[12]

IX. Objection 1. So far as the cycles themselves are concerned, one can well ask what kinds of events are needed to confirm the existence of a cycle.

(*a*) If we find Plato in the ancient world, a genuine Platonist in the medieval, and another Platonist of the same stripe in the modern (perish the thought! for he would never be published in the journals, and editors would take his books to pieces even before the critics had had a chance at him), then this would not, in my view, constitute a cycle, but a fortuitous set of separate events.

(*b*) If there were a pair, say Plato and Aristotle, in the Greek world, and an analogous pair, say St. Bonaventura and St. Thomas in the medieval, and in the modern another pair, such as Goethe and Kant (as Spengler thought, juggling chronology a little meanwhile), this could only give testimony to a cycle in the dimmest way; much better, it would betoken that the far-reaching use of proportions by a philosopher tends to breed a relatively more literal-minded use of terms in the next generation of thinkers—assuming Aristotle, St. Thomas, and Kant to be more literal. But then, the use of analogies in St. Bonaventura and Goethe is at best only analogous to their use by Plato, and the differences in the manner of their thinking still outweigh their common use of the device. With this at hand as evidence, then, cycles could only be predicated in the vaguest way. Spengler would say, however, that these pairs were parts of cycles of vast historical sweep, involving all sorts of cultural structures and events and changes; but McKeon, despite his oft-reiterated insistence on "circumstances," rarely gave any but the slimmest concrete instances of the actual circumstances accompanying the cycles in philosophic thought.

(*c*) Instead of building sequences gradually I look to the only possibility holding much merit. To be a phase in a genuine cycle, there would have to be an entire school or other series of philosophers in each given period, and one would follow the other in a pattern set by the first to appear, and thereafter the sequence of the first would have to be repeated, or nearly so. One finds that this holds, but only to a sharply limited extent; for when we say that both the Alexandrians and the Renaissance writers were concerned mainly with formulations in language and were followed in this by modern symbolic logicians, we must at the same time admit that the three sets of pistic concerns were very differently arranged: preservation of the past, expansion of the future, and the construction of ideal, unambiguous systems of symbols.

The Known

Thesis X, that there are no simple answers except in limited and temporary contexts, finds no opposition from me.

Thesis XI concerns the degree of precision that we are empowered to discover in—or impute to—the terms of any system under scrutiny. This I concede, and would merely add some remarks. If its author works his way through genera and species, we must permit him his broad terms as well as his strict and very strict ones; and more than that, we must seek to discover his usages even when he gives explicit accounts of his plan for imposing his terms; for he may not be altogether correct in this description. If, on the other hand, he uses his language analogically, as does Hobbes most of the time, or Hegel, or indeed dozens of other excellent thinkers, then this must be taken into account.

A philosopher can employ several methods spread through several texts, and even within a single text this is also possible, though less likely. In Plato's *Timaeus,* a set of analogies suitable for the whole cosmos gives place to one suited to its least parts, their relatively unpredictable movements and combinations,[13] and this in turn is superseded by a method compounded to deal with parts and wholes (of the human body) at the same time.[14] Reading the *Timaeus,* then, without constant attention to these changes and their implications leads to mistakes such as Plato tried to guard against, but which flow freely from the pens of those accustomed to a linear treatment such as Euclid employed. Kant is one of the most generous philosophers in his informing the reader concerning the method he has selected and the method against which his choice is to be pitted. The approach is critical, overall, as opposed to both skeptical and dogmatic, but within that broad field it can be metaphysical or transcendental, and in either case the philosopher follows a dozen distinctions to narrow the part of the field under discussion, and with them the ways his terms are given their meanings. There are expositions and deductions, there is an analytic method and a synthetic, there are what might be called the leading statements and the ancillary *Anmerkungen,* all having different though related purposes and all setting up propositions having slightly different epistemic values. Kant wrote that he was never satisfied until he had turned an idea on its side and found all its possible connections; and surely this is quite as important for understanding him as are his remarks about the critical method and the Copernican Revolution. Because a method is, in effect, a pathway from concept to concept, it cannot exist without concepts; but neither can concepts be deployed without a method, which does not merely drop them as a pigeon would drop a pebble and then move on. Kant's method, like all others, gives each concept its character, sets its relations to other concepts, or finds that it can be used in a limited context and then discarded. Elaborate superordinations and subordinations are widely practiced, for Kant is not the only philosopher to use this device; and failure to notice leaves the reader mired in misconceptions and feelings of annoyance.

Thesis XII has to do with the expertness with which a philosopher upholds his position.

XII. Objection. Is the real issue the truth of philosophy as written, or is it the truth that it subsequently acquires in its positioning on an array or matrix? Is not a matrix itself neither verifiable nor unverifiable, except in the loose sense that appropriately consistent individual terms in the system can also be made appropriate (in another way) to the genera and species that identify the otherwise empty matrix nodes? Is not this double appropriateness, however, difficult to settle by any traditional tests for truth: correspondent, coherent, pragmatic, or subjective? The heart of my objection to McKeon's practice is that there must then be a test combining that for truth and also, but only incidentally, for uniqueness of worth, two independent criteria. The reason for this is that a system possessing truth is unique unless other systems possess true propositions in much the same number and rank of generality.

The upholding of the truth of a system is also twofold: by the constructive statements and by the refutations it puts forward against opposing systems. But the truths are established by the constructive proofs, which rest on its principles (carefully distinguished by McKeon; see chapter 7) and at the same time are solutions of the dilemmas of common discourse. If, upon closer inspection, it turns out that the original proposition and its supposed contrary proposition to be refuted are not in strict logical conflict, so much the better; both systems can be enriched by the partial absorption of the other's statements. I believe that in McKeon's view all refutations would ultimately be absorbed into the arrays or matrices, though not into a single system already roosting on four nodes. Refutation would no longer be an immediate logical issue, only a rhetorical one, a pistic one. It would arise out of an almost predictable response to each set of entries in matrix nodes other than one's own, and it would become not much more than a game. So any given philosopher cannot help but make a contribution, differing only in detail from others. The basic proviso would be that an Aristotle would compose objections to Heraclitus, say, in harmony with Aristotle's own system rather than with that of Democritus or Plato or Friedrich Nietzsche; the objections and refutations are part of the system, not mere brickbats flung at random.

In this way the array or matrix, while encouraging an equality among philosophies, would dissipate the energies of real debate because the issues are now no longer those of real correctness but only of expertness of statement and defense of the right to a special perch on the matrix. Would not adopting such a device, then, tend to devitalize philosophy? I mention this paradox, which is decidedly not borne out personally in view of McKeon's own enormous intellectual energy, which he threw so instintingly into the fray on behalf of his philosophical reform.

Conclusion

Early in this book I spoke of McKeon as comparable to Immanuel Kant in his intelligence and have tried to exhibit something of McKeon's sweep, sharpness of focus, his resourcefulness and profundity, though I am fully aware of differences in the very marrow of their philosophizing. He may have written down a system or a substantial portion of it, but meanwhile, before anything more is brought before the public, we may judge him on what he published and on the way it was published, as well as on his extraordinary classroom sessions. The essays reveal him not only as a peerless scholar but as one of the originators in the philosophy of discourse, not a rearguard doxographer. His scholarship was synergic, it implied a mastery of so many arts and subject matters that he could take a single proposition and test it in a multiplicity of contexts—its terms, its grammatical cohesiveness and relations with its neighbors, its place in various discursive sequences, its historical ante-

cedents and successors, the character of its literary medium, and ultimately its truth.

Even so, I have not suppressed doubts that came to my mind either
from early or from later contacts with the philosopher or his publications, and it seems justifiable now to set down more succinctly points
that have often troubled me about his way of doing philosophy. These
are general reservations, unattached to any particular theses of his.

Most of his writings fare much better after several readings. It is
hardly captious to say that I have often wished, as I know others have,
that McKeon would "come right out and say what he means." He always did, however; he was frank, he explained over and over what he
was trying to do, but he could not, or would not, be simple, even while
he was saying that he aimed at simplicity. He paid a great price for universality in his philosophic genera—his categories—and for subtlety in
his differentiation of their species. The subtlety involved devising a
structure in which distinctions did not rest upon headings of two, three,
or four columns under which were placed groups of concepts, nor did
he in his mature thought use branching charts whose subbranches were
always tied with their same superordinate terms; instead he used more
elaborate methods of cross-classification that allowed different combinations of terms to be more flexibly applied. But this is often wearying
when made to operate on topics where it seems not wrong but still not
urgently needed.[15]

If it could be taken for granted that the whole subject matter of philosophy is words and their relations, then whatever use is made of them
by whatever method would be permissible so long as the method remains consistent. If, however, words are simply vehicles for thoughts or
indicators of things and *their* relations, then texts would not be the
single best source for gaining an understanding. I remember chancing
on a book decades ago on labor relations, carrying the dedication: "For
the Education of R. P. McK." The recipient of this helpful inscription
was once asked how one would gain an understanding of violence, and
he replied that it would be necessary to read several different philosophic accounts of it. Mark Twain said, though, that anyone carrying a
cat by the tail would have sixty or seventy times more information
about that than anyone else. It is not that McKeon got so much of his
material from careful reading alone, for as I have insisted, he was also a
man of extensive practical experience. I believe it more probable that in
his objective reading about the cat he would feel neither its annoyed

fury nor much of the pain of the boy with the lacerated thigh and arm. The cat would be thinking of other and better ways to be carried, and the boy about the definition of pain and its possible opposites. McKeon had a passion for philosophizing, for justice and world harmony, and for much else; but the passion is hidden under the classic impersonality that apparently sets aside experience if it is private, thoughts if they are unique, feelings if they are strong.

Every philosopher feels, as he must, that he is writing a mere prologue to the work to come, but in addition to McKeon's excessive complexity and cerebral abstraction, I find cause for a third complaint: his writing simply suggests what should be done. It is perfectly legitimate for a philosopher—or anyone—to hope that others will follow and take up his labors; it is obligatory for him to recognize that he has not dealt with every aspect of his chosen topics, and that some of them have been left untouched altogether; it is insightful to recognize that there are weaknesses here and there in his conclusions, and that, given another lifetime, he could do better. Had he but world enough, and time, he would still do no more than sketch what should be written in full; but it appears to me that McKeon, especially in his later phases, became unusually programmatic. The nature of his philosophy turned into one of pointing out ambiguities not to be resolved now as test instances but that could be resolved in the future, if and when certain restatements and other devices were applied. The particular problems and their solutions were left till a later date and no doubt for other hands. This gives even more of an air of detachment to a man who a colleague once said was one of the very few philosophers he knew who could tie his own shoes.

Finally, I would like to have seen a proof, start to finish, that the four approaches that McKeon ultimately distinguished are equivalent in worth. He was perfectly clear in his own mind that this was true, but the writings to which I have had access show this equivalence only by juxtaposing the quartet of distinctive lines of thought; and my request in a class, in 1947 (when McKeon posited only three approaches) did not elicit what I thought would constitute such a proof. If no a priori argument can be furnished, would not some future philosopher, starting from the same general descriptions, be able to show some one of them to be in fact superior to the rest? And would it not have been wise for McKeon to have demonstrated in advance that this project could not succeed? I remember a student of McKeon's at Columbia who was identified as one "who doesn't recognize the holoscopic method," which at that time meant casting into oblivion most of the history of philosophy, leaving only the staunchest, strictest Aristotelians safe. There are bound to be those who would discard one or more of the four types and acknowledge one superior or at best a couple of superior approaches. Against these persons some concerted proof, not an assertion or exhibition in parallel columns would be desirable, indeed required.

In point of fact, two kinds of proof, not one, would be needed. The first would relate to things as they are, to show that on theoretic grounds reality is sufficiently amorphous—or else has so many interconnected structures—that four quite different types of description would fit it. Another kind of proof altogether would show that the desired ends of practical philosophy, such as massive cultural cooperation under the aegis of a strengthened United Nations, or even the cooperation of scientists and of philosophers only, would prosper more vigorously were it to foster and be fostered by the plural philosophies distinguished by McKeon. At first blush it would seem likely, for the inevitable reaction to a monolithic system has always been first minor schism and then downright opposition; a disagreeable situation at best, a deplorable one at the other extreme, first for the schismatics, then for officialdom. There can be no question that the four *Ursysteme* are mutually at odds with each other if one takes a single representative from their number and places it in a dominant, domineering position, letting the others pass as no more than heresies. But to give them equal status, and enforce but one exceptional doctrine, namely that each thinker should try mightily and persistently to seek accommodations with all the others no matter how diligently he pursued his own track, would relieve the feelings of opposition, the tensions, the controversies, quarrels, and acts of vengeance. But all this stands in need of a proof tighter than the present one.

A few words on McKeon's possible influence are in order, but they must be general, as it is still early, and the work of such elevated thought as his comes to the attention of a wider public rather slowly.

Without any doubt the most obvious point about his influence—or that of anyone advocating a pluralism resembling his, for that matter—lies in this, that a commitment to a pluralism is a kind of monistic devotion as much as to its original propounder it will be an individual discipleship. It cannot be otherwise, even though McKeon himself seemed reluctant to adopt any fashionable devices for securing a large following. On the other hand, it appears almost equally inescapable that to follow out a pluralistic doctrine to the letter would be far less likely to weld the neophyte to a single philosophy brooking no divisions, no latitude of beliefs, no choices among solutions to the prescribed problems; and with that, it might be less likely for him to engage in the professional struggles and partisan favoritisms that have marred so much of twentieth-century philosophic activity.

The question could arise, What if all the original texts interpreted by the analyst (be he historian, commentator, critic, or whatnot) were destroyed immediately upon completion of his manuscript? How much of his report could we trust upon the evidence of his own criteria, stated and unstated? For my part, I think McKeon's avowed pluralism would be very persuasive on the mere face of it, as a point of departure for the writing of detailed studies, far more so than the methods implicit in the history by Bertrand Russell, for instance, or in the histories written from a pragmatist's or phenomenologist's viewpoint, or certainly that of a logical positivist. (I am talking about premises, not mastery of details.) McKeon's preferences, of which he certainly had many, did not and could not blind him to the merits of the existing systems and kept his mind open to the virtues of possible systems to come.

McKeon's unremitting care to be accurate, by breaking up each argument into its component propositions, the propositions into their terms, and his relating at every stage the parts and the wholes, would, of course, be a second qualification, and moreover one carrying rhetorical conviction to the reader seeking an authority who could be trusted for both facts and interpretations. I remember a class discussion in which the students were to summarize the main speech of Thrasymachus in *Republic* I (343a–44c). Several of us gave as his main contentions his starting points; others, his conclusion. Disagreement was rife over the testy Sophist's harangue. McKeon then laid out all the propositions of the speech one by one, showing at each point if and where verbal shifts were occurring so that although there was a unity of sorts, the entire sequence was dialectically unsound. It was a lesson in joining every part together before trying to judge the speech in its entirety. It is on this, I think, that the most trustworthy histories are built.

Another thought experiment, as Einstein would call it, consists of wondering what effect McKeon's writings would have were every future philosopher required to read his essays on or applying pluralism. In a sense, accommodation, compromise, would govern the new writings produced by these younger persons. If, however, one reads McKeon's own works to the end in each case, he is found to have created a large number of ideas, which although they have the weight of historical erudition as a basis (much as a scientist has his laboratory experiments), they still deal with the circumstances, trends, and possibilities themselves in a variety of fields, some of which have been recounted in this book. It is perhaps a question of the rhetoric of exposition; had McKeon not begun so very many of his writings with references to past thinkers, he might be better known at present as an innovator in higher education, an apostle of diplomacy, a prophet of world government, a drill sergeant of philosophic and scientific methods, and more besides.

Throughout this book there have been indications that, as with most philosophers, certain divisions had to exist in McKeon's thinking, divisions arising from the nature of thought and life itself. Of these I mention three. A mathematician in love with his calculations must have other loves as well, a statistician cannot always practice with his formulas, a doctor his health regimens, and so on. I have tried to show that in addition to the coolness and impartiality in almost all McKeon's published work there was another side, related to the first yet sufficiently different that it bears noticing again, as perhaps having some effect upon his persona in print. McKeon was an enthusiast for certain sports, and quite proficient, though these facts would never be reflected in his essays. Or would they? The essays reveal a healthy nature, a balance of disposition, and a range of interests for which one must go far to find a duplicate. I have no way of knowing whether it was his study of Greek philosophy that instilled in him the aim of a strong constitution inhabited by a keen but massive intellect, yet it seems reasonable to suppose that such a study would at any rate encourage the cultivating of that classic ideal.

One would not suppose from the readings that McKeon disliked or even disapproved of many philosophers, but I have hinted that private communications often contained germs of the kinds of objections he leveled against Wilhelm Dilthey and, in the same published essay, against a contemporary and for a time a colleague, Eliseo Vivas.[16] One evening McKeon inveighed against a certain book on ethical values by a prominent British scholar as being "full of the God-damnedest distinctions," and once he spoke of a famous philosopher whose opinions he respected, and frequently referred to, as a "wordy bird." In a way, however, this strengthened his espousal of plural philosophies and their dispassionate analysis, much as the person with a tic must if he can develop an unusual degree of self-control. The pluralism must be made to work at all costs, because it is the last best hope. But a man's favorites and his Dr. Fells are still part of him.

I have been told by Zahava K. McKeon that at the time of his death her husband was working on some of the writings of F. J. E. Woodbridge, his former teacher, an imposing figure in the School of Graduate Studies at Columbia University. From reading some of those writings and from attending a course of his on the theory of nature, I have always taken Woodbridge for a much simpler, less versatile intellect than McKeon, but with much intuitive sense, one who looked directly at nature more readily than at ways to talk about it. Yet it is difficult to be sure that the particular doctrines of his former mentor were what commanded McKeon's attention again late in life, for they would have fitted neatly into one line of an array. Instead, it might have been his mentor's determined simplicity.

Tradition has it that toward the end of his life Aristotle turned more and more to the study of myths, certainly at opposite ends from the intricate, mainly literal, highly differentiated treatises that he had formerly penned. Another tradition has St. Thomas, in his last months, putting all his failing energies into the composing of hymns. Kant, for his part, kept elaborating right to the end. It would be merely speculative to suppose that McKeon was coming to a point where his seemingly unquenchable thirst for diversification and nuance had finally been slaked, and instead of the endless loving search for the utmost in comprehensiveness he had turned this love to the unity of some one sheer, plain nature, of which it could be said that to be at all is to be intelligible. The fact is, however, that this was not his motive; Richard McKeon loved wholeness more, and in the late weeks of his long and greatly productive life he did not cease to look for a more diversified totality.

Notes

Chapter 1. Reminiscences of the Years 1932–49

1. Based as it is almost entirely on my own recollections, this chapter is no biography, and I have had recourse only to an old *Who's Who in America* to check one or two dates and professional titles. I shall not be describing Mc-Keon's work as administrator or consultant on foreign affairs in any detail, for I would have to call upon hearsay and speculation.

2. The philosopher's full name was Richard Peter McKeon, but he regularly dropped the middle name in his publications and, I believe, in programs of meetings and similar professional functions. Occasionally he included his middle initial.

3. Publication facts of many writings of McKeon are in notes to subsequent chapters, especially those for chapter 2.

4. In connection with Kant, McKeon made a remark significant later on when he said, rather offhandedly: "Do not worry at first whether space and time are really subjective forms in the mind, but worry instead about what Kant *means* when he says they are." This remained a key to much of McKeon's own thinking, and twenty years later he included similar admonitions in his published work, for example in "Imitation and Poetry," in *Thought, Action, and Passion* (Chicago: University of Chicago Press, 1954), pp. 216–17.

5. The teaching might indifferently be titled forced thinking or depth reading. To give an example: if Aristotle had a string of, say, five arguments, what is the principle of order behind them all? Is it an application of the four causes? How, then, is one to account for the fifth argument—does it reuse one of the four? If not, and if the fitting of the other four was rather strained, then what is the foundation, rendered in purely Aristotelian terms? Parts versus wholes? Substances versus accidents? Kinds of motion? These lay at the heart of Aristotle's procedure—if indeed he had a procedure and was not simply tacking together some dusty lecture notes, as some maintain.

Before World War II it was the fashion for students at Chicago to imitate these exegetical sessions. Groups of students would rent an apartment or house near the campus and then conduct "colloquia" or whatever to discuss, with a leader, the salient features of some text. They could not duplicate McKeon's orderliness. I was an invited guest in the audience at one such session on St. Augustine's *Concerning the Teacher,* presided over by someone who happened to be a staff official of the university. I forget his name; perhaps it is just as well. His "method" consisted of random questioning and incessant badgering, with scarcely an inkling of the well-composed discourse on language and instruction constituting Augustine's text. In chapter 8 I shall explain and illustrate the coinage, "McKeonesque."

6. At an American Philosophical Association meeting some years—I will not say exactly how many—after I left Chicago, McKeon told me, rather mournfully, that philosophy students' docility was greater then than formerly, when he could expect some sharp questioning, indeed a good fight. Now, he said, the students, though hardworking and intelligent, were less inclined to disagree. McKeon was a complex man, and I had no clear picture of him as one who courted controversy. Certainly he preferred the clash of ideas to the clash of persons.

7. McKeon once told a friend of mine, a very trustworthy man indeed, that shortly before World War II he had written a mystery novel. I have not followed this lead any further.

Chapter 2. Conspectus

1. In this chapter my chief purpose is to trace some of the external features of McKeon's writings without losing the main lines in a morass of detail. A helpful listing of the books and nearly all articles is in *Richard McKeon: A Bibliography of His Published Works* (Chicago: University of Chicago Press, 1980). This unsigned leaflet was presented to McKeon on the occasion of his eightieth birthday. He himself kept a year-by-year mimeographed list that included references to all his reviews in addition to the articles and books; the reviews were not included in the other booklet. Up to 1966 (the last year included in my copy of his mimeographed list), McKeon had published ninety-three reviews of books written in Latin, French, German, Italian, and English. Both lists have been of inestimable help. A listing with some additions and corrections has been published in *The Journal of the History of Ideas,* vol. 47 (1986), pp. 654–62.

About the reviews I say little, partly because a fair judgment of them requires that one read the many books under review, partly because I spent a number of years in climes where the journals were not readily available. Paul Goodman once said that McKeon's reviewing of these books simply *showed* that he "had the situation well in hand."

2. New York: Noonday, 1952. This small book has been reprinted, together with several essays by McKeon, by the University of Chicago Press under the editorship of Zahava K. McKeon in 1989. I give page references to this edition of all its contents as well as to the original paginations. *Freedom and History, and Other Essays* will be signaled hereafter as *FHOE.*

3. Most books and papers merely mentioned in this chapter will be treated at greater length in subsequent chapters.

4. *The Philosophy of Spinoza: The Unity of His Thought* (New York: Longmans, Green, 1928).

5. *Selections from Medieval Philosophers,* 2 vols. (New York: Scribner, 1929, 1930).

6. See note 28, this chapter.

7. *Sic et Non: A Critical Edition* (Chicago: University of Chicago Press, 1976–77).

8. *The Edicts of Asoka* (Chicago: University of Chicago Press, 1959).

9. Chicago: University of Chicago Press, 1954.

10. It is as shortsighted to call most of these works essays as it is to call *Tonio Kröger, Death in Venice,* and *Mario and the Magician* short stories, for these novellas all possess in concentrated form the range and depth of ideas one would expect to find in novels of considerable length. I use the word "essay" in default of a better term. Several pieces to which I am alluding are sixty or more pages in length, but "monograph" does not fit because it refers to an independent publication. "Memoir" in the sense of an extended account of research might do, except that in the scholarly sense it ordinarily refers to research in the mathematical and physical sciences. "Disquisition" might be used, providing it not be taken in the slighting sense that it has attracted to itself. Many of McKeon's papers, moreover, are slender, and it is only the larger efforts that should be called by this name.

11. Again, see the listing in note 28 of this chapter. The longer articles take up either a science or some important topic cutting across the sciences.

12. In *Proceedings and Addresses of the American Philosophical Association* vol. 25 (1951–52), pp. 18–41.

13. "Moses Maimonides, the Philosopher," in *Essays on Maimonides: An Octocentennial Volume* (New York: Columbia University Press, 1941), pp. 2–8.

14. "Thomas Aquinas' Doctrine of Knowledge and Its Historical Setting," *Speculum: A Journal of Mediaeval Studies,* vol. 3 (1928), pp. 425–44.

15. "The Relation of Logic to Metaphysics in the Philosophy of Duns Scotus," *The Monist,* vol. 49 (1965), pp. 519–50.

16. "Introduction to the Philosophy of Cicero," in *Brutus, On the Nature of the Gods, On Divination, On Duties,* Hubert M. Poteat, trans. (Chicago: University of Chicago Press, 1950), pp. 1–65.

17. In *Thought, Action, and Passion* (Chicago: University of Chicago Press, 1954).

18. In *Modern* (sic) *Philology,* vol. 34 (1936), pp. 1–35.

19. "Renaissance and Method in Philosophy," in *Studies in the History of Ideas,* vol. 3, edited by the Department of Philosophy of Columbia University (New York: Columbia University Press, 1935), pp. 37–114.

20. In his "Criticism and the Liberal Arts: The Chicago School of Criticism," in *Profession 82* (New York: Modern Language Association of America, 1982), pp. 1–18, McKeon, looking back upon at this essay on imitation (see note 18) nearly fifty years later, held that he had really differentiated four types of poetic theory: the Platonic, the Aristotelian, the Democritean, and the Sophistic. But this was long after he had given up his attempt to reduce the history of philos-

ophy to the interplay of Platonic and Aristotelian tendencies alone and had settled on the four root traditions just named and *their* interplays. See chapter 4 for more on the difficulties encountered when philosophies are classified.

21. Throughout, McKeon analyzed histories of various kinds, and a sample of his classification is a segment from a longer account in his "Democracy, Scientific Method, and Action," in *Ethics,* vol. 55 (1945), pp. 235–86: "The materials of universal history [seeking to bring history to some unity] were organized in two ways: according to lines of development and according to successive kinds of rule. The historians of Rome—Polybius, Diodorus Siculus, Florus, Appian, Justin—traced the long series of events which culminated in imperial Rome; the Alexandrian scholars developed a scheme of periodizing history, which was given canonical statement by Claudius Ptolemy, according to the four monarchies of the world: the monarchies of the Assyrians and Babylonians, the Medes and the Persians, the Macedonians and the Diadochi, and finally, the Romans. The one tended to a progressive, the other to a cyclical, theory of history, and when they were fitted to Christian documents, both created problems for Christian doctrine, which persisted in the Renaissance and modern theories of history. Following earlier suggestions in Hippolytus, Origen, and Eusebius, Jerome found authority in the Book of Daniel to repeat the sequence of the four monarchies and to continue it in the Incarnation, the Last Judgment, and the Kingdom of God, thereby bequeathing to the Middle Ages a problem concerning the parallelism of the coming end of the last and current monarchy with the unhappy fates of the preceding monarchies, which was still serious when Sleidan filled in the medieval extension of the history in his *De quatuor summis imperiis.* Eusebius, Jerome, and Augustine similarly divided the history of the world into six ages" (p. 276).

22. In *Modern Philology,* vol. 41 (1943), pp. 65–87, and (1944), pp. 129–71.

23. *Ethics,* vol. 65 (1954), pp. 1–33.

24. *Journal of Philosophy,* vol. 48 (1951), pp. 653–82.

25. *Review of Metaphysics,* vol. 13 (1960), pp. 539–54.

26. Autobiographical statements in print by McKeon are neither plentiful nor personal. There are some comments, however, in "A Philosopher Meditates on Discovery," in *Moments of Personal Discovery,* R. M. MacIver, ed. (New York: The Institute for Religious and Social Studies, 1952; distributed by Harper and Brothers), pp. 105–32. A broader, slightly more consistently personal account, but still limited to intellectual pursuits, is an untitled chapter in *Thirteen Americans: Their Spiritual Autobiographies,* Louis Finkelstein, ed. (New York: The Institute for Religious and Social Studies, 1953; distributed by Harper and Brothers), pp. 77–114. A third piece that might by extension be called autobiographical is in *Philosophers on Their Own Work,* André Mercier and Maja Svilar, eds. (Bern and Frankfort am Main: Herbert Lang, 1975), pp. 99–112. The article is preceded by a list of posts held by McKeon and honors he received and followed by a long but still incomplete bibliography of his publications.

27. In chapter 8 I shall present a more systematic outlay of kinds of misrepresentations, actual and projected.

28. The fullest and most erudite is a remarkable series of articles appearing in learned journals, to some degree summarized in a one-hundred-page mimeographed account of Aristotle's philosophy at large that was circulated, almost surreptitiously for a time, on the University of Chicago campus. A shorter version of the latter served as the introduction to the anthology edited by McKeon from the Oxford eleven-volume translation; this appeared as *The Basic Works of Aristotle* (New York: Random House, 1941, and reprintings). Briefer introductions to smaller portions of the texts were printed in *Introduction to Aristotle* (New York: Modern Library, 1947; rev. ed., Chicago: University of Chicago Press, 1973).

I cannot find space to summarize the longer articles in this book. Aristotle emerges from them as a serious, coherent, consistent thinker of great power and originality moved by two unlike but compatible tendencies: to differentiate problems in relation to the varied subject matters he encounters, seeking to view them in their own terms; and to make full and appropriate use of general truths in regard to being, discovered and defended in the work commonly known as the *Metaphysics*. These truths relate to the four causes and the distinction between principles, causes, and elements in any science; the principles of contradiction and excluded middle; the various meanings of unity and plurality and of potentiality and actuality; the nature of being as substance and of substance as form, matter, and their compound; the four categories of motion.

The four articles devoted wholly to the Stagyrite are "Aristotle's Conception of Moral and Political Philosophy," *Ethics,* vol. 51 (1941), pp. 253–90; "Aristotle's Conception of Language and the Arts of Language," *Classical Philology,* vol. 41 (1946), pp. 193–206, and (1947), pp. 21–50, an exposition of great subtlety dealing with various levels of discourse, logical, rhetorical, and poetic; "Aristotle's Conception of the Development and the Nature of Scientific Method," *Journal of the History of Ideas,* vol. 8 (1947), pp. 3–44, devoted chiefly to metaphysical considerations applied to the special sciences; "Rhetoric and Poetic in the Philosophy of Aristotle," in *Aristotle's "Poetics" and English Literature,* Elder Olson, ed. (Chicago: University of Chicago Press, 1965), pp. 201–36.

Essays in which Aristotle's thought plays an important part are "Literary Criticism and the Concept of Imitation in Antiquity" (see note 18, above); "Aristotelianism in Western Christianity," in *Environmental Factors in Christian History,* John Thomas McNeill, Matthew Spinks, and Harold R. Wiloughby, eds. (Chicago: University of Chicago Press, 1939), pp. 206–31; "The Development of the Concept of Property in Political Philosophy: A Study of the Background of the Constitution," *Ethics,* vol. 48 (1938), pp. 297–366; "Aristotle and the Origins of Science in the West," in *Science and Civilization,* R. G. Stauffer, ed. (Madison: University of Wisconsin Press, 1949), pp. 3–29; "Philosophy and Method," *Journal of Philosophy,* vol. 48 (1951), pp. 653–82 (this article was subsequently issued as a separate monograph); *Freedom and History: The Semantics of Philosophical Controversies and Ideological Conflicts* (New York: Noonday, 1952); "The Hellenistic and Roman Foundations of the Tradition of Aristotle in the West," *Review of Metaphysics,* vol. 32 (1979), pp. 677–715;

"Plato and Aristotle as Historians: A Study in the History of Ideas," *Ethics,* vol. 51 (1940), pp. 66–101; republished in *Thought, Action, and Passion* as "Truth and the History of Ideas," pp. 54–98.

McKeon divulges some of his attitude toward Aristotle in "The Battle of the Books," in *The Knowledge Most Worth Having,* Wayne C. Booth, ed. (Chicago: University of Chicago Press, 1967), pp. 191–94. He has always borrowed more from Dewey than from Aristotle, he says, but Dewey and Aristotle shared much, if account be taken of changing circumstances (p. 193).

29. *Essay Concerning Human Understanding,* Book IV, chap. 17, sec. 2.

30. "Aristotelianism in Western Christianity" (see note 28, above) explains much of this history; see also "The Hellenistic and Roman Foundations of the Tradition of Aristotle in the West" (note 28, above).

31. "Criticism and the Liberal Arts: The Chicago School of Criticism" (see note 20, above). The "classical" part of this essay supplements "Literary Criticism and the Concept of Imitation in Antiquity" (see note 18, above).

32. "Between Two Generations: The Heritage of the Chicago School," in *Profession 82,* pp. 19–26. Dean Booth never associates the "School" with any one philosophy but describes the intellectual convictions of McKeon and Ronald S. Crane (chairman of the department of English at Chicago during the years in question) as being pervasive among an enlarging group of scholars and critics. He also reviews briefly some books written by adherents to all or most of McKeon's principles regarding criticism and education.

33. Chicago: University of Chicago Press, 1952. An abridged edition, omitting the less general essays, was published as *Critics and Criticism: Essays in Method* (Chicago: University of Chicago Press, 1957), with a new preface by the same editor in which he vigorously denied any exclusive attachment to Aristotle. "The only critical philosophy that underlies all the essays in the volume," he says, "is contained in the very un-Aristotelian attitude toward criticism, including the criticism of Aristotle, which they have called 'pluralism'" (p. iv). The essays by McKeon published in the complete edition are "Literary Criticism and the Concept of Imitation in Antiquity," "Aristotle's Conception of Language and the Arts of Language," "Rhetoric in the Middle Ages," "Poetry and Philosophy in the Twelfth Century: The Renaissance of Rhetoric," and "The Philosophic Bases of Art and Criticism." Only the last, a remarkable study to be discussed in chapter 7, can be found in the abridged edition. When Crane's chairmanship of the department of English came to an end, its temper changed rapidly. Virtually all university departments are pluralistic in the sense of being staffed by persons of different persuasions; what set McKeon, Crane, and their followers apart was that each one of these men was committed to pluralism and could deal with a variety of critical and philosophic studies.

McKeon wrote a little about the "Chicago School" (his quotation marks), recounting its intellectual adventure connected with *Critics and Criticism,* in "Philosophy as a Humanism," *Philosophy Today,* vol. 9 (1965), pp. 151–67; see especially pp. 159–62, the section devoted to discussion and controversy, which says that discussion among the original collaborators was replaced by controversy from outside reviewers. This was no doubt true, except that one or two of McKeon's fellow authors had penned severe denunciations of some contemporary critics discussing certain classics.

34. This trio of terms formed the title of an undergraduate course that McKeon dominated for many years after World War II at the University of Chicago.

35. An example of the latter is the fact that until the Sophists, almost none of the Presocratics said anything concrete about method in the fragments remaining. McKeon sought to reconstruct what he could of their methods—whether their terms were being used literally or analogically, whether they conceived of divisions in their philosophies, and so on. This required examining their concepts closely so that with the (presumed) method in hand he could return to those concepts, illuminating them accordingly.

36. McKeon rarely boasted in his classes, but I did hear him say that Plato had been interpreted one-sidedly by philologians and also, but differently, by philosophers, and that we would remedy this by bringing the two different disciplines together.

37. McKeon liked to revert to Duns Scotus's observation that a glass rod feels double when the fingers touching it are crossed but is seen to be single; on the other hand, a rod in a tumbler of water appears to be broken but to the fingers is sound enough. Which, then, of our senses should we trust?

38. McKeon's use of concepts was by no means always literal; sometimes it was heavily disguised, as when principles, causes, and elements (Aristotle, *Metaphysics*, Book V, chaps. 1, 2, and 3) are rearranged and become the epistemic, constitutive, and pistic aspects of an evaluation of a large group of thinkers ("An American Reaction to the Present Situation in French Philosophy," in *Philosophic Thought in France and the United States: Essays Representing Major Trends in Contemporary French and American Philosophy*, Marvin Farber, ed. [Albany: State University of New York Press, 1950], pp. 337–62).

39. *Phaedrus* 265d–e.

40. For his course Science and Metaphysics he took typical Platonic pairs of opposites for dealing with questions of truth and falsity: being-not being, same-other, motion-rest (from the *Sophist*), while those that Aristotle regularly used are the ten categories, not treated as contraries at all but supplementing each other.

41. In the *Gorgias*, Plato has the enigmatic Callicles pour contempt upon packs of slaves who merely say something; these are not legal ordinances (*nomima*, 489c). Similarly, not everyone concocting speculations is constructing a philosophy worthy of detailed analysis, much less of adoption.

42. One example, paraphrased from Aristotle: the spleen in animals with horns and hooves is rounded: goat, sheep, and others like these, unless its large size has caused it to elongate somewhere, as in the ox. In polydactylous animals the spleen is long: for instance pig, man, and dog. In animals having solid hooves the spleen is partway between the two and has the qualities of both: in one place it is broad, elsewhere narrow: as in horse, mule, and donkey (*Parts of Animals* III, xii. 673b32–674a4). Rather parallel to this is a passage, chosen almost at random, from McKeon's "Imitation and Poetry" (in *Thought, Action,*

and Passion, pp. 138–39): "'Imitation' may be defined relative to the objects imitated or to the persons involved in the imitation, and four fundamentally different means are found. . . . If imitation is defined relative to the object of imitation, the proper object of imitation may be conceived to be a transcendent value which determines and controls all things, including actions and arts. This is the mark of the Platonizing dialectical concept . . . in which two kinds must be distinguished, a better which is the imitation of reality and a worse which is an imitation of imitations, that is, changing sensible things. If, on the other hand, nature is conceived to consist of particular finite things exercising natural function . . . the proper object of imitation in art is found in things and particularly in the actions of men. . . . If imitation is defined relative to the persons involved in the imitation, the emphasis may fall on the skill of the artist or on the nature and sensibility of the audience."

43. McKeon once said to me (in 1947 or early 1948) that he did not consider the work he had done on comparing systems to be philosophy in the usual sense: "But I *have* a philosophy," he added, "and I have written it out."

44. Jay Hambidge, *Elements of Dynamic Symmetry* (New York: Brentano's, 1926; reprint, New York: Dover, 1967). The so-called Golden Section and closely related Fibonacci Series of numbers were fundamental to Hambidge's attempt to chart essential spatial relations between parts of an art work and between parts and whole. It was, in effect, a formal interpretation of a painting, but when a student began with a Hambidge diagram on his canvas, rectangles, diagonals, and curves chopping it up neatly, his resultant painting of a landscape or portrait figure was usually labored and emotionally ineffectual, though it would be unfair to confuse post hoc with propter hoc.

45. See note 5, above.

46. The difficulty in reading McKeon's works will doubtless be a short-term deterrent; the long modifier-laden sentences may have kept many from reading Kant and Hegel in their time, but some decades later hosts of readers mastered the turnings of their prose, if that is the word for it. The études of Paganini and Liszt are now deftly fingered by more and more violinists and pianists respectively than in the mid-nineteenth century.

47. Kant, with his four basic "titles," Quantity, Quality, Relation, and Modality, almost never changed their order in his critical writings. W. E. Johnson kept to his sequence throughout his logic, elaborating upon his root formulas: *if p then q; if q then p; not both p and q; either p or q.* It may be that McKeon, in varying the order of Problematic and the rest as special inquiries suited, felt that to retain a single order would convey a harmful notion of rigidity.

48. "Literary Criticism and the Concept of Imitation in Antiquity," *Modern Philology,* vol. 34, p. 13.

Chapter 3. A Learned Apprentice

1. This may not have been a fair evaluation. Others have thought the M.A. thesis quite interesting for its own sake and also as a harbinger of things to come.

2. New York: Longmans, Green, 1928. During those years, Columbia and other universities required that the Ph.D. dissertation be published—a heavy burden on most students, as the publishing (in "hot" type) had to be done at their own expense unless they were fortunate enough to have a contract, as did McKeon, from a publishing house. The general use of photo-offset by which ordinary typing and drafting could be cheaply, presentably reproduced was still some years in the future.

3. One could contrast Descartes with Spinoza by saying that for the former "I think, therefore I am," is the basis of the method, whereas it is for Spinoza "I think, therefore God is."

4. "Causation and the Geometric Method in the Philosophy of Spinoza," *Philosophical Review,* vol. 39 (1930), pp. 178–89, 275–96.

5. "The Background of Spinoza" in *Entretiens in Jerusalem on Spinoza—His Thought and Work: Proceedings of a Conference of the International Institute of Philosophy, September 6–9, 1977* (1980), pp. 1–40.

6. "Spinoza on the Rainbow and on Probability," in *Harry Austryn Wolfson Jubilee Volume* (Jerusalem: American Academy for Jewish Research, 1965), pp. 533–59.

7. In almost none of McKeon's writings with which I am familiar is there any significant reference to the biography of a man, certainly not as a necessary clue for accounting for the structure of his thought.

8. *Selections from Medieval Philosophers* (New York: Charles Scribner's Sons), vol. 1, *Augustine to Albert the Great* (1929), and vol. 2, *Roger Bacon to William of Ockham* (1930).

9. Symptomatic of McKeon's stress on the individuality of each philosopher's thinking was a reference he once made to a well-known French history of medieval philosophy: "Dry and doctrinaire, and devoted to showing that all medieval philosophers said the same thing."

10. Leibniz was an exception. In an entry headed "That the opinions of the theologians and of the so-called scholastic philosophers are not to be wholly despised," he says, "I know that I am advancing great paradox in pretending to resuscitate in some sort the ancient philosophy. . . . Our moderns do not do sufficient justice to Saint Thomas and to the other great men of that period." *Discourse on Metaphysics, Correspondence with Arnauld, and Monadology,* George R. Montgomery, trans. (Chicago: Open Court, 1931), pp. 17–18.

11. "A Note on William of Ockham," *Speculum: A Journal of Mediaeval Studies,* vol. 2 (1927), pp. 455–56.

12. "Thomas Aquinas' Doctrine of Knowledge and Its Historical Setting," *Speculum: A Journal of Mediaeval Studies,* vol. 3 (1928), pp. 425–44.

13. "The Empiricist and Experimentalist Temper in the Middle Ages: A Prolegomenon to the Study of Mediaeval Science," in *Essays in Honor of John Dewey* (New York: Henry Holt, 1929), pp. 216–34.

14. "Utility and Philosophy in the Middle Ages," *Speculum: A Journal of Mediaeval Studies,* vol. 8 (1933), pp. 431–36.

15. In *Studies in the History of Ideas,* vol. 3, ed., Department of Philosophy, Columbia University (New York: Columbia University Press, 1935). This essay contains a fairly long account of Abailard's theory of language.

16. With Blanche B. Boyer: Peter Abailard, *Sic et Non: A Critical Edition* (Chicago: University of Chicago Press, 1976–77).

17. Ernest A. Moody, *The Logic of William of Ockham* (New York: Sheed and Ward, 1935), p. 16 n. This was a pioneer study, showing (along with much else) that Ockham rather than others was the true disciple of Aristotle, purging the interpretation of the *Organon* of neoplatonic influences introduced by the *Isagoge* of Porphyry.

Chapter 4. The Structural Dialectic of Philosophic Discourse

1. This chapter should be called dialectical rather than logical, although dialectic is properly part of logic and deals chiefly with the discussion and possible resolution of philosophic difficulties. Logic is also the analysis of terms, propositions, and other types of arguments in addition to the dialectical.

2. I am told that in later decades McKeon sometimes used the word "quadrants" to designate his 4 × 4 arrays.

3. It must be remembered that in publications McKeon almost never printed an array as a chart. I have endeavored to simplify his prose expositions by using this device. Plato very explicitly describes one such array, the Divided Line (*Republic* VI, 509d–511e), but he has several dozen others, though rarely advertising them as such. For a valuable study that should lay to rest any notion of carelessness in the dialogues in this respect, see Robert S. Brumbaugh, *Plato's Mathematical Imagination: The Mathematical Passages in the Dialogues and Their Interpretation* (Bloomington: Indiana University Press, 1954). Of the arrays falling outside my present classification into squares and oblongs, one or two were printed as charts. See McKeon's "Rhetoric and Poetic in the Philosophy of Aristotle," in *Aristotle's "Poetics" and English Literature,* Elder Olson, ed. (Chicago: University of Chicago Press, 1965), p. 221, for an unusual, very ingenious triangular diagram to distinguish and interrelate Aristotle's arts and sciences.

4. A paper illustrating an array headed by two philosophers and grouping others as variants and mixtures, also dealing with the range of meanings accorded by Plato to "imitation," is "Literary Criticism and the Concept of Imitation in Antiquity," in *Modern Philology,* vol. 34 (1936), pp. 1–35.

5. Charting pure approaches will make it far easier to understand the deviants. Like it or not, philosophic thinking is necessarily carried on with some recourse to both groupings and separations of terms and of propositions— identities and distinctions marking kinds or levels of existences. These can be illustrated visually because of analogies between conceptual and spatial relations. The mixed methods are handily charted by crossed lines and other markings.

6. An ably-written book examining logical positivism and other trends in recent thought is *Metaphysics and the New Logic* (Chicago: University of Chicago Press, 1942), by Warner Arms Wick, a former pupil and then a colleague of McKeon's. This work borrows and analyses the concepts of holoscopic and meroscopic at some length.

7. It is troubling to think of Aristotle as a *way* of getting from Plato to Democritus or vice versa, hence to conceive of him as balancing claims of the two might be wiser. See *On Generation and Corruption* I. 2. 316a5–14, b24–33; *Physics* II. 2. 193b23–94b15; *On the Soul* I. 1. 403a25–b18.

8. "The Philosophic Bases of Art and Criticism," *Modern Philology*, vol. 41 (1943), pp. 65–87, and (1944), pp. 129–71, shows the Platonic approach (not that of Plato himself, except in an incidental sense) as a catchall; see especially pp. 159–60.

9. Published in *Studies in the History of Ideas*, vol. 3, ed., Department of Philosophy, Columbia University (New York: Columbia University Press, 1935), pp. 37–114. See especially pp. 81 and 106–7. The essay also included Martin Luther, whom I omit here because his inclusion raises other questions of organization.

10. One might also complain that when Erasmus rejects logic he is rejecting not quite what Abailard thought of as logic, so that again the two men are arguing about quite different things. But that does not vitiate McKeon's basic point about the plurality of approaches—in fact, it supports it.

11. *Journal of Philosophy*, vol. 48 (1951), pp. 653–82. This essay could well have been titled "Philosophy: Methods and Principles."

12. Cf. inter alia Aristotle's *Metaphysics* I. 4. 985b5–10, where he refers to Leucippus and Democritus as postulating a solid or full and a void (both equally real) as material causes. Two chapters later (6. 987b3–9) he says, "Plato, on the other hand, taking into account the *thought* of Socrates, came to the belief that, because sensible things are always in a state of flux, such inquiries into definitions and universals were concerned with other things and not with the sensibles. . . . He called things of this other sort 'ideas,' and believed that sensible things exist apart from Ideas and are named according to Ideas" (*Aristotle's Metaphysics: Translated with Commentaries and Glossary*, Hippocrates G. Apostle, trans. [Bloomington: Indiana University Press, 1966]). In one of his longest and best articles on that philosopher, "Aristotle's Conception of the Development and the Nature of Scientific Method," *Journal of the History of Ideas*, vol. 8 (1947), pp. 3–44, McKeon treats his method under three special headings: in connection with the theories of Aristotle's predecessors, with the nature of things, and with the validation of propositions. Under the first heading (pp. 3–19) he takes up Aristotle's objections to Plato and Democritus for opposite reasons, primarily reducible to this, that Plato had stronger theories but was weak in dealing with facts of experience, while Democritus could manage the facts but lacked full theoretical explanations. McKeon then raises several of Aristotle's own questions: Whether to trust the senses? What distinctions should be made and how rigid can they remain? What devices establish the meanings of terms? Whether causes should be employed as explanations? How may one distinguish between form and matter and between whole and part? and How can principles be selected appropriate to subject matters?

13. Philosophers are often content to list what they consider sufficient numbers of items, not attempting to prove that these are all possible ones. Kant and Hegel are outstanding exceptions, since for them completeness of a set of concepts is of paramount importance.

14. *Logic,* part 1 (Cambridge: At the University Press, 1921), p. 1. Johnson goes on to distinguish the proposition from the judgment, which in this case is an instance of this element taken as an act of thought, not as symbolism.

15. *Collected Papers of Charles Sanders Peirce,* vol. 2, *Elements of Logic,* Charles Hartshorne and Paul Weiss, eds. (Cambridge: Harvard University Press, 1932), par. 2.44, p. 269 n.

16. McKeon never published a separate exposition of his matrices, and the present discussion has been based upon lecture notes taken by me 'and some others in 1948 and 1949, especially the latter year. Several of his printed essays shortly after that time make some use of these squares.

17. There is, as McKeon insisted, no way of combining all nine entries of the minor of the X matrix (or the others) into one, to make a single grand logical element that is simultaneously faithful to objects, persons, and symbols; hence there is no way of summing them all together in the major, and no theory superior to all other theories of logic. (Node 1 in the upper left corner evidently sums everything, but only because the nodes on a line in the minor are taken separately.) Each theory must therefore be measured against others and compared point for point in terms of generality, precision, and the other desiderata. If this be true of the elements, it is also true of the methods (Y matrix) and principles (Z matrix).

18. McKeon seemed ready to experiment with squares having five nodes on a side, in "Creativity and the Commonplace," *Philosophy and Rhetoric,* vol. 6 (1973), pp. 199–210; but five concepts will tend to break up into two unequal groups. A square with twenty-five nodes, moreover, would be exhausting to both writer and reader, and three such matrices even more perplexing.

19. Responses to this paper, or rather, to McKeon's theory of discourse in general, were offered on that occasion by Father Robert Harvanek, S.J., Wayne C. Booth, and me, and McKeon gave a brief summary afterward, as part of a rescue mission, since the critics had had but a day or two to ponder the principal essay. I have been told by Zahava K. McKeon that this paper went through several metamorphoses on its way to mimeographing and delivery, and there is much evidence that even then her husband was never fully satisfied with it. Yet it must be considered definitive in the sense of being the last readied by his hand on the subject; apparently no other unpublished essay supersedes it. This 1966 paper has now been published in a single-volume printing with several others, *Freedom and History and Other Essays* (*FHOE*) by the University of Chicago Press, and will subsequently be printed in a multivolume collection of all of McKeon's published essays as well.

20. Methods and Principles as headings are a pair reminiscent of the older Y and Z matrices. Subject matter was displayed in the X matrix, but is now called Selections. The four kinds of Interpretations are new.

21. The operational or sophistic type of philosophy had been present in earlier work. Papers published the year after the 1951 essay on philosophy and its three methods and principles already add this new kind, which up to that time had been sequestered under other headings, chiefly, I think, the Platonic. See, for instance, "Philosophy and Action," *Ethics,* vol. 62 (1952), pp. 79–100,

especially pp. 86–87, 96, 99. But neither "operational" nor "actional" were accorded positions in the all-embracing squares until 1966.

Chapter 5. Metaphysical Bearings

1. *Psyche,* vol. 8 (1927), pp. 55–77.

2. *The Philosophy of Spinoza: The Unity of His Thought* (New York: Longmans, Green, 1928), part 1, chap. 4, pp. 130–57.

3. Historians have deemed the contest unequal, a distinguished experimental chemist and physicist on one side and an armchair philosopher and lens grinder on the other. McKeon shows, however, that Spinoza's credentials in the physical sciences were excellent and he was held in high respect among leading scientists of the day (ibid., pp. 130–33).

4. "The Science of Criminology," part 3 of *"Crime, Law, and Social Science: A Symposium,"* with Beardsley Ruml and Karl N. Llewellyn, *The Columbia Law Review,* vol. 34 (1934), pp. 291–309.

5. *The Journal of Philosophy,* vol. 27 (1930), pp. 673–90.

6. *The Monist,* vol. 49 (1965), pp. 519–50.

7. My information came chiefly from notes borrowed from other undergraduates who had copied them from two graduate students enrolled in the course.

8. In "Propositions and Perceptions in the World of G. E. Moore," a contribution to *The Philosophy of G. E. Moore,* Paul A. Schilpp, ed. (Evanton, Ill.: Northwestern University, 1942), pp. 453–80, McKeon implied differences in the value of the three approaches: "There is . . . a double dislocation in Mr. Moore's world. First, there is a dislocation from things to perceptions: one might be led to expect that, in a brave realistic world, *knowledge* about things would be constructed from examination of things; instead Mr. Moore demonstrates the *existence* of things from examination of knowledge. Second, there is a dislocation from cognitions to assertions: one might be led to expect that analysis of propositions might be directed to the clarification of *true* cognitions; instead Mr. Moore's analysis is directed to clarification of ambiguous statements or the destruction of false philosophic questions and puzzles" (p. 467). McKeon is not saying that either the epistemic or the linguistic approach is altogether false, but only that Moore misses an opportunity.

9. *The Review of Metaphysics,* vol. 13 (1960), pp. 539–54.

10. There are two welcome summaries, pp. 549–50 and 552–54.

11. For these terms, see McKeon's *Selections from Medieval Philosophers,* vol. 2 (New York: Scribner, 1930), in the glossary, pp. 502–3, and in the selection from St. Thomas Aquinas, *Disputed Questions on Truth,* Q. 1, art. 1, I reply, pp. 163–66. Also Ernest A. Moody, *The Logic of William of Ockham* (New York: Sheed and Ward, 1935), pp. 45–46, 118, 123–24.

12. No special list of categories is recommended in the essay, but in his course, Science and Metaphysics, and also Advanced Logic, McKeon paid special attention to the six categories of Plato in the *Sophist,* the ten of Aristotle,

those of Descartes, Locke, Spinoza, Kant, (occasionally) Hegel, Peirce, Whitehead.

13. Another of McKeon's papers pertaining to metaphysics should be quoted here: "The Future of Metaphysics," a chapter in *The Future of Metaphysics*, Robert E. Wood, ed. (Chicago: Quadrangle Books, 1970), pp. 288–308, in which McKeon says, "I shall try . . . to show that metaphysics is *actual* today, *contingent* not in necessary forms of thought but on circumstantial developments of culture, in which it is both *impossible* as an apodeictic science of connections and *necessary* to provide the ordering principles of *possible* intersecting communications and interrelated communities" (p. 293). I do not find such a strong bond with cultural changes in McKeon's earlier studies.

14. *The Journal of Philosophy*, vol. 48 (1951), pp. 653–82. Its great successor, "Philosophic Semantics and Philosophic Inquiry," has now been published in *Freedom and History and Other Essays*, Zahava K. McKeon, ed. (Chicago: University of Chicago Press, 1989), pp. 242–56. Noted as *FHOE*.

15. George Boole, in his *An Investigation of the Laws of Thought*, published as volume 2 of his *Collected Works* (Chicago: Open Court, 1940), p. 163, required of the principles of a system that they be (*a*) complete—no material relations in them that are not fully exposed to the reader; (*b*) accurate—no relations implied where these were not intended by the author; and (*c*) independent—no possibility of deducing one principle from the others. At no point does McKeon lay out a list of universally applicable criteria for all sets of definitions and axioms. Instead, he differentiates types of principles to fit different systems, and their criteria would vary accordingly. Boole's requirements would fit the Democritean approach, with its simple principles and logistic method of combining them to expose for the reader all important implications that can be wrung from them.

16. The four methods are well expounded in a work by one of McKeon's pupils, Michael J. Buckley, S.J., in *Motion and Motion's God: Thematic Variations in Aristotle, Cicero, Newton, and Hegel* (Princeton, N.J.: Princeton University Press, 1971), a learned, clearheaded account of the ways physics (specifically kinetics and kinematics) has been linked to theology. Broader in scope, less detailed, with some new terminology but rich in applications, is Walter Watson's *The Architectonics of Meaning: Foundations of the New Pluralism* (Albany: State University of New York Press, 1985), a fine introduction to all sixteen of the headings of McKeon's later semantic theory.

17. McKeon delayed for long including the Sophists as furnishing a distinct and coequal approach, although he made much of them in his classroom expositions of Plato and earlier philosophers. These men, he said, "stalk through a dozen dialogues" ("Plato and Aristotle as Historians: A Study of Method in the History of Ideas," *Ethics*, vol. 51 [1940], p. 69; also printed in his *Thought, Action, and Passion* [Chicago: University of Chicago Press, 1954] as "Truth and the History of Ideas," p. 56).

18. I had puzzled over this point from time to time through the decades, not because it was one on which McKeon's whole philosophy would stand or fall— there is no such single point—but because it was a matter of interest to test this philosophy in its own terms, much as one would ask Locke what his own simple

ideas had been and whether "simple idea" is simple, or Hegel whether he achieved the Absolute as an outgrowth of the very last phases of his thinking. I had reached conclusions pertinent to McKeon's earlier, simpler schemata that satisfied me, but I was glad to have Zahava K. McKeon (quoting her husband's statements) confirm some tentative conclusions that I had arrived at regarding the latter and perhaps save me from mistakes had I tended to veer off from the profile offered just now.

Chapter 6. Discourse, Controversy, and Resolution in Society

1. "The Development of the Concept of Property in Political Philosophy: A Study of the Background of the Constitution," *Ethics*, vol. 48 (1938), pp. 297–366. Some time in the late 1940s McKeon told me that he had received more correspondence over this than over any of his other papers to date. With many regrets, I shall not review the highly detailed article, for reasons of space.

2. *Ethics*, vol. 61 (1951), pp. 105–35.

3. In this chapter, rather than attempting much analysis or criticism, so broad is the range of materials to be discussed and numerous the papers devoted to them, I shall follow one of McKeon's own favorite manners of exposition, that of picking out what he considered the most salient points and then linking them together, sometimes commenting briefly as he summarized or quoted, sometimes letting his references speak for themselves.

4. *Philosophy and Phenomenological Research*, vol. 7 (1956), pp. 143–63. Reprinted in *Freedom and History and Other Essays*, Zahava K. McKeon, ed., pp. 103–125. Chicago: University of Chicago Press, 1989.

5. But in "Symposia," the Presidential Address of the Fiftieth Annual Meeting of the Western Division, American Philosophical Association, May 1952, published in the *Proceedings and Addresses of the American Philosophical Association, 1951–1952*, vol. 25, pp. 18–41, McKeon advocates a truly Platonic dialectic for settling problems (p. 35). See also note 10 below.

6. In his Concluding Remark in "Discussion—Freedom and Value," *Atti del XII Congresso Internazionale di Filosofia* (Florence: Sansoni, 1961), pp. 500–506, McKeon places crossed monologues ("a series of speeches which employ the same words—like 'freedom' and 'value'—but which do not use them in the same senses and do not raise common issues" [p. 303]) between dialogue and controversy. This is a valuable intermediate, but in any urgent situation it is unlikely to have much practical significance, and no doubt McKeon omitted it in most accounts because it raised needless dialectical complications.

7. *Ethics*, vol. 65 (1954), pp. 1–33.

8. This is McKeon's word, a fairly unaccustomed usage for him since he almost never labeled a concept with a privative prefix. It might be mentioned that in this UNESCO essay he went back to a basic dichotomy, with the help of this prefix (using such a privative *demands* that it be a dichotomy!), though elsewhere he had distinguished three kinds of philosophy, of which the dialectical was one. The change from three to two must have been for temporary purposes of simplification of issues.

9. McKeon lists his positions with UNESCO and his activities to the time

of writing on p. 299 of his "Knowledge and World Organization," in *Foundations of World Organization: A Political and Cultural Appraisal*, Lyman Bryson, Louis Finkelstein, Harold D. Lasswell, and R. M. MacIver, eds. (New York: Eleventh Symposium on the Conference on Science, Philosophy, and Religion, distributed by Harper and Brothers), pp. 289–329.

10. In "Symposia" (see note 5 above) McKeon says: "If philosophers could construct some such method [of common or group thinking] to explore the intervals of the many loves which divide them, as well as all other men, and which make them mutually unintelligible and mutually indifferent, our discussions, and those of the world, might return to circumstances in which the inspirations of poetry, wine, love, and religion [all of these being at the heart of Plato's *Symposium*, an account of which commences McKeon's essay] confirm and strengthen what reason is able to discover and establish, and in which the satisfaction of desires and the defense of traditional ideals do not automatically take the form of opposition to action for the common good" (p. 36).

11. *Ethics*, vol. 54 (1944), pp. 235–62.

12. These four are described first in general terms and then with reference to Plato, Aristotle, Spinoza, and Machiavelli (and some of their followers) respectively.

13. *Ethics*, vol. 67 (1957), pp. 89–99. Reprinted in *Freedom and History and Other Essays*, pp. 88–102.

14. This trio of epithets seems casual enough, but I hazard that it stems from Aristotle's division of syllogism into scientific, where the aim is utmost precision and truth to facts, dialectical, where back-and-forth discussion to winnow out evident falsehoods is the desideratum, and rhetorical, in which syllogisms and quasi-syllogisms are used to persuade various kinds of audiences. This is never to say that all such series in McKeon's writings stem from the classics, but certainly the collection of Greek (and to a lesser extent the Roman) writers is one good place to seek for likely precedents.

15. In *Great Moral Dilemmas in Literature, Past and Present*, R. M. MacIver, ed. (New York: Harper and Brothers, 1956), pp. 113–33.

16. *Ethics*, vol. 70 (1960), pp. 187–203.

17. Originally published in *Teachers College Record*, vol. 61 (1961), pp. 564–75. This paper is oddly divided there, and I suspect that the subtitles were supplied by a hand other than McKeon's, with the intention of taming some of the complexities. A year later, it was also published in *Ethics and Bigness*, Harland Cleveland and H. D. Lasswell, eds. (New York: Harper and Brothers, 1962), pp. 471–87. References in my chapter are to the earlier publication.

18. *Ethics*, vol. 51 (1941), pp. 253–90.

19. New York: Longmans, Green, 1928, part 2, chaps. 3 and 4.

20. *The Early Works of John Dewey, 1882–1898*, Jo Ann Boydston, ed., vol. 3 (Carbondale: Southern Illinois University Press, 1969), which reprints Dewey's *Outline of a Critical Theory of Ethics;* see especially pp. 300, 302.

21. *Leviathan: Or the Matter, Forme, and Power of the Common-wealth, ecclesiastical and civill* (New York: E. P. Dutton, 1914), part 1, chap. 13, p. 64.

22. See, for instance, his remarks in "The Development and the Significance

of the Concept of Responsibility," in *Revue internationale de philosophie*, vol. 34, fasc. 1 (1957); *FHOE*, pp. 62–87: "The [second World War] itself was an extension in armed conflict of differences concerning the nature of human communities and concerning the use of power, which had been based ideologically on what purported to be philosophical principles" (p. 1; *FHOE*, p. 62). The peace afterward reflected "a more complex conflict of ideologies . . . which despite ambiguities in their statement, have become rigid" Cf. "The Philosophic Problem," in *New Perspectives on Peace*, George B. Huszar, ed. (Chicago: University of Chicago Press, 1944), p. 199: "Most discussions of war and peace in particular are conflicts of two unacknowledged philosophies. . . . The chief philosophic problem to be solved if peace is to be secured and maintained is the translation of such tacit philosophic disputes into terms explicit enough for the kind of consideration which may lead to rational agreement." It is impossible to disagree, yet I wonder if it represents either the clearest insight into the multiple causes of war or the firmest path to peace. I am uncomfortable with any treatment of these issues as if they arose in a debating society.

23. New York: Noonday, 1952. Reprinted in *Freedom and History and Other Essays*, pp. 160–241.

24. When McKeon changes the adjectives "dialectical," "logistic," and "problematic" to nouns, the first becomes "dialectic," the second remains the same in shape and sound, while the third becomes "inquiry."

25. *Ethics*, vol. 68 (1958), pp. 98–115. The previous year a French version had been published in *Annales de philosophie politique*, vol. 1 (1957), pp. 1–32.

26. In *Foundations of World Organization: A Political and Cultural Appraisal*.

27. In addition to "Ethics and Politics" and "The Development and the Significance of the Concept of Responsibility," reviewed in this chapter, one might mention the following papers that speak more than in passing of particular nations or regimes: "Philosophical Presuppositions and the Relations of Legal Systems," *University of Chicago Law School Conference on Jurisprudence and Politics* (April 1955), pp. 3–19; "Human Relations and International Obligations," *Journal of Philosophy*, vol. 53 (1956), pp. 29–55 (concerning India); "The Ethics of International Influence," *Ethics*, vol. 70 (1960), pp. 187–203 (concerning the Soviet Union).

28. *Revue internationale de philosophie*, vol. 34 (1957), pp. 1–32. Reprinted in *Freedom and History and Other Essays*, pp. 62–87.

29. In *Ethics and Social Justice*, Howard E. Kiefer and Milton K. Munitz, eds. (Albany: State University of New York Press, 1970), pp. 300–322. Reprinted in *Freedom and History and Other Essays*, pp. 37–61.

30. McKeon's silence regarding types of governmental constitutions is the exact opposite of Aristotle's discussion in the middle books of his *Politics*, which take up types of city-states and their mixtures.

31. *Talks* (July 1949, pp. 10–18) a publication of the Columbia Broadcasting System.

32. *Ethics*, vol. 55 (1945), pp. 235–86.

33. Ibid., p. 239. I have changed punctuation slightly to suit the deletion.

34. The word "dialectic" is from *dialegesthai*, also translated as "discussion."

McKeon's usage in the present context is much closer to Aristotle's (*Topics* I. 1) than it is to any of Plato's, let alone anyone else's. As I have indicated earlier, his use of "dialectic" here should not be confused with the different meaning he gives it in the array on semantics.

35. Cf. Plato, *Gorgias* 471e–72a; *Crito* 46a–47c, for characterizations of voting. I believe that the four levels of grounds of voting that McKeon gives are deliberately based upon Plato's Divided Line.

36. This list is closed in the sense of its being circular, but open in the sense that one can with little trouble enlarge it to double or triple the length that I have proposed or else, at will, reduce it to half.

37. In *The Knowledge Most Worth Having,* Wayne C. Booth, ed. (Chicago: University of Chicago Press, 1967), pp. 173–202.

38. *Journal of General Education,* vol. 15 (1964), pp. 239–49.

39. He could do this as proven in the introduction (pp. 1–29) to his *Thought, Action, and Passion,* which to the ordinary observer contained four essays on rather widely differing topics, together with an appendix on Thomas Mann. He managed to give a dialectical coherence to the book that would be the envy of authors printing any collection of their papers. I do not mean that he would state an undifferentiated lumpish unity of a group consisting of a couple of apples, the Declaration of Independence, and a Ford car; but it is still true that he had, as Wallace Stevens would put it, a blessed rage for order.

40. *Kritik der Urteilskraft,* Einleitung, footnote to table of faculties.

41. See note 22 above.

42. The one empire to which McKeon believed history bore unimpeachable witness as embracing all the then civilized regions of the world, and thus resembled closely this superorganization, was not the empire of Alexander or that of Charlemagne or Napoleon but the Roman Empire.

43. Among them are "Economic, Political, and Moral Communities in the World Society," *Ethics,* vol. 57 (1947), pp. 79–91; "Les fondements d'une déclaration internationale des droits de l'homme," *Synthèses,* vol. 2 (1947), pp. 274–87; "Philosophie et liberté dans la cité humaine," *Les études philosophiques,* n.s., vol. 3 (1948), pp. 163–79 (English translation in *Ethics,* vol. 59 [1949], pp. 155–61); "World Community and the Relations of Cultures," in *Perspectives on a Troubled Decade* (New York: Harper and Brothers, 1950), pp. 801–15); "Knowledge and World Organization" (see note 9, above).

44. See preceding note. Also published as "Conflicts of Values in a Community of Cultures," *Journal of Philosophy,* vol. 47 (1950), pp. 197–210.

45. *The Principles of Biology,* 2 vols. (New York: D. Appleton, 1904), vol. 1, pp. 90, 93, 99.

Chapter 7. The Arts: Principles and Methods

1. *Phaedrus* 245a; *Ion* 533e, 534c.
2. *Ion* 525b–c.
3. *Critical Inquiry,* vol. 5 (1979), pp. 511–21.

4. *Current Issues in Higher Education, 1964,* G. Kerry Smith, ed. (Washington, D.C.: Association for Higher Education, National Education Association of the U.S.), pp. 36–64.

5. *Humanistic Education and Western Civilization: Essays for Robert M. Hutchins,* Arthur A. Cohen, ed. (New York: Holt, Rinehart and Winston, 1964), pp. 159–81.

6. These "fields" have their origins in Cicero. See section on rhetoric as a verbal art, this chapter.

7. New York: Noonday, 1952. Reprinted in *Freedom and History and Other Essays,* Zahava K. McKeon, ed. (Chicago: University of Chicago Press, 1989), pp. 160–241. An expanded schema underlies a later essay, "Has History a Direction? "Philosophical Principles and Objective Interpretations," in *La compréhension de l'histoire,* Nathan Rotenstreich, ed. (Jerusalem: Israel Academy of Sciences and Humanities, 1968), pp. 29–32, 38–39, 63–101, 159–62. This also was reprinted in *Freedom and History and Other Essays* (pp. 126–59), and will be noticed at greater length than McKeon's book of 1952 as presenting a somewhat richer context for history.

8. In his *Thought, Action, and Passion* (Chicago: University of Chicago Press, 1954), pp. 102–221 and pp. 239–85 (more than McKeon's usual proportion of footnotes).

9. "Plato and Aristotle as Historians: A Study of Method in the History of Ideas," *Ethics,* vol. 51 (1940), pp. 66–101; reprinted as "Truth and the History of Ideas" in *Thought, Action, and Passion,* pp. 54–88.

10. *The Philosophy of Spinoza: The Unity of His Thought* (New York: Longmans, Green, 1928). The only possible exception to this is the large group of articles on Aristotle listed in chapter 2, note 28. Even these, taken together, omit important parts of Aristotle's system: the heavens, the earth sciences, biology, kinds of political systems, the virtues, vices, and friendship.

11. On occasion, especially in the longer papers on Aristotle, McKeon would list the important places where a term occurred, but he accompanied these with explications and distinctions.

12. *Modern Philology,* vol. 41 (1943), pp. 65–87; and (1944), pp. 129–71. Republished in *Critics and Criticism, Ancient and Modern,* Ronald S. Crane, ed. (Chicago: University of Chicago Press, 1952), pp. 463–545. Again republished in *Critics and Criticism (Abridged Edition): Essays in Method,* Ronald S. Crane, ed. (Chicago: University of Chicago Press, 1957), pp. 191–273. I follow the pagination of the original journal printing, adding the references to the abridged edition. Superior vision is needed for the many long and detailed footnotes in all three printings. Or a strong glass.

13. *Modern Philology,* vol. 41 (1943), pp. 68–87; and Crane, *Essays in Method,* pp. 194–218.

14. *Modern Philology,* vol. 41 (1944), pp. 129–53; and Crane, *Essays in Method,* pp. 218–50.

15. In Aristotle's broad sense "practical" includes both politics (embracing ethics as well) and the productive sciences, while in his narrow sense it applies only to politics and ethics.

16. *Modern Philology,* vol. 41 (1944), pp. 153–71 also Crane, *Essays in Method,* pp. 250–73.

17. For additional details see McKeon's "Rhetoric and Poetic in the Philosophy of Aristotle," in *Aristotle's "Poetics" and English Literature,* Elder Olson, ed. (Chicago: University of Chicago Press, 1965), pp. 201–36. For a close translation of the *Poetics,* with many excellent interpretive aids and acknowledging indebtedness to McKeon, see Kenneth A. Telford, *Aristotle's Poetics: Translation and Analysis* (Chicago: Henry Regnery, 1961).

18. See note 8, above.

19. This section briefly retraces much of the ground in "Literary Criticism and the Concept of Imitation in Antiquity," in *Modern Philology,* vol. 34 (1936), pp. 1–35, giving less attention to the broader contexts in which "imitation" appears, especially in Plato.

20. Plato's dialectic allows countless variations, seconded by the operational method, which is, after all, a protean philosophy without even the analogies that serve as the parameters for Platonism. The precision of Aristotle's exposition, on the other hand, and the rigidly conceived combinations in Democritus preclude these deviations from a central doctrine.

21. Published as an appendix in *Thought, Action, and Passion,* pp. 223–27.

22. McKeon has omitted the article customarily used in translating the title, *Der Zauberberg.*

23. "A Generalized Pell Equation," with H. H. Goldstine, *Travaux de l'Institut mathématique de Tbilissi,* vol. 8 (1940), pp. 165–71.

24. *The Thomist,* vol. 24 (1961), pp. 211–56.

25. These and closely related essays were printed in various journals and official publications beginning in 1947 and running for several years thereafter. Some had UNESCO in their titles, others did not.

26. *Phaedrus* 278e–79b.

27. Ibid., 271a–74a.

28. During a brief visit in the spring of 1935 to the Columbia campus (he was on vacation from Chicago), McKeon voiced his lingering doubts to me about the "intellectual approach" to philosophy. The March day was clouded and blustery, which may well have been a joint cause; at any rate, he quickly added that he felt his approach justified.

29. *Profession 82* (New York: Modern Language Association of America, 1982), pp. 1–16; especially pp. 5–16, a segment written in the late 1930s.

30. *The Classical Tradition: Literary and Historical Studies in Honor of Harry Caplan,* Luitpold Wallach, ed. (Ithaca, N.Y.: Cornell University Press, 1966), pp. 365–73.

31. *Great Expressions of Human Rights,* R. M. MacIver, ed. (New York: Harper, 1950), pp. 29–41.

32. *Proceedings and Addresses of the American Philosophical Association,* vol. 25 (1951–52), pp. 18–41. Reprinted as "Love and Philosophical Analysis" in *Thought, Action, and Passion,* pp. 30–53.

33. *Classical Philology,* vol. 41 (1946), pp. 193–206; and vol. 42 (1947), pp. 21–50.

34. See note 17, above.

35. Cicero, *Brutus, On the Nature of the Gods, On Divination, On Duties,* Hubert M. Poteat, trans. (Chicago: University of Chicago Press, 1950), pp. 1–65.

36. *Philosophy and Rhetoric,* vol. 6 (1973), pp. 199–210.

37. *Speculum: A Journal of Mediaeval Studies,* vol. 17 (1942), pp. 1–32. Reprinted in *Critics and Criticism, Ancient and Modern,* pp. 260–96.

38. *Modern Philology,* vol. 43 (1946), pp. 217–34.

39. *Studies in the History of Ideas,* vol. 3, ed. Department of Philosophy, Columbia University (New York: Columbia University Press, 1935), pp. 37–114.

40. *Developments in the Early Renaissance,* Bernard Levi, ed. (Albany: State University of New York Press, 1972), pp. 158–223.

41. For McKeon's most detailed accounts of Aristotle's theory of structures and methods of the sciences and their instruments, see (1) "Aristotle's Conception of the Development and the Nature of Scientific Method," *Journal of the History of Ideas,* vol. 8 (1947), pp. 3–44; (2) "Aristotle's Concept of Language and the Arts of Language," *Classical Philology,* vol. 41 (1946), pp. 193–206, and vol. 42 (1947), pp. 21–50. Heaviest emphasis on rhetoric in the latter is on 33–34, 42–44, 48–49 of the 1947 volume.

42. *Rhetoric* I. 1. 1354a1.

43. Originally printed in *Philosophy and Rhetoric,* vol. 6 (1973), pp. 199–210, and reprinted in Richard McKeon, *Rhetoric: Essays in Invention and Discovery,* Mark Backman, ed. (Woodbridge, Conn.: Ox Bow Press, 1987), pp. 25–36. References are to pages in that book.

44. "Places" or "commonplaces" is the usual translation for *topoi,* which stands as title for Aristotle's treatise on dialectical reasoning (in his meaning, not Plato's), following the account of demonstrative or scientific reasoning in the *Posterior Analytics.* A commonplace is a general rule applicable in arguments about propositions offered, whose probability derives not from their intrinsic structure and content but from the fact that common or expert opinion has held them to be true. One such commonplace, the first of hundreds stated in the *Topics,* is to see if your opponent has asserted that something belongs only as an accident to something else, when in fact it belongs in some other way, as a definitory essence, a genus, or a permanent property. A rule of this kind applies to ordinary discussion, though its use may help to refine the discussion sufficiently that it may merge with the scientific; but the safeguards required for scientific propositions are far more rigorous.

45. See note 30, above.

46. *Démonstration, vérification, justification: Entretien de l'Institut international de philosophie, Liège, septembre 1967,* pp. 37–55.

47. *Perspectives in Education, Religion, and the Arts,* Howard E. Kiefer and Milton K. Munitz, eds. (Albany: State University of New York Press, 1970), pp. 329–50.

48. *The Prospect of Rhetoric,* Lloyd F. Bitzer and Edwin Black, eds. (Englewood Cliffs, N.J.: Prentice-Hall, 1971), pp. 44–63.

49. Traditionally, rhetoric was concerned with actions that had been done, were being done, or might in future be done; these are always in the nature of things particular, whereas dialectic deals with universals.

50. *The Future of Metaphysics,* Robert E. Wood, ed. (Chicago: Quadrangle Books, 1970), pp. 288–308.

51. For a summary of McKeon's own position, see also chapter 5, note 13.

52. *Selections from Medieval Philosophers,* vol. 2, *From Roger Bacon to William of Ockham* (New York: Scribner, 1930), p. 311.

Chapter 8. Theses and Distortions

1. The list is partly a falsification, as are all attempts at paraphrase and condensation. A doctoral candidate once prepared a fifty-item précis of the system of John Dewey, and McKeon rejected it peremptorily, not because it was done badly but because it was done at all. The fluidity of Dewey's own dialectic would make him one of the worst prospects for this kind of condensation, though he himself first wrote "My Pedagogic Creed," an itemized summary, in 1897, reprinted in *The Early Works of John Dewey, 1882–1898,* Jo Ann Boydston, ed. (Carbondale and Edwardsville: Southern Illinois University Press, 1972), vol. 5 (1895–98), pp. 84–98.

2. Plato, *Cratylus,* 384b–c.

3. These twelve theses and their respective distortions were originally sketched at a meeting on McKeon's work in 1966, and were discussed with him afterward. Verbal alterations since then have been few and slight. It has been said long ago that the history of an idea is the history of its misinterpretations, but this teasing aphorism need not hold, and especially when the misstatements are laid before the public in advance.

4. These distorted versions seem philosophically dubious on the face of them, but as Hobbes remarks, "For it is most true that *Cicero* saying of them somewhere: that there can be nothing so absurd, but may be found in the books of Philosophers" (*Leviathan,* part 1, chap. 5). One need not be a full-fledged professional to come under this stricture, though it may happen in some cases. Because of the complexities of this issue, further citations of distorting writers are pointless. The published literature (except for short reviews) on McKeon has not been extensive to date (spring 1989), and much criticism of his enterprise has been made in those reviews, one or two of them so wide of the mark as to make reference to them unnecessary. I wish to say, however, that his closer followers have committed extremely few errors. Indeed, McKeon has enjoyed an enviable list of dedications and acknowledgments in books by pupils who have grasped very clearly what he was teaching. See, for instance, Robert S. Brumbaugh, *Plato's Mathematical Imagination* (Bloomington: Indiana University Press, 1954), for its McKeonian reconstructions of arrays in the dialogues; and note the preface, p. vii.

5. One must assume here that properly speaking a philosophy is a work of reason if only because it contains linguistic forms intelligibly connected, and because if nonrational powers have any relation to philosophizing it is in the subsidiary sense of providing motivations for carrying out the rational operations. Pareto thought otherwise, but that was because his reasoning was wrong, not necessarily his motives.

6. That this is untrue to McKeon's own spirit is attested by a sentence or two from "The Philosophic Bases of Art and Criticism" in *Modern Philology*, vol. 41 (1943), p. 171: "[This paper] may pretend to adequacy in treating what has been said about art and beauty, for being a dialectic of what medieval philosophers used to call second, as distinct from first, intentions, it accounts for the literal modes, as well as the dialectical mode in which it is couched, without distortion or prejudice." The enterprise is thus not a different kind of thing and uses the same terms as the traditional analysis of art, beauty, and the rest—the list could go on much longer—and simply considers familiar problems from a new standpoint. We should, however, be careful to assume that his work is worth doing, that it adds to the sum of human knowledge, by the very fact that it is a synthesis, a classification, and a mutual adjustment of doctrines. It makes combinations where they have not existed explicitly before.

7. For an admittedly compressed example, see McKeon's introduction to *The Basic Works of Aristotle* (New York: Random House, 1941), pp. xi–xxxiv. At no point does he fall back upon the spirit of the times, the shaky science of the Hellenic world, the slave-based society, or even the peculiarities of the Greek language as excuses for Aristotle's thought or its possible shortcomings. Nor is there any attempt at psychoanalysis. Grasp of Aristotle's very complex methods—which must be derived from the text, mainly in what is done rather than what is stated about what is done—enables McKeon to integrate the parts of the system that to many in modern times have seemed sketchy, unconnected, and crankily contradictory. If philosophy is integral love of truth in regard to first principles, then it is a slipshod defense of a philosopher to show him in difficulties and then try to extricate him by pleading his life and times.

8. As a principle, this thesis might not warrant inclusion, but for consistency's sake it is vital, since McKeon's theory rests upon an interpretation of philosophy itself and hence is subject to whatever limitations he would lay upon other interpreters, save only some enforced lack of texts. A good instance of this is in "Aristotelianism in Western Christianity," in *Environmental Factors in Western Christianity*, John Thomas McNeill, Matthew Spinks, and Harold R. Willoughby, eds. (Chicago: University of Chicago Press, 1939), pp. 206–31. Here three radically different versions of Aristotle's system, each having some claim to correctness, are shown in their impact upon the Dark and Middle Ages.

9. As an aside in his course on the history of philosophy (Columbia University, spring 1934), McKeon said that there were a dozen great philosophers, or if one were feeling especially sanguine, perhaps two dozen.

10. Their difficulty would be compounded by the remark that McKeon made in a class (winter 1949) when he first expounded his 4×4 matrices. He referred, obliquely, to the fact that he was "two years away from the Ph.D." when first he had formulated them. Why he dropped them for a quarter century before bringing them to a semipublic attention I do not know. Even so, earlier papers, such as "The Philosophic Bases of Art and Criticism" (see note 6, above) had made use of matrices, though the reader unacquainted with their construction would doubtless never divine their structural origins.

11. It would be a nice question, of the sort that modern British Platonic

scholars delight in, whether McKeon's versatility in the exegesis of men as different as St. Augustine, Hobbes, Bosanquet, Ockham, and Strawson emerged out of conscious attention to the arrays and matrices, or the matrices were developed to justify the variety of philosophies that McKeon found fruitful and consistent. My supposition is that they grew side by side, but I cannot document this point.

12. I would not have included this last had not a student once said that he had heard of McKeon that "everything goes."

13. That this leads to a further problem, whether McKeon's impartial semantics does not paralyze the mind for decisive action, was long known to the philosopher himself, and many of his titles reflect this concern: "The Problems of Education in a Democracy," in *The Bertrand Russell Case,* Horace M. Kallen, ed. (New York: Viking, 1941), pp. 91–130; "Philosophic Differences and the Issues of Freedom," *Ethics,* vol. 61 (1951), pp. 105–35; "Philosophy and Action," *Ethics,* vol. 62 (1952), pp. 79–100. McKeon often said that one of the profoundest influences upon him was that of John Dewey, hardly a man to slight positive action. What emerges from the matrices and arrays seems not to be alternative answers to the question whether action is necessary, or what sort of action to take, but rather a variety of reasons why action is justifiable and necessary, and how it is linked to human nature and its ultimate aims. It should not be forgotten, McKeon once said, that even though Socrates became lost in meditation on his way to a party, he proved a most effective celebrant once he got there; and moreover that to do philosophy during a lull in battle still requires toughened feet (*Symposium* 174d–75c; 220a–d).

14. McKeon emphatically did not wish to see philosophy subside into a thermodynamic *Wärmetod* of bland acceptance. Sherlock Holmes put aside the Copernican versus the Ptolemaic controversy as irrelevant to his tracking of murderers, but this would make little sense to a strict follower of McKeon, for whom all points of view on all subjects sooner or later deserve consideration.

15. See McKeon's "Literary Criticism and the Concept of Imitation in Antiquity," *Modern Philology,* vol. 34 (1936), p. 35.

16. One of McKeon's most important contributions to classical scholarship was based upon his insistence that in the dialogues Plato throws nothing away—each one embodies a philosophic art in which all parts contribute to the rich unity of the work, but these parts are not necessarily of equal weight. A reader should also be warned against the tendency to erect casual gestures into illustrations of the forms, casual names into divisions between being and becoming.

17. Many, if not most, of the theses proposed in this chapter will be found stated in a late essay by McKeon, "The Circumstances and Functions of Philosophy," in *Philosophers on Their Own Work,* André Mercier and Maja Svilar, eds. (Bern and Frankfurt am Main: Herbert Lang, 1975), vol. 1, pp. 99–112; this is a partly autobiographical account of the order in which McKeon took up his studies in New York and Paris, but it moves into more general reflections on philosophies, their parts, and their antagonisms.

Chapter 9: Concessions, Queries, Objections, Refutations

1. The essay, "Philosophic Semantics and Philosophic Inquiry," posited *knower, knowable, known,* and *knowledge,* relating them with extreme ingenuity in various combinations that to retain here would carry this chapter far beyond its proper confines.

2. Aristotle communicated this handily enough when he remarked (*Metaphysics* I. 4. 985a14–16) that his forerunners (he was thinking chiefly of Empedocles in the passage) were like untrained men rushing into battle and striking a few good blows, but without science; and everyone suspects that Aristotle thought of himself as the best damned drill instructor in Athens or Pella or any city between them. McKeon did not share this view of his own predecessors; he rejected the plan of trying to build an edifice from the dry bones of their systems; it had been done too often before. Although he offered a number of lectures from time to time on the history of historians of various periods—mainly the doxographers and grammarians of the post-Aristotelian period—he did not, in my own experience, give a thoroughgoing review of thinkers who in one way or another had anticipated him in the belief that the usual game of philosophy was almost played out and that true reform consisted not in finding more principles and building new systems but in discovering ways to accommodate already-existing systems to each other—what he sometimes called the irenic aspects of discussion.

3. In Plato's dialogues Gorgias, Polus, Laches, Ion, Hippias, and some others are all at or near the top of their respective professions in the arts but cannot seem to come to terms with the real significance of what they are able to practice. The same difficulty impedes Theaetetus, a brilliant young mathematician.

4. As an example, "evolution" is part of and derived from "change," a metaphysical notion.

5. The lack of concern for detail makes a so-called interest in the arts of little value. A young student at the University of Chicago was complaining that philosophers never said anything of interest outside of the history of philosophy and mentioned a fellow student, a graduate in the department, and at one time an adherent of sorts of McKeon's. She had said to him, "Say something interesting about anything else—sculpture, for instance." "Sure," he replied. "A sculpture is a whole having parts." "Is that all you can say?" "Isn't that enough?" At the other extreme, incidentally, was a professor of philosophy and department head at another midwestern university who said to me, "I don't like modern art. I like pictures of boats. I want the painting to look like a boat, and if it looks like a boat, I don't care about any art theory criticizing or supporting it."

6. *Tractatus Logico-Philosophicus,* C. K. Ogden, trans. (New York: Harcourt Brace, 1922), 5.64, 5.641.

7. I remind the reader that the four were the dialectical, the logistic, the aporetic or problematic, and the sophistic, sometimes called the operational. With the last I have trouble, if by "operational" is meant the work of such men as Eddington and P. W. Bridgman, for they seem to be little in accord with the

old Sophists. If, as Protagoras is quoted as saying, man is himself the measure, then the pointer readings prominent in the writings of the astronomer and the physicist strike me as being in direct opposition, for the measures on dials are made into truth and are not the source of a probabilism. The devices represent man's most determined efforts to get beyond the relativist perceptions of eye, ear, and hand.

8. F. H. Bradley, *The Principles of Logic,* 2d ed., 2 vols. (London: Oxford University Press, 1922), vol. 2, book 1, chap. 4.

9. In his spring 1934 course in the history of medieval and modern philosophy, McKeon said pointedly that if they were properly and individually interpreted, philosophers generally would be found to have made sense. What he made of Plato and of Aristotle by his patient study treating them as philosophers, not reporters or diarists or pulpiteers or improvisers, led him into interpretations flying in the face of much respected commentary on them; this was true as well of most of the other figures whose work McKeon expounded. Since the days of Lewis Campbell, T. I. Case, and Wincenty Lutoslawski, the prevailing opinion has been that the dialogues are sketches of different phases of Plato's thought, written under varied influences, and that the same thing must be said of Aristotle's treatises. It has also been popular to show inconsistencies in Spinoza's *Ethics,* a task easily accomplished when ignoring his differentiation of a method of derivation of essences stemming from God and a method of synthesis adapted to what he calls the common order of nature, the movements and combinations of bodies. The labors of Vaihinger, Adickes, Kemp Smith, and other commentators to show that Kant's ideas in the *Critique of Pure Reason* are almost irremediably ill-suited to each other could also be cited.

10. *On the Soul* III. 5. 430a10–25. A very clear exposition of this most perplexing passage is in *Aristotle's On the Soul (De Anima): Translation with Commentaries and Glossary,* by Hippocrates G. Apostle (Grinnell, Iowa: Peripatetic Press, 1981), p. 51, and commentary, pp. 156–68.

11. The reader is warned against confusing the O system with the notion of the personal self mentioned in connection with thesis 4. To Frege, his highly impersonal account of the foundations of arithmetic is still part of his O system (though it would not have been to Schroeder, whose O system contained his modified and expanded Boolean algebra).

12. In the winter of 1946 McKeon gave a public lecture in which he discussed these cycles. Several students pooled their scant purses to hire a stenographer, and carbons of the transcription circulated for a time, but to my knowledge nothing was published.

13. *Timaeus* 47e.

14. Ibid., 69a–b.

15. Several pages at the beginning and end of McKeon's untitled essay in *Thirteen Americans: Their Spiritual Autobiographies,* Louis Finkelstein, ed. (New York: Harper, 1953), pp. 77–114, could be used as an example of the author's impulse to overshadow a clear narrative with carefully-wrought distinctions. A single quotation may suffice: "The account of one man's difficulties in speculation about principles, in deliberation about means, and in inquiry about conse-

quences, is significant only if . . . the statement of his arguments has a bearing on ideas and aspirations as they are at once shared by other men of the time or tradition and involved in timeless principles or inspirations" (p. 78).

16. "Imitation and Poetry," in *Thought, Action, and Passion* (Chicago: University of Chicago Press, 1954); there is a long footnote, pp. 277–85, devoted to a somewhat harsh reply to Professor Vivas. I understand, however, that at about the same time McKeon nominated Vivas for a vice-presidency or presidency of an important learned society, a gesture not dictated by qualms of conscience, I believe, but through McKeon's instinctive way of looking at different sides of a proposition or a person.

Bibliography

I. Books and Articles by Richard McKeon

This list contains only those works explicitly referred to in the present book, slightly less than half of McKeon's total published articles and more than half of his books. In addition to those printed in letterpress, I include one piece that up to the present (August 1989) has remained in mimeographed form, but has had strong influence on students and others fortunate enough to have obtained copies. With the improvements in xerography in recent decades one can assume that copies of copies have been made, and that distribution by now of this general introduction to Aristotle (untitled) is far wider than was originally planned. The essay, "Philosophic Semantics and Philosophic Inquiry," has been posthumously published but is also listed for the year of its original delivery, 1966.

The entries are in chronological order, reflecting the tendency of much of this study.

1928

"A Note on William of Ockham." *Speculum: A Journal of Mediaeval Studies*, vol. 2, pp. 455–56.

"Spinoza and Experimental Science." *Psyche*, vol. 8, pp. 55–77.

"Spinoza and Medieval Philosophy." *Open Court*, vol. 42, pp. 129–45.

The Philosophy of Spinoza: The Unity of His Thought. New York: Longmans, Green.

"Thomas Aquinas' Doctrine of Knowledge and Its Historical Setting." *Speculum: A Journal of Mediaeval Studies*, vol. 3, pp. 425–44.

1929

Selections from Medieval Philosophers. Vol. 1, *Augustine to Albert the Great*. New York: Charles Scribner's Sons.

"The Empiricist and Experimentalist Temper in the Middle Ages: A Prolegomenon to the Study of Mediaeval Science." In *Essays in Honor of John Dewey*, pp. 216–34. New York: Henry Holt.

1930

Selections from Medieval Philosophers. Vol. 2, *Roger Bacon to William of Ockham*. New York: Charles Scribner's Sons.

"*De Anima:* Psychology and Science." *Journal of Philosophy*, vol. 27, pp. 675–90.

"Causation and the Geometric Method in the Philosophy of Spinoza." *Philosophical Review*, vol. 39, pp. 178–79, 275–96.

1933

"Utility and Philosophy in the Middle Ages." *Speculum: A Journal of Mediaeval Studies*, vol. 8, pp. 431–36.

1934

"The Science of Criminology." Part 3 of *Crime, Law and Social Science: A Symposium*, with Beardsley Ruml and K. N. Llewellyn. *Columbia Law Review*, vol. 34, pp. 291–309.

1935

"Renaissance and Method in Philosophy." In *Studies in the History of Ideas*, edited by the Department of Philosophy of Columbia University. 3 vols. Vol. 3, pp. 37–114. New York: Columbia University Press.

1936

"Literary Criticism and the Concept of Imitation in Antiquity." *Modern Philology*, vol. 34, pp. 1–35.

1938

"The Development of the Concept of Property in Political Philosophy: A Study of the Background of the Constitution." *Ethics*, vol. 48, pp. 297–366.

1939

"Aristotelianism in Western Christianity." In *Environmental Factors in Christian History*, edited by John Thomas McNeill, Matthew Spinks, and Harold R. Wiloughby, pp. 206–31. Chicago: University of Chicago Press. Republished Port Washington, N.Y.: Kennikat Press, 1970.

1940

With H. H. Goldstine, "A Generalized Pell Equation." *Travaux de l'Institut mathématique de Tbilissi*, vol. 8, pp. 165–71.

"Plato and Aristotle as Historians: A Study of Method in the History of Ideas." *Ethics*, vol. 51, pp. 66–101.

1941

The Basic Works of Aristotle. New York: Random House.

Mimeographed Introduction to Aristotle's Philosophy (originally intended for *The Basic Works of Aristotle;* the printed introduction in that volume is a much condensed version).

"Aristotle's Conception of Moral and Political Philosophy." *Ethics,* vol. 51, pp. 253–90.
"Moses Maimonides, the Philosopher." In *Essays on Maimonides: An Octocentennial Volume,* pp. 2–8. New York: Columbia University Press.
"The Problems of Education in a Democracy." In *The Bertrand Russell Case,* edited by John Dewey and H. M. Kallen, pp. 91–130. New York: Viking.

1942

"Propositions and Perceptions in the World of G. E. Moore." In *The Philosophy of G. E. Moore,* edited by Paul A. Schilpp, pp. 453–80. Evanston, Ill.: Northwestern University.
"Rhetoric in the Middle Ages." *Speculum: A Journal of Mediaeval Studies, vol. 17: pp. 1–32.*

1943

"The Philosophic Bases of Art and Criticism." *Modern Philology,* vol. 41, pp. 65–87, 129–71.

1944

"Discussion and Resolution in Political Conflicts." *Ethics,* vol. 54, pp. 235–62.
"The Philosophic Problem." In *New Perspectives on Peace,* edited by George B. Huszar, pp. 96–226. Chicago: University of Chicago Press.

1945

"Democracy, Scientific Method, and Action." *Ethics,* vol. 55, pp. 235–86.

1946

"Poetry and Philosophy in the Twelfth Century: The Renaissance of Rhetoric." *Modern Philology,* vol. 43, pp. 217–34.

1946–47

"Aristotle's Conception of Language and the Arts of Language." *Classical Philology,* vol. 41, pp. 193–206, and vol. 42, pp. 21–50.

1947

Introduction to Aristotle. New York: Random House, Modern Library.
"Aristotle's Conception of the Development and the Nature of Scientific Method." *Journal of the History of Ideas,* vol. 8, pp. 3–44.
"Economic, Political, and Moral Communities in the World Society." *Ethics,* vol. 57, pp. 79–91.
"Les fondements d'une déclaration internationale des droits de l'homme." *Synthèses,* vol. 2, pp. 274–87.

1949

"Aristotle and the Origins of Science in the West." In *Science and Civilization,* edited by R. G. Stauffer, pp. 3–29. Madison: University of Wisconsin Press.

"Should Communists Be Allowed to Teach in Our Schools?" *Talks* (a publication of the Columbia Broadcasting System; July), pp. 10–18.

1950

"Introduction to the Philosophy of Cicero." In *Brutus, On the Nature of the Gods, On Divination, On Duties,* translated by Hubert M. Poteat, pp. 1–65. Chicago: University of Chicago Press.

"An American Reaction to the Present Situation in French Philosophy." In *Philosophic Thought in France and the United States: Essays Representing Major Trends in Contemporary French and American Philosophy,* edited by Marvin Farber, pp. 357–62. Buffalo: University of Buffalo Publications in Philosophy.

"World Community and the Relations of Cultures." In *Perspectives on a Troubled Decade,* pp. 801–15. New York: Harper and Brothers.

"The Funeral Oration of Pericles." In *Great Expressions of Human Rights,* edited by R. M. MacIver, pp. 29–41. New York: Harper and Brothers.

"Philosophy and the Diversity of Cultures." *Ethics,* vol. 60, pp. 233–60.

1951

"Philosophy and Method." *Journal of Philosophy,* vol. 48, pp. 653–82. Also published as a separate unbound booklet.

"Philosophic Differences and the Issues of Freedom." *Ethics,* vol. 61, pp. 105–35

1952

"A Philosopher Meditates on Discovery." In *Moments of Personal Discovery,* edited by R. M. MacIver, pp. 105–32. New York: The Institute for Religious and Social Studies, distributed by Harper and Brothers.

Freedom and History: The Semantics of Philosophical Controversies and Ideological Conflicts. New York: Noonday.

"Philosophy and Action." *Ethics,* vol. 62, pp. 79–100.

"Knowledge and World Organization." In *Foundations of World Organization: A Political and Cultural Appraisal,* edited by Lyman Bryson, Louis Finkelstein, Harold D. Lasswell, and R. M. MacIver, pp. 289–329. New York: Eleventh Symposium of the Conference on Science, Philosophy and Religion, distributed by Harper and Brothers.

"Symposia." In *Proceedings and Addresses of the American Philosophical Association 1951–1952,* vol. 25, pp. 18–41.

Critics and Criticism, Ancient and Modern, edited by Ronald S. Crane. Chicago: University of Chicago Press. (Reprints the following essays by McKeon: "Literary Criticism and the Concept of Imitation in Antiquity" [1936], pp. 147–75; "Aristotle's Conception of Language and the Arts of Language" [1946–47], pp. 176–231; "Rhetoric in the Middle Ages" [1942], pp. 260–96; "Poetry and Philosophy in the Twelfth Century: The Renaissance of Rhetoric" [1946], pp. 297–318; "The Philosophic Bases of Art and Criticism" [1943], pp. 463–545.)

1953

Untitled contribution to *Thirteen Americans: Their Spiritual Autobiographies,* edited by Louis Finkelstein, pp. 77–114. New York: The Institute for Religious and Social Studies, distributed by Harper and Brothers.

1954

Thought, Action, and Passion. Chicago: University of Chicago Press. (Reprints, with some changes, "Symposia" [1952] as "Love and Philosophical Analysis," pp. 30–53; "Plato and Aristotle as Historians: A Study of Method in the History of Ideas" [1946] as "Truth and the History of Ideas," pp. 54–88; "The Funeral Oration of Pericles" [1950] as "Freedom and Disputation," p. 89–101; these are preceded by an introduction, pp. 1–29, and followed by a new essay, "Imitation and Poetry," pp. 102–221, together with an appendix, "Remarks on the Occasion of the Seventieth Birthday of Thomas Mann," pp. 223–27.)

"Dialectic and Political Thought and Action." *Ethics,* vol. 65, pp. 1–33.

1955

"Philosophical Presuppositions and the Relations of Legal Systems." In *University of Chicago Law School Conference on Jurisprudence and Politics,* pp. 3–19. Chicago: University of Chicago Press.

"Dialogue and Controversy in Philosophy." In *Entretiens philosophiques d'Athènes,* pp. 161–78. Athens: Institut international de philosophie.

1956

"Dialogue and Controversy in Philosophy." Reprinted in *Philosophy and Phenomenological Research,* vol. 17, pp. 143–63.

"The Choice of Socrates." In *Great Moral Dilemmas in Literature, Past and Present,* edited by R. M. MacIver, pp. 113–33. New York: Institute for Religious and Social Studies, distributed by Harper and Brothers.

"Le pouvoir et le langage du pouvoir." *Annales de philosophie politique,* vol. 1, pp. 1–32.

1957

"Power and the Language of Power." *Ethics,* vol. 68, pp. 143–63. (Translation of "Le pouvoir et le langage du pouvoir.")

"The Development and the Significance of the Concept of Responsibility." In *Revue internationale de philosophie,* vol. 34, pp. 3–32.

"Communication, Truth, and Society." *Ethics,* vol. 67, pp. 89–99.

"Aristotle's Conception of Scientific Method." In *Roots of Scientific Thought: A Cultural Perspective,* edited by Philip P. Wiener and A. Noland, pp. 73–89. New York: Basic Books. (Reprint of parts of "Aristotle's Conception of the Development and the Nature of Scientific Method" [1942].)

Critics and Criticism (Abridged Edition): Essays in Method, edited by Ronald S. Crane, pp. 191–273. Chicago: University of Chicago Press. (Reprints "The Philosophic Bases of Art and Criticism" [1943–44].)

With A. N. Nikam, *The Edicts of Asoka.* Chicago: University of Chicago Press.

1960

"The Ethics of International Influence." *Ethics,* vol. 70, pp. 187–203.
"Being, Existence, and That Which Is." *Review of Metaphysics,* vol. 13, pp. 539–54.

1961

"Medicine and Philosophy in the Eleventh and Twelfth Centuries." *The Thomist,* vol. 24, pp. 211–56.
First Lyman Bryson Lecture. "Ethics and Politics." *Teachers College Record,* vol. 62, pp. 564–75.

1962

Republication of "Ethics and Politics." In *Ethics and Bigness,* edited by Harlan Cleveland and Harold D. Lasswell, pp. 471–87. New York: Harper and Brothers.

1964

"Love and Wisdom: The Teaching of Philosophy." *Journal of General Education,* vol. 15, pp. 239–49.
"The Liberating Arts and the Humanizing Arts in Education." In *Humanistic Education and Western Civilization: Essays for Robert M. Hutchins,* edited by Arthur M. Cohen, pp. 159–81. New York: Holt, Rinehart and Winston.
"The Future of the Liberal Arts." In *Current Issues in Higher Education, 1964,* edited by G. Kerry Smith, pp. 36–44. Washington, D.C.: Association for Higher Education, National Education Association of the U.S.

1965

"Rhetoric and Poetic in the Philosophy of Aristotle." In *Aristotle's "Poetics" and English Literature,* edited by Elder Olson, pp. 201–36. Chicago: University of Chicago Press.
"The Relation of Logic to Metaphysics in the Philosophy of Duns Scotus." *The Monist,* vol. 49, pp. 519–59.
"Spinoza on the Rainbow and on Probability." In *Harry Austryn Wolfson Jubilee Volume,* pp. 533–59. Jerusalem: American Academy for Jewish Research.
"Philosophy as a Humanism." *Philosophy Today,* vol. 9, pp. 151–67.

1966

"The Methods of Rhetoric and Philosophy: Invention and Judgment." In *The Classical Tradition: Literary and Historical Studies in Honor of Harry Caplan,* edited by Luitpold Wallach, pp. 365–73. Ithaca, N.Y.: Cornell University Press.
"Philosophic Semantics and Philosophic Inquiry." Typescript, mimeographed. Published posthumously, 1989.

1967

"The Battle of the Books." In *The Knowledge Most Worth Having,* edited by Wayne C. Booth, pp. 173–202. Chicago: University of Chicago Press.

"Discourse: Demonstration, Verification, and Justification." In *Démonstration, Vérification, Justification: Entretiens de l'Institut international de philosophie, Liège, septembre 1967*, pp. 37–55. Louvain: Nauwelaerts.

Reprint of "An American Reaction to the Present Situation in French Philosophy." In *Philosophic Thought in France and the United States: Essays Representing Major Trends in Contemporary French and American Philosophy*, edited by Marvin Farber. 2d ed. Albany: State University of New York Press.

"Has History a Direction? Philosophical Principles and Objective Interpretation." In *La compréhension de l'histoire*, edited by Nathan Rotenstreich. Jerusalem: Israel Academy of Sciences and Humanities. (Pp. 29–32, the paper; 38–39, 63–101, 159–62, discussions.)

1970

"The Future of Metaphysics." In *The Future of Metaphysics*, edited by Robert E. Wood, pp. 288–308. Chicago: Quadrangle Books.

"Philosophy and History in the Development of Human Rights." In *Ethics and Social Justice*, edited by Howard E. Kiefer and Milton K. Munitz, pp. 300–322. Albany: State University of New York Press.

"Philosophy of Communications and the Arts." In *Perspectives in Education, Religion, and the Arts*, edited by Howard E. Kiefer and Milton K. Munitz, pp. 329–50. Albany: State University of New York Press.

1971

"The Uses of Rhetoric in a Technological Age: Architectonic Productive Arts." In *The Prospect of Rhetoric*, edited by Lloyd F. Bitzer and Edwin Black. Report of the National Development Project Sponsored by the Speech Communication Association. Englewood Cliffs, N.J.: Prentice-Hall. (Pp. 44–63, paper; 182–85, discussion.)

1972

"The Transformations of the Liberal Arts in the Renaissance." In *Developments in the Early Renaissance*, edited by Bernard Levi, pp. 158–223. Albany: State University of New York Press.

1973

Introduction to Aristotle. 2d ed. Chicago. University of Chicago Press. (Revised and enlarged version of the 1947 Modern Library volume.)

"Creativity and the Commonplace." *Philosophy and Rhetoric*, vol. 6, pp. 199–210.

1975

"The Circumstances and Functions of Philosophy. In *Philosophers on Their Own Work*, edited by André Mercier and Maja Svilar, vol. 1, pp. 95–142. Bern and Frankfurt am Main: Herbert Lang.

1976–77

Peter Abailard, *Sic et Non: A Critical Edition*, with Blanche B. Boyer. Chicago: University of Chicago Press.

1979

"The Hellenistic and Roman Foundations of the Tradition of Aristotle in the West." *Review of Metaphysics,* vol. 32, pp. 677–715.

1982

"Criticism and the Liberal Arts: The Chicago School of Criticism." *Profession 82,* pp. 1–18. New York: Modern Language Association of America.

Posthumous

1987

Rhetoric: Essays in Invention and Discovery, edited by Mark Backman. Woodbridge, Conn.: Ox Bow Press. (Reprints "The Uses of Rhetoric in a Technological Age: Architectonic Productive Arts" [1971], pp. 1–24; "Creativity and the Commonplace" [1973], pp. 25–36; "Discourse, Demonstration, Verification, and Justification" [1969], pp. 37–55; "The Methods of Rhetoric and Philosophy: Invention and Judgment" [1966], pp. 56–65; "Symbols, Myths, and Arguments" [1955], pp. 66–94; "Philosophy of Communications and the Arts" [1970], pp. 95–120; "Rhetoric in the Middle Ages" [1942], pp. 121–66; "Poetry and Philosophy in the Twelfth Century: The Renaissance of Rhetoric" [1946], pp. 167–93; "A Philosopher Meditates on Discovery" [1952], pp. 194–220.)

1989

Freedom and History and Other Essays, edited by Zahava K. McKeon. Introduction by Howard Ruttenberg. Chicago: University of Chicago Press. (Reprints the following by Richard McKeon: [the untitled] Spiritual Autobiography [1953], pp. 3–36; "Philosophy and History in the Development of Human Rights [1970], pp. 37–61; "The Development and the Significance of the Concept of Responsibility" [1957], pp. 62–87; "Communication, Truth, and Society" [1957], pp. 88–102; "Dialogue and Controversy in Philosophy" [1956], pp. 103–25; "Has History a Direction? Philosophical Principles and Objective Interpretations" [1968], pp. 126–59; "Freedom and History" [1952], pp. 160–241; "Philosophic Semantics and Philosophic Inquiry" [delivered 1966, not published by author], pp. 242–56.)

II. Other Works

Aristotle. *Aristotle's Metaphysics.* Translation and commentaries by Hippocrates G. Apostle. Bloomington: Indiana University Press, 1966.

Aristotle. *The Nicomachean Ethics.* Translation and commentaries by Hippocrates G. Apostle. Dordrecht, Holland: D. Reidel, 1975.

Aristotle. *Categories and Propositions (De Interpretatione).* Translation and commentaries by Hippocrates G. Apostle. Grinnell, Iowa: Peripatetic Press, 1980.

Aristotle. *Aristotle's Posterior Analytics*. Translation and commentaries by Hippocrates G. Apostle. Grinnell, Iowa: Peripatetic Press, 1981

Aristotle. *Aristotle's On the Soul (De Anima)*. Translation and commentaries by Hippocrates G. Apostle. Grinnell, Iowa: Peripatetic Press, 1981.

Aristotle. *Aristotle's Politics*. Translation and commentaries by Hippocrates G. Apostle. Grinnell, Iowa. Peripatetic Press, 1986.

Aristotle. *Works*. 22 vols. Loeb Classical Library. Cambridge: Harvard University Press, 1926–65.

Boole, George. *The Collected Works*. Vol. 2, *An Investigation of the Laws of Thought*. Chicago: Open Court, 1940.

Booth, Wayne C. "Between Two Generations: The Heritage of the Chicago School." In *Profession 82*. New York: Modern Language Association of America, 1982.

Bradley, F. H. *Appearance and Reality: A Metaphysical Essay*. 2d ed. Oxford: At the University Press, 1897.

Bradley, F. H. *The Principles of Logic*. 2d ed. 2 vols. Oxford: At the Clarendon Press, 1922.

Brumbaugh, Robert S. *Plato's Mathematical Imagination: The Mathematical Passages in the Dialogues and Their Interpretation*. Bloomington: Indiana University Press, 1954.

Buckley, Michael J., S.J. *Motion and Motion's God: Thematic Variations in Aristotle, Cicero, Newton, and Hegel*. Princeton, N.J.: Princeton University Press, 1971.

Dewey, John. *Experience and Nature*. 2d ed. La Salle, Ill.: Open Court, 1929.

Dewey, John. *The Early Works of John Dewey 1882–1898*. Vol. 3. Edited by Jo Ann Boydston. Carbondale, Ill.: Southern Illinois University Press, 1969.

Edwards, Paul, ed. *The Encyclopedia of Philosophy*. 8 vols. New York: Macmillan and Free Press, 1967.

Hambidge, Jay. *Elements of Dynamic Symmetry*. New York: Brentano's, 1926.

Hobbes, Thomas. *Leviathan*. New York: E. P. Dutton, Everyman Library, 1914.

Johnson, W. E. *Logic*. 3 vols. Cambridge: At the University Press, 1921–24.

Kant, Immanuel. *Kritik der Urteilskraft*. Edited by Karl Vorländer. Hamburg: Felix Meiner, 1924.

Leibniz, Gottfried. *Discourse on Metaphysics, Correspondence with Arnauld, and Monadology*. Translation by George R. Montgomery. Chicago: Open Court, 1931.

Locke, John. *An Essay Concerning Human Understanding*. Edited by Alexander Campbell Fraser. 2 vols. Oxford: At the Clarendon Press, 1894.

Lucretius. *On the Nature of Things*. Translation and commentary by Cyril Bailey. Oxford: At the Clarendon Press, 1947.

Moody, Ernest A. *The Logic of William of Ockham*. New York: Sheed and Ward, 1935.

Peirce, Charles Sanders. *Collected Papers*. Edited by Charles Hartshorne and Paul Weiss. Cambridge: Harvard University Press, 1931–35.

Plato. *Works*. 12 vols. Loeb Classical Library. Cambridge: Harvard University Press, 1931–35.

Spencer, Herbert. *The Principles of Biology*. 2 vols. New York: D. Appleton, 1904.

Telford, Kenneth A. *Aristotle's Poetics: Translation and Analysis*. Chicago: Henry Regnery, 1961

Watson, Walter. *The Architectonics of Meaning: Foundations of the New Pluralism*. Albany: State University of New York Press, 1985.

Wick, Warner A. *Metaphysics and the New Logic*. Chicago: University of Chicago Press, 1942.

Whitehead, Alfred North. *Process and Reality: An Essay in Cosmology*. New York: Macmillan, 1929.

Index

Abailard, Peter, 50, 52, 184; his *Sic et Non*, 14, 43
Acceptance, two kinds of, 177
Action(s): common and advantageous, 99; free, principle of, 102; and passion, 121; and reality, a kind of, 60; and statements, sequences of, 164–65
Adjustments: semantic, 185; social, 43
Adler, Mortimer J., 10
Agreement(s): general, 162; on principles, impossible, 94–95, 101
Allenby, Edmund, General, 6
Alternatives, in arguments, 188–90
Ambiguity(ics): detecting, 200; "productive," 114; resolution of, 180; rooting out, 97; stimulation of, 126
American Philosophical Association, xv, 9, 206n.6
Analogy(ies): chain of, 49; between democracy and science, 117; and metaphors, 168; in Plato and Aristotle, 55; rigid, 52, 122, 131; from science to politics, 118; set of, 183; of states to kinship groups, 111–15. *See also* Method(s); Term(s)
Analysis: whether genetic, 128; problematic, 129; and synthesis, 60
Apostle, Hippocrates G., 5, 8
Applications, of synergic methods, 173
Approach(es): Aristotelian and Platonic, 91; "comfortable," 91; eight, 58; epistemic, 80; four, 122, 160, 181, 229n.7; linguistic, 80–81; mixed, 181; operational, 69–70; Platonic, 48; "pure," 47; Sophistical-Operational, added, 132; three, stemming from

Kant, 164; unitary and collational, 72. *See also* Method(s); System(s)
Aquinas, Saint Thomas, 10, 20, 22–23, 33, 64, 150, 168; and hymns, 204
Architecture, 167
Argument(s): accounting for, 205n.5; analysis of, 121, construing of, xiv; logistic, 87; negative: exploratory and confirmatory, 177; and propositions, terms, 202; structure of, 6
Aristotelian(s), 46; good, 174; strict, 19, 201
Aristotelianism, superficial view of, 19–20
Aristotle, 1, 2, 10, 11, 19, 22, 31, 33, 52, 94, 104, 105, 107, 108, 112, 114, 133, 137, 140, 143, 145, 146, 155, 168, 179, 183; and analogies, "pedagogic," 55; as anatomist, comparative, 29; and *aporia*, 55; articles on, by McKeon, 209n.28; the "bad," 19–20; on being, intelligibility of, 22; on bodies, falling, 19; on commonplaces, 225n.44; on Democritus, 215n.12; on demonstration, dialectic, rhetoric, 152–53; on dialectic, 45; as a duffer, 20; essentialist theory in 107–8; on facts, their correlation, 29; on forerunners, 229n.2; his four-cause theory, 128; four causes in Plato, whether he sees, 27; the "good," 20–21; and habits, moral, 145; on Heraclitus, 198; and history, 139; on imitation, 148; and inquiry as method, 133; and "literal" criticism, 142; and McKeon, discussion by, 19, 93, 180; mapped on X matrix, 63; and measure

Aristotle (*continued*)
of motion, 77–78; as mediator, 54, 55; and medieval period, early, 20; as meroscopic, 47–48, 76; and metaphysics, false, 19; and method, 47, 50; and motion, kinds of, 77, 78; and myth, 204; on natural objects and poetry, 141; on nature and art, 144–45; his philosophy, flexible yet precise, 180; and place, theory of, 76–77; on poems, 140; principles of, 55; procedure of, 205n.5; his questions, four, of inquiry, 86, 156, 215n.12; read in his own terms, 205n.5; on rhetoric, 194–95; and science, whether impeded, 20; simplification of, 153; and soul, 72–73; on spleens, animal, 211n.43; status of, as compromising and compromised, 48; subtleties of, 153–54; his times, not stressed, 227n.7; and tragedy, rules for, 19; and truth, theory of, 180; writings by, instrumental: *Categories,* 53; *On Interpretation,* 63; *Organon,* 6, 26, 53; *Posterior Analytics,* 20, 26, 63; *Prior Analytics,* 63; *Rhetoric,* 20, 26, 141, 154; *Topics,* 20, 26, 54, 152; writings by, practical: *Nicomachean Ethics,* 6, 26; *Politics,* 6; writings by, productive: *Poetics,* 21, 141; writings by, theoretic: *Metaphysics,* 26; *Physics,* 6, 26, 76, 136; *On the Soul,* 6

Array(s): and art, 125; columns of, 53, 57; commonplaces of, 69; earliest, 67; four by five, 52; four by four, 68; inclusion in, 198; of inquiry, 186, justifying many philosophers, 175; lacuna in, 184; limitations of, 51–52; logic of, 53; and matrices, 65, 137, 173, 227n.10; modifications of, 48; new, 57, 68; observations on, 51–52; omnibus, 17, 46, 50, 58; in Plato, 56; not printed as charts, 214n.3; not a priori, 54; semantic, 69, 88; special, 17, 46, 50, 52; structures of, 54; three-columned, 50; three by three, 52, 57, 79, 82, 83; three by two, 55, 67, 120; and *Ursysteme,* 179; vague headings of, 67. *See also* Matrix(ces)

Art(s), 125, 131, 146; architectonic, 151, 153, 155; of common action, 127; concepts of, 125–26; as expression, four approaches to, 147; hierarchy of, 126; humanizing, 126; liberal, 127–28; as nothing but art, 142; object made by, 125; and religion and science, 123; rhetorical, a practical, 194; and sciences, 133, 140, 182; in society, 127–28; technology of, 179; theories of, 125–50; universal, 155; of words, 195

Artist(s): aim of, 102; and critic, 141; and symbol or act, 146; theory of, in Mann, 149–50

Aspects, formal, of thought, 52–53

Associations: "amorous," 120; philosophical, 19

Assumption, of superiority to system, 192

Atomist(s), 48; McKeon not an, 92; types of, 55

Audience, universal, 194, 195

Augustine, Saint, 1, 2, 33, 78, 94, 100, 145, 154, 183; *Concerning the Teacher,* 206n.5; and six ages of world, 208n.21; and truth, 28

Austin, John L., 80, 95

Author: his changes in complexity, 166; and external circumstances, 184

Autrecourt, Nicholas of, 4, 64

Avicenna, 12, 81

Bacon, Sir Francis, 2, 110, 111, 140, 141, 157, 183

Barrett, William, 7–8

Baumgarten, Alexander Gottlieb, 33, 126, 146

Beard, Charles A., 123

Beauty: of art and nature, 140; and pleasure, 126; and truths, 149

Beethoven, Ludwig van, 86, 125

Behaviorism, and laryngeal motions, 73

Being: as article of faith, 51; and becoming, 27; categories of, 155; intelligibility of, 22; modes of, 69; insights into, 193; qua being, 71; as substance, 209n.28; Supreme, 71; and Thought, modes of, 86; truths of, 209n.28

Benjamin, A. Cornelius, 9

Bentham, Jeremy, 122, 108

Berkeley, Bishop George, 3, 79, 177

Biography, of an author, 41

Bodies, 55; and space, 77

Boethius, Manlius Torquatus Severinus, 157, 184
Bohr, Niels, 164
Bonaventura, Saint, 1, 145, 150, 156; and Saint Thomas, 195
Boole, George, 55; on principles, 218
Booth, Wayne C., 21–22, 210n.32, 216n.19
Bosanquet, Bernard, xiv, 11
Boyle, Sir Robert, 37, 72
Bradley, F. H., xiv, 11, 31, 65, 189, 190; his *Appearance and Reality,* 15, 177; and symbolic logic, 189
Bridgman, Percy W., 69
Brumbaugh, Robert S., 8, 226n.4
Building, and painting, 186
Buridan, Jean, and *insolubilia,* 73

Campanella, Tommaso, 111, 180
Carnap, Rudolf, 9, 137; contrast, with McKeon, 24; and logistic split, 85; and philosophic syntax, 84; and questions, nonempirical, 75; and reality, 76; and *Scheinprobleme,* 75; and semantics, 85
Cassiodorus, 3
Catchwords, and types of philosophies, 64
Category(ies), 82; of being and method, 155; of language and action, 88; lists of, 217n.12, 218; reflects truth, 172, and tragedy, 148
Causes, four, 128, 160
Centuries: twelfth, 20; thirteenth, 21, 138, 154, 191; fourteenth, 20, 74, 138, 154, 191; fifteenth, 154; sixteenth, 154, 180; seventeenth, 42, 109, 145, 157; eighteenth, 109, 143, 147, 157; nineteenth, 42, 105, 143; twentieth, 169, 179, 183, 202; advances and regressions of, 105; linguistic philosophers of, 163; rowdy, 138; style in, 31
Change: exaggerated notion of, 173; social, its stages, 128
Chesterton, G. K., 2
"Chicago School," 10, 90, 210n.32, 210–11n.33; basis for, 21–22; and McKeon's opinion of, 22
Cicero, 19, 26, 33, 94, 100, 141, 145, 151; on commonplaces, 155; and ele-

ments for rhetorical mastery, 153; and five commonplaces, 157; influential in Middle Ages, 154, methods of, 153; and Roman writers, 154; and rhetoric, 153; treatment of Aristotle, 153, 159
Class, of all propositions about propositions, 73–74
Classification(s): in equilibrium, 188; of previous systems, 178
Cohen, Morris R., 9
Coleridge, Samuel Taylor, 46, 141
"Colloquium," of students, 2056n.5
Columbia College, 1, 13, 119
Columbia University, 4, 9, 36, 46, 75, 200–201, 204; and dissertations, publishing of, 213n.2; and Philosophy, Department of, 5
Combinations: in modes of inquiry, 69; possible, of approaches, 181
Commonplaces, 60, 160, 194; in Aristotle, 225n.44; of history, 157; metaphysical, 69; of rhetoric and dialectic, 152. *See also* Topic(s)
Communication, 143, 157; and actions, 185; and associations, communities, 98; and dialectic in society, 95–98; and experiment, physical, 164; fourfold functions of, 101–2; improvements in, 179; and instrument for truth, 101; when lacking, 111; meanings of, 101; means of, 96; reliance upon, 164; useful in crises, 157; between writer and reader, 119
Community: effects of, on science, 116, world, idea of, 122
Computers, cybernetic basis of, 182
Concepts: abstract, 49; and action, 125; of arts, 125; important, listing of, 25–26; and methods, 28, 46–47, 76–79; need to interpret, 24; numbers of, unlimited, 54; Platonic, 76; as principles, 28; simple, 48; as stations on path, 49; structuring, 85; traditional, 25. *See also* Method(s)
Concerns, pistic, 196
Concessions, queries, objections, refutations, 176
Conflict(s): minimal resolution of, 95; philosophical, 33, 197–98
Conjunction, and combination, 54, 189

Connections: not explicit, 41; latent, 138; between types of thinking, 51
Consistencies, as aim of philosophy, 170
Content, and expression, 147
Context(s): historical, 187–88; metaphysical, of art, 146; original, 174; plural, cause confusion, 174
Contradiction, principle of, 191, 209n.28
Contrasts, four-term, three-term, two-term, 16
Controversy, 111; replaces dialogue, 96
Course, one- and fifty-drachma, 167
Crane, Ronald S., 22; and "Chicago School," 210nn.32–33
Creation: and criticism, 141; and imagination, 144
"Creativity," as commonplace, 154, 157
Criteria: application of McKeon's own, 170; of historian, 202; recognized, 104
Criticism: and concepts, 125; and creation, 141; literary, 10; practical, 149; theoretic and practical, 143
Critics, and philosophers, 139–43
Critics and Criticism: Ancient and Modern, 22, 210nn.32–33
Croce, Benedetto, 36, 94, 146
Cube, matrices, whether combinable into, 65
Culture(s): lessening of tensions between, 97; metaphysics of, 164; uncovering interrelations between, 123, 167
Cumming, Robert D., 11
Cycle(s): in history of philosophy, 136, nature of phase in, 195–96
Cycloid, as pattern for writing, xv

Dark Ages, 20, 50, 127
Data: and facts, 129; unordered democracy of, 67
Definition(s), 6; properties and applications of, 188; and property, genus, accident, 152
Democracy: no definition of, 147; and essay titles, 115; and right, 114; whether unscientific, 116–17
Democritus, 41, 55, 104, 105, 107, 108, 114, 137, 151, 198; and matter, 54; as meroscopic, 48; on nature, 145
Demonstration, 20, 114
Departments, pluralistic, 210n.33

Department of Philosophy. *See under* Columbia University; University of Chicago
Descartes, René, 2, 33, 157, 183; atomism of, 55; and geometry, 78; as holoscopic, 78; and self-referring formula, 73, 74; and Spinoza, 213n.3
Determinants, Leibnizian, 58
Dewey, John, xi, 2, 12, 15, 21, 26, 31, 33, 79, 94, 100, 103, 116, 146, 166; and action, 228n.13; his circle of terms, 118–19; and education, 118–19; *Experience and Nature*, 15; on individual and society, 103; and McKeon, contrasted, 103–4; precis of, 226n.1; on self-realization and desire, 103; as teacher of McKeon, 19
Diagonals, 58
Diagrams, early philosophical, 46–47
Dialectic, 56; adjustments of, between dialogues, 66; Aristotle's view of, 45; as column head, 54; and communication, 95–98; degeneration of, 96; and democracy, 117; freezing of, 124, 131; and indifference, 126; method of, 87; and methods, imposter, of Plato, 55; mixed, 145; mode of criticism, 142; Platonic, 45, 50, 140, 146; and rhetoric and poetic, 144; varieties of, and practice, 97. *See also* Method(s)
Dialectician: his attitude toward Carnap, 75–76; convictions of, 98; in Plato, 56
Dialogue(s): Platonic, 113; as poem, 141; replaced by controversy, 96; speakers in, 50. *See also* Dialectic; Hegel; Plato
Dichotomy, 48, 150
Differences, between thinkers, 70; philosophical, 185
Dilemmas: of common discourse, 197; metaphysical, 183
Dilthey, Wilhelm, 130–32; and experience, 164; method of, 132; objections to, 131, 203
Disagreements, between persons, 185
Discipleship, individual, 201–2
Discourse: kinds of, 160; its limits widened, 194; unity of, 83
Discussion: and dialectic, 111; free, 111; irenic aspects of, 229n.2; ordinary, and science, 225n.44

Dissension, causes of, 110

Distinctions, 33, 52, 181; conceptual and methodological, 55; dichotomous, 48; four-term, 54; root, 34; Scotist, 75; semantic, 162; and transformations, 94; trichotomous, 48–56

Distortions, 28; freedom from, 83; minimal, need for, 171; origins of, 167

Divergencies, apparent, between Plato's dialogues, 66

Divisions: McKeon's earliest, 55; in McKeon's later thinking, 203; tripartite, 53. *See also* Distinctions

Doctrine(s): Christian, 208n.21; classifying of, 57; coequal, relations between, 188; in common, 58; dissemination of, 113; dogmatic, 124; extractions from systems, 67; McKeonian, McKeonistic, McKeonesque, described, 167–68; of rights, 113; no single, 94; statement of, 83

Dogmatism, 169; ridding philosophy of, 187

Doubt, eternal, 207; not suppressed, 199

Earle, William, 11

Edman, Irwin, xii; as lecturer, 2; and use of blackboard, 4

Education, 118–21; administering of, 167; in arts, 127–28; definition of, 120; general, four meanings of, 119; higher, reforms in, 124; liberal, 119; and love, 120; McKeon's studies in, 94, 118; theory of, 43

Ego, transcendental, 184

Einstein, Albert, 3, 202; and generalized formulas, 77; as mixture of types, 77

Elements, methods, principles, 64

Elephant, four reports of, 191

Eliot, T. S., 142

Eloquence, and wisdom, 158

Empedocles, 194–95

Empire, Roman, 222n.42

Empiricism, 163; and empiricists, British, 112

Encyclopedia of Philosophy, The, 15

Ends: common, 115; kinds of, 188–89

Entities, order of, 43

Epicureans, and pleasure, 188–91

Epistemology, 2; McKeon's interest in, 18

Erasmus, 50

Erudition, and experiments, 203

Ethico-political, realm of, 111

Ethics, and politics, four relations between, 104–105. *See also under* Spinoza

Euclid, 138; and linear treatment, 250

Evaluation, in epistemic, constitutive, and pistic terms, 211n.38

Exigesis(es): classroom, 11, 16; sessions of, xiii; and theory of communications, 93

Existence, 86; categories of, 75; posterior in metaphysics, 81

Experience: common, 115; and That Which Is, 83

Experiment, as communication, 164

Exploration: of common purposes, 109; open, 131

Expression: and communication, 143, 144; theories of, 148. *See also* Communication

Fact(s), 86; and cause, 159; historical, and array, 50–51; modes of, 69, 86; and simples, composition with, 132–33

Fishnet, image of, 132

Fitzgerald, George Francis, 3; his contraction, 78

Flexibility, way to restore, 67

Forms: in logic, 60; and matter, 209n.28

Foundation, monistic, for pluralism, 94

Free, what things are, 107

Freedom, 127; and democracy, 105; for dialectician and others, 106; existentialist view of, 107; grounds of, four views, 108; kinds of, 62; limitations upon, 112; nature of, and four methods, 108; and power, 105–11; principle of, 123; of thought, speech, action, 103

Functions, 88; organic bases of, 73; polemic, educational, and irenic, of philosophy, 121–22

Gandhi, Mahatma, 115

Geisteswissenschaft, 130–32

Gewirth, Alan, 5, 8, 11

God, illumination by, 42

Goethe, Johann Wolfgang von, 131; and Kant, 195

Goodman, Paul, 7, 206n.1
Goods: determining, 128; four senses of, 100
Gorgias, 141, 194–95
Government: its agencies, 117; representative, 112
Grammar, 51, 126; and rhetoric, dialectic, logic, 154; of sciences, 81
Grammarian-historians, 4
Greeks: their science, xiv; as originators, 64–65, 137; and poetry, 139
Grene, Marjorie, 9

Hambidge, Jay, and dynamic symmetry, 30; effects of, 212n.44
Hartshorne, Charles, 9, 10
Harvanek, Father Robert, S. J., 216n.19
Headings: analogically used, 4; generic, 171–72; separate, 53; three philosophical, 54
Hegel, Georg Wilhelm Friedrich, 3, 19, 23, 55, 94, 96, 97, 126, 146, 166, 181, 196; and Idea, prior to culture, 130; and Jena, 184
Heidegger, Martin, 23, 31, 171
Heraclitus, 186, 198
Hierarchies, 84, 88, 192; in Plato, 56; of values, 141
Hilbert, David, 175
History(ies): as an art, 105–6, 128–30; cultural, 23, 133; cycles in, 71, 195; dialectical, logistic, problematic, 106, 129; epochal, causal, disciplinary, 129; of logic, 66; metaphorically understood, 168; of philosophy, 54, 65, 69, 120, 129, 133, 136, 139, 162, 166, 177; of philosophy, conceptual, 43, of philosophy, as the problem, 178; and poetry and philosophy, 83; progressive and cyclical, 208n.21; questions asked in, 68; simples of, 133; "spirit of," 168
Hobbes, Thomas, 33, 48, 103, 104, 109, 110, 183, 184; and analogical language; his *Leviathan,* 10; and nature as work of art, 141
Holoscopic, 31, 53; its altered meanings, 48; concepts, 47; its examination of meroscopic, 90; explained, 46; no label for loose thinking, 48; method, 49,

reapplication of, 87. *See also under* Concepts; Hegel; McKeon; Method(s); Plato
Homilectics, 127, 128
Horace, 140, 141
Hugh of St. Victor, 51
Hume, David, 3, 7, 33, 48, 79, 87, 100, 112, 133, 146, 147, 183, 190
Husserl, Edmund, 137, 162
Hutchins, Robert Maynard, 10, 22, 124

"I," and living self, 184
Ibsen, Henrik, 93
Ideals, as facts, 123
Ideas: simple, 15; structured, 114; system of, 182; traced from sensations, 73; too vague for metaphysics, 71
Illinois Philosophy Conference, 68
Images, quasi-mathematical, 4
Imagination, and creation, 143
Imitation: concept of, applied, 144; and historical cycles, 145; definition of, 212n.42; and imagination, 144, 148–49; and methods, 144; in poetics, 131; and poetry, four aspects of, 147; theory of, 143; a useful concept, 147
Implication, and counterimplication, 189
Imputation, internalized, 112
Independence, undisciplined, 136
Indeterminacy, 192–93
Indifference, principle of, 126, 144
Inquiry, 55, 57; array of, 186; meanings of, 133; philosophic, 65; problem of, 90; questions regarding, 86; scientific, 116, 165; simplistic literal, 122; square of, 69, 86; types of, 83
Integration, levels of, 63
Intellect, active, 193
Intentions, first and second, 191, 227n.6
International Institute of Philosophy, 111
Interpretation(s), 69, 87; dogmatic, 173; of facts and values, 126; importance of, 1; kinds of, 88; of philosophy, 170; sole principle of, 174
Invention, recovery, presentation, 127
Inversions, material and formal, 63, 67
Involution, double, 146
Irony, in Mann, 149
Isocrates, 150–51

Jaeger, Werner, 172
James, William, 12, 64, 137
Johnson, Dr. Samuel, his kick, 176
Johnson, W. E., xiv, 11, 63; four root formulas of, 212n.47
Justice, defined, 114

Kant, Immanuel, 10, 13, 33, 79, 93, 94, 122, 138, 147, 157, 162, 183; his *Critique of Pure Reason,* 26; and duty, 188–91; and Hegel, 215n.13; interpretation of, 205n.4; on judgement of beauty, 140; latest elaborations of, 204; and three kinds of metaphysics, 163; many methods of, 139; and multiple methods, 196–97; precursors of, 3; on thesis, antithesis, synthesis, 120; and thing-in-itself, 80; and four "titles," 212n.47
Kemp Smith, Norman, 172
Knowable, knower, knowledge, known, 160, 177, 229n.1
Knower: and known, 82; and world, 184
Knowledge: and action, 110; dissemination of, 167; as power, 110; as prudence, 108; of realities, 165; structured by symbols, 71; theoretic and practical, 43; of all things, 74; and What Is, 82
Known, and unknown, 155

Labor relations, book on, 199
Language: arts of, 51; a philosopher's native, 41; practical use of, 110
Law, 169; civil and divine, 112; McKeon's studies in, 94; McKeon's writings in, xi; natural, 114
Lawrence, T. E., 6
Leibniz, Gottfried, 3, 55, 58, 157, 183; determinants of, 58; his opinion of "ancient philosophy," 213n.10
Levels: four, for presenting theories, 75; four, of intellectual cooperation, 97; two, of individuals, societies, sciences, 121
Liberal arts, 127–28
Likenesses, and disagreements, 90
Liszt, Franz, 212n.46
Locke, John, 3, 10, 19, 27, 183

Logic, 2, 51, 69, 125, 162; of arrays, 53; of cause and effect, 140; demands for, to be dropped, 96; demonstrative, 50; of discovery, informal, 194; forms of, 60; function of, 126; history of, 66; leading thinkers of, 180; medieval, 41; modern, 7; and occupation of vertical lines, 66; philosophic, 11; of physical and value entities, 82; Polish, 185; proof by, 181; symbolic, 55; theories of, 63, 216n.17; two-valued, 177
Logician-historians, 4
Logicians: symbolic, 196; task of, 62–63
Logistic: as column head, 54; method of, 87. *See also under* Method(s)
Logos, for arts and sciences, 182
Longinus, 142, 146; and judgments, 141
Lorentz, Hendrik Antoon, 3, 78
Love: and knowing, doing, making, 120; and wisdom, 121
Lucretius, 48, 55, 65, 133, 154; his *De rerum natura,* 15
Lully, Ramon, 33, 157

McKeon, Muriel Thirer, first wife of Richard, 7, 12
McKeon, Richard. *See also* McKeon, Richard, writings of
—His approach(es) to philosophy: advantages and disadvantages of, 29–30; his affiliations, not printed, 91; aim of, 175; analogies, use of, 4; assumption, its principal, 28; not atomistic, 92; attacks, sparsity of, on others, 130; biographical references, lack of, 213n.7; its categorization, dislike of, 9; changing, 45, 172; whether a contradiction in, 157; and covering of tracks, 67; four, efforts to expound, 180; four, whether embraced, 91; four, summary of, 93; whether historical, 18–19; history, treatment of, 128; ideas, traces changes in, 148; independence of, 10; McKeonian, genuine, 23; whether medievalist, 44; metaphilosophy, rejects, 91; its method, 28, 92, 129, 131; original and scholarly, 1; philosophical and historical, whether equal, 137; whether Platonic, 90; practical, 9; pragmatic

McKeon, Richard (*continued*)
 and utopian, 115; its preferences, philosophic, 90–93; its principles, reflexive, 92; its problems, chief, 136; its procedure, 30; programmatic character of, 200; psychological reasons in, 66, "pure," its meanings, 169; reservations on, general, 199–201; and sense, that philosophers make, 28; and simplification, possible, 204; whether sophistic, 90; as spectator, 191; starting-point of, 130; and system-builders, 27; and systems, study of, 193; and system, whether writing, 198; and texts as facts, 29; and trivium, his analogical use of, 4; and *Urphilosophen,* whether standing above, 91
 —His career: its development, stages in, 67; diplomacy, apostle of, 203; earlier and middle, 166; middle, 52; Navy, service in, 8, 99; some courses taught: Advanced Logic, 11, 217n.12; General History of Philosophy (Philosophy 162), 2–4; Hobbes, 10; *Physics* (Aristotle), 6; *Politics* (Aristotle), 6; *Republic* (Plato), 6; *On the Soul* (Aristotle), 6; *Timaeus* (Plato), 6; teaches Science and Metaphysics, 4, 11, 46, 75–79, 211n.40, 217n.12; professional life of: administration, of military program, 12–13; administrative capabilities, 1, 205n.1; at Columbia, 1, 4, 5; commissions, service on, 99; deanship, 5, 8–9, 99; Greek, professor of, 5; Charles F. Grey Distinguished Service Professor, 12; history, professor of, 5; philosophy, professor of, 5, 12; retirement of, 12; UNESCO, positions in, 113, 219n.9
 —Personality and mind of: his anecdotes, 7; his apartment, 7; his appearance, 2, 9; austerity of, 8; complexity of, 206n.6; conferences, his attendance at, 12; as conversationalist, xii, xiii, 8; diversification, search for, 204; his doubts, regarding "intellectual approach," 224n.28; epitaph for, 124; as experienced, 98; family of, 99; frankness of, 199; helpfulness of, 8; as host, 7; his intellectual energy, 198; his nature of, healthy, 203; a neoteric, 124;

and oppositions, welcoming of, xv; optimism of, 163; and philosophy, whether disillusioned with, 151; practical nature of, 167; rural vacations, attitude toward, 7; speeches, his love of, 92; sports, his skill in, 2, 203; temperament of, xii–xiii; as autobiographer, 18, 208n.26, 230n.15; and languages: facility in, 3, 12, 42
 —Powers of: able to cross disciplines, 34; erudition of, 94, as originator, 198; his subtlety, 199; his sweep, 198; versatility of, 12; analyses of Hamlet, 13; Near Eastern Institute, proposal for, 12; numbers, his work in theory of, 18; short stories, lectures on, 13, Stravinsky, his conversation on, 13; studies of Bacon, outlining of, 10; his doctorate, 36; engineering, early interest in, 12; Europe, his sojourn in, grasp of texts, 23; his ideas, system of, 167; interests, later, 11, 43; as leader, 102; learning of, 124, 216; M.A. thesis, his estimate of, 36; materials, his early mastery of, 9; name, his full, use of, 205n.2; Navy, training in, 12; outdoing of, whether possible, 23; scholarship of, 198; social problems, interest in, 18; speed, of reading, 10; studies, medieval, 42; texts, mastery of, 92; travels of, 7, 98–99
 —And public: his antagonists and defenders, 167; book dedication, 199; debate, formidable in, 176; defense of, by followers, reluctance to seek, 201–2; future influence of, possible, xi, 201–3; judgment of, 93; literature on, not extensive, 226n.4; misinterpretation of, easy, 8–22, 23; and others, 169; and predecessors, 229n.2; and public, wide, 30
 —And students: papers by, his comments on, docility of, lament over, 206n6; favoritism, lack of, xiii; letters from, to McKeon, xiv; loyalty of, to McKeon, 8; as servicemen, his wartime correspondence with, 11
 —As teacher: as anatomist, 27; chapel talk by, 1; class notes, 10; classroom, procedures of, 5–7, 57; concepts, dis-

tinguishing of, 120; concepts, physical, plans for treating, 76; as cryptanalyst, 28; diagramming, skill in, 38; diagrams, blackboard, 4; exegesis(es), courses in, 56; disagreements with, foolhardy, 176; discussion(s), class, 1, 8; lectures of, xiii, 1, 11; methods, drill sergeant of, 203; phrases of, characteristic, xiii; praise by, rare, 5–6; preparation of, 5; and private asides, 170–71; questioning by, 5–6, 11; speaking, manner of, 2; style, of teaching, changes in, 11; theories, own, new emphasis on, 11; tenet of, a basic, 100; tests, for meaning, 38; texts, his correlations of, 29; and theology, cosmology, epistemology, 71; theories of, 1, 25, 179; and theses, order of, 175; his thinking, divisions in, 203; thought, a turn in, 150–65; Thrasymachus, his method of interpreting, 202; truth, existence of, not denied, 188

—Topics, specific: Aristotle: attitude toward, 210n.28; differs from, on systems, 93; discusses, most, 180; essays on, 19; and four approaches, 180; interpretation of, vitalized, 180; method of, 215n.12; studies of, 20; writings on, 10; Aristotelian and neo-Aristotelian: whether can be considered, 18–22, 91, 93; art: conclusions on, 126; feeling in, 125; practitioners of, 18; steps not taken in, by McKeon, 125–26; "Chicago School," 18–22; McKeon, whether a member of, 21–22; earnestness, regarding choices, 91; "circumstances, insistence upon," 195; and classical ideal, 203; and cultural change, 21; and cycles, 145; on cycles in history, 71, 195–96; concepts, his much-used, listed, 25–26; concepts, new use of, 8, 25; constitutions, silence on, 221n.30; Dewey, difference from, 103–4, 118; and dialogue, conductor of, 56; Dilthey, whether McKeon refutes, 130–32; discourse, his theory of, 24; distinctions, his, 32, 181, 183; distortion, his aim at minimal, 185; division, his method of, 166; divisions, his earliest, 55; education, experimental, his

part in, 119, 203; epistemology, interest in, 18; freedom, discussions of, 105; historical procedures of, 178; human being, two-level view of, 99; Kant, and McKeon compared, 13, 198; and contrasted, 163–64; on letter C, 27; and matrices, exposition of, 57–58, 216n.16; metaphysics, his interest in, 18, 71; and method, early emphasis on, 43; method, historical, of McKeon, 131; method, as operationalist, 93; method, his use of, 24, 27; and peace, essays on, 18; work for, 122, 124, 191; philosophers, his fourfold distinction between, 107–9; his number of great, 227n.9; philosophies, his alternants in, 190–91; approaches to, schematized, 143; his arrays of, earlier, 75; four aspects, of cognition, 177; methods, historical, equivalence of, 129; own, 212n.43; pattern of, capacious, 29; philosophy of, protean, 176; and plurality of moral orders, 104; principles, types of, 218n.15; prototypical, 64; theories, types of, 47–48; Plato, his conception of, 55–56; pluralism, 110, 133, 165, 202; politics, no complete philosophy of, 123; silence on topics of, 110; principles, his, 116; self-evidence of, 92; problems, common, 131; reality, three kinds of, 60; reasons, rejection of psychological and social, 183–84; rhetoric, laments misuses of, 157–58; and predecessors in, 159; writings, late, on rhetoric, and rhetoric of Isocrates, 149–150; and rhetoric, late writings on, 156; Bertrand Russell, contrast with, 24; Gilbert Ryle, contrast with, 25; schema, determination of, 142; semantics, concern for, 85; impartiality, whether paralyzing, 22n.13; array of, left unpublished, 88; and Spinoza: criticism of, 38; interpretation of, 36–41; papers on, 38; plans for revision of book on, 37; system, closed, 180–81; stress on whole, 43; talk, two-fold explanation of, 96; task, regarding commensurable, 192; theory, uniqueness of his, 180; unity, two kinds of, in his work, 38; *Ursysteme,* his use of,

McKeon, Richard (*continued*)
179; war, whether caused by words,
104, 221n.22; wholeness, his love of,
204; and Wittgenstein, 25; and Woodbridge, last labors on, 204; and world
government, prophet of, 203; world
peace, 110; world problems, 122, 155;
world, homogenized, rejected, 162
McKeon, Richard, writings of, xiv, 4, 81,
198; listings of, 206n.1; general characteristics of, 14–18; literary arrangement
of, 33–35; order of, 18, 95; in first period, 179; later, 43; *Nachlass,* 30, types
of, 150; monothematic and collational,
81, preservative and interpretive,
16–17
—Books, remarks on, 9, 14; mystery
novel, 206n.7; "philosophy in the
Middle Ages," appearance of, 44
—Essays, remarks on: amplification of,
15; arranging, difficulty of, 34–35;
arts, papers on, 18; authorship of, primary, 14, 15; and book reviews,
206n.1; chronological order of, 18;
chronological reading of, 34; collational, 17; complexity of, 23, on culture, 18; dialectical connections of, 18;
earlier and later, 166; early, give no unified source, 196; edition of, planned,
15; on education, 18; on ethics, 103–
5; interconnections of, 15; on metaphysics, 18; and "monograph," "memoir," "disquisition," as descriptive of,
207n.10; monothematic, 17, 72, 74;
patterns of, 23, 119; on philosophy,
general, 18; on philosophy, Greek, 17;
political, first, 94; popularity of some,
33; reading of, 34; surveying, problem
of, 18; their topics, spectrum of, 14–
15; as sources for study of author, 14
—Individual books discussed: *Freedom
and History: The Semantics of Philosophical Controversies and Ideological Conflicts,*
14, 17, 97, 106–7, 129–30; *The Philosophy of Spinoza: The Unity of His
Thought,* 14, 19, 36, 43, 103, 136; *Selections from Medieval Philosophers,* 2, 14,
16, 31, 41–45; *Thought, Action, and
Passion,* 14
—Individual essays discussed: "Aristotle's
Conception of Language and the Arts

of Language," 151; "Aristotle's Conception of Moral and Political Philosophy," 103; "The Background of Spinoza," 39; "The Battle of the Books,"
119–20, 124; "Being, Existence, and
That Which Is," 17, 81–83; "Causation
and the Geometric Method in the Philosophy of Spinoza," 38–41; "Communication, Truth, and Society," 101–2;
"Creativity and the Commonplace,"
151, 154–56; "Criticism and the Liberal Arts: The Chicago School of Criticism," 21, 207n.20; "*De Anima;* Psychology and Science," 72–74;
"Democracy, Scientific Method, and
Action," 116–18; "The Development
and the Significance of the Concept of
Responsibility," 111–13; "Dialectic and
Political Thought and Action," 17, 97;
"Dialogue and Controversy in Philosophy," 96–97; "Discourse, Demonstration, Verification, and Justification,"
156, 160; "Discussion and Resolution
in Political Conflicts," 99–101; "Ethics
and Politics," 103–5; "The Future of
the Liberal Arts," 126; "The Future of
Metaphysics," 163–65; "Has History a
Direction? Philosophical Principles and
Objective Interpretations," 132–33;
"Imitation and Poetry,' 130–32, 143–
49; "Introduction to Aristotle" (unpublished), 14, "Introduction to the Philosophy of Cicero," 16, 151; "Knowledge and World Organization," 110;
"The Liberating Arts and the Humanizing Arts in Education," 127–28; "Literary Criticism and the Concept of Imitation in Antiquity," 16; "Love and
Wisdom: The Teaching of Philosophy,"
120–21; "Moses Maimonides, the Philosopher," 16; "The Methods of Rhetoric and Philosophy: Invention and
Judgment," 151, 156, 159; "Propositions and Perceptions in the World of
G. E. Moore," 80; "The Philosophic
Bases of Art and Criticism," 11, 17,
139–43; "The Philosophic Problem,"
121–22; "Philosophic Differences and
the Issues of Freedom," 94; "Philosophic Semantics and Philosophic Inquiry," 17, 68, 85–90, 132, 156, 158,

160, 180; "Philosophy and History in the Development of Human Rights," 113–15; "Philosophy and Method," 17, 52–56, 68, 85–86; "Power and the Language of Power," 109–10; "The Relation of Logic to Metaphysics in the Philosophy of Duns Scotus," 74; "Remarks on the Occasion of the Seventieth Birthday of Thomas Mann (June 6, 1945) Made at a Dinner Given to Him in Chicago (June 29, 1945)," 149–50; "Renaissance and Method in Philosophy," 50, 52, 151; "Rhetoric in the Middle Ages," 43; "The Science of Criminology," 72; "Spinoza on the Rainbow and on Probability," 39–40; "Symposia," 97, 151; "The Uses of Rhetoric in a Technological Age: Architectonic Productive Arts," 158–59, 197; "World Community and the Relations of Cultures," 123–24

—His Style, 30–35; care for, 176; alterations, of terms, 32; anaphora, and antithesis, 32; "artistry" of, 32; capitalization, 31; epithets, use of, 39; in late essays, 32–33; impersonal, 200, irony in, possible, 118; prose, 23, 53, 212n.46; and figures, related, 4; reading of, not easy, 16, 199; its rhythm, 32; its substructures, not described, 16; and technical terms, 25; tendencies in arrangment: citations, no unanalyzed, 136; exposition, method of, 136; organization, principles of, xv; paragraphing, 32; proportions, in subjects treated, 17–18; summaries, use of, 33

McKeon, Zahava K., second wife of Richard, 37, 204; on development of essay on semantics, 219n.19; and profile of McKeon's approach, 218n.18; as teacher and author, 12

Maimonides, Moses, 12

Man: and group, 103; as living creature, 130; as rational animal, 19; as whole, 128

Mankind, moral aims of, 191–92

Mann, Thomas, 126, 149–50; *Tonio Kröger,* 207n.10

Marx, Karl, 55, 94, 130

Mathematics, xi, 165, 169, 183

Matrix(ces), 11, 46, 125, 171–72; advantages of three, 66; no bar to progress, 187; no boundaries to, 175; not certainties, 186; combination of, impossible, 216n.17; defect of, 67; and determinants, 169; and diagonals, 58, 137–38; and distances between doctrines, 187; and doctrines, location of, 61–62; and doctrines, resolution of, 187; expansion of, 194; explanation of, unpublished, 216n.16; first appearance of, 57; flexibility of, 65; four by four, 67, 83, 227n.10; general and neutral, 177; glossary of terms used in, 59; as gridlocks, 62; inclusion in, 198; interpretations of, 66, 137–38; lines equal in, 188; major of, 58; minor of, 65; nodes on, 173, 174, 197; as peirastic devices, 186; placement on, 191; in Plato, 33; and possibilities, 85; questions regarding, 63–67; summary of, 62; and textual readings, 227n.11; three, 69; usefulness of, limited, 187; and *Ursysteme,* 179; X, Y, and Z types, 64, 69. *See also* Array(s); Square(s)

Matter, and form of text, 34

Meaning(s), 11, 60, 97–98; devices to demolish, 95; different, 99; dubious, 87; unambiguous, 141; univocal, 87, 193; width of, xiv

Mediation, by problematic method, 54

Memory, and invention, 154–55

Meroscopic, 31, 47, 53; alteration of meaning of, 48, 87; and divisions, 48; explained, 46. *See also under* Aristotle; Concepts; Democritus; McKeon, Richard; Method(s)

Metaphors, and analogies, 168

Metaphysical Society of America, 81

Metaphysics, 34, 69, 125, 162; as actual and contingent, 218n.13; aims of, 83; approaches to, 82; Aristotelian, 71; of culture, 164; and future of rhetoric, 164, 165; implications of, 90; insecurity of, 165; knowledge of, 71, 182; and linguistic approach, 80–81; making of, 182; and moral science, 165; necessity for, 100; need for change of, 179, Platonic, 71, pluralistic, 164; and principles, 71; and retreat from certainty, 165; revised view of, 162; of science, 168; as science of being qua being, 71,

Metaphysics, (*continued*)
76; of substance and essence, 165; as
truths of intellect and language, 71. *See
also under* Aristotle; Being; McKeon,
Richard; Plato
Method(s), 69, 87; advertized, 173–74;
analogical, 140, 142; analytic, 50; application of, 143–44; Aristotelian, 76;
"balanced," 48; commitment to, 65;
and concepts, 46–47; failure to adhere
to, 28–29; and fitting to concepts, 49,
197; consistently employed, 49; Democritean, as catchall, 50, 61; dialectical,
55, 144; differences in, 64; of Dilthey,
151; diverging, 190; examination by,
90–91; four, 87, 143, 144, 147; functions of, 28; geometrical, 38–40; holoscopic, 47–48, 91; Kantian, 139,
196–97; logistic, as calculative, 54; and
selection, 186; McKeon's early emphasis on, 43; and matrices, 216n.20; meroscopic, 47–48; nature of, 49; operational, 63, 143, 144; and physics,
concepts of, 76–79; Platonic, 50, 76;
and principles, 92, 137, 160; problematic, placing of, 54, 55; purity of, 65;
right, 95; stages of, 66; and submethod, 139; supervenient, 29; synergic, 173; taken together, 63; three,
53, 68; two-part, 27; two, three, four,
64; and Y matrix, 61. *See also under*
Concepts; Holoscopic; McKeon, Richard; Meroscopic; Plato; Principle(s)
Middle Ages, 20, 34, 50, 127, 154, 179;
misconception of, 41–42
Mill, John Stuart, xiv, 3, 11, 27, 33, 94,
100, 112, 127
Mixtures, of four philosophies, 65
Modes, circumstantial, 83; of inquiry,
four kinds of, 86, 154; special, 82
Monologues, crossed, 219n.6
Moore, G. E., 80; dislocation in, 217n.8
Morris, Charles W., 9, 146
Motion: four categories of, 209n.28; in
Plato's cosmos, 78; uniform, 77

Nachlass, 175
Nagel, Ernest, 5
Nations: contacts between, 112; harmony
of, 110; problems of, 111

Neo-Aristotelian: affiliations of, 90–91;
meanings of, 93
Neoterics, 119
Neurologist, and cybernetics, 182–83
Newton, Sir Isaac, 53, 76–79, 96
Nietzsche, Friedrich, 23, 183, 198;
twenty Nietzsches, 102
Nizolius, Marius, 33, 50, 157
Node(s): four, 69; interpertations of, 67;
lines of, 57; and matrix, 65, 83, 171,
173, 174, 198; as metaphysical, 62;
multiplication of, 60; number of, 83;
whether philosophic, 62; occupation
of, 187; rejection of, 92, selection of,
186; shared, 58; as squares of chessboard, 65; and trios of letters, 58; two,
determine line, 67; uses of, 57
Novel, changes in, 149

Object(s): art, 125; mathematical, 183;
and persons, symbols, 216n.17
Objection(s): described, 176; in private
communications, 203
Oblongs, 4, 51–52, 68
Observation, interpretation, integration,
23
Ockham, William of, 2, 20, 64, 171, 183;
his Razor, 41; and senses of word, 133;
and soul, repudiation of, 72; on terms,
width of, 175
Opinions: ordinary, 165; respect for, 95;
right, in politics, 117; and speakers, in
Plato, 56; truth of, 152
Opposites, pairs of, Platonic, 211n.40;
tensions in, 201
Opposition(s), and agreements, 43, 56
O system, 193–94

Paganini, Nicolò, 212n.46
Paleoterics, 119
Paradoxes: in use of laws, 114; *tu quoque,*
179
Paralogisms, 164; four types of, 114; of
science and community, 116
Part(s): coherent with others, 47; least,
48, 196; and whole, 64
Patterns, need to reconstruct, 23
Peace, 33, 221n.22; marches for, 8; two
kinds of, 122; universal, 110, 167
Peer Gynt, 176

Peirce, Charles S., 31, 63, 79
Person: as agent, 102; and mind, 62; and philosophy, 193; responsibility toward, three kinds, 112, 185
Persuasion: dialectical, logical, rhetoric, 96; means of, 151; ranked above philosophy, 150–51
Philology, united with philosophy, by McKeon, 24
Philosopher(s): ambivalent position of, 97; American, 3; and beauty, 139; and critics, 141; disagreements between, 63–64; and doctrines, 185; and experience, 184; and expertness, 197; and gaps, 181; grouping of, 48; health of, 66; history, their ignorance of, 19; latest, 178; linguistic, 163; major, 174; making sense by, 230n.9; medieval, 10, 42; meroscopic, 48; and method, advertising of, 173–74; and methodic inconsistencies, 28–29; and neurosis, 66; and nodes, sharing of, 58; pluralities of, 95; and politics, 123; and predecesors, 175; purposes of, 41, 43; and rule, suitability for, 97; succession of, 133; systematic, 182; task of, 99; transition between, 42; and truth, partial, 192, and *Ursysteme,* mixing of, 88; and wars of words, 96; writings of, 90
Philosophy(ies): arrival of, late, 66; its assimilation to past, 168; Cartesian, 37; character of, 29; and culture, history of, 133; cycles in, 195; change of, need for, 179; devitalization, its possible, 198; dialectic of, 229; disappearance of, 169; divisions of, threefold, 68; equality of, 198; formation of, 57; functions of, three, 121; future of, 163; game of, played out, 229n.2; German, 131; grasp of, 175; Greek, study of, 203; and history, 137, 143; history of, 54, 64, 65, 68, 69, 120, 133, 139, 154, 162, 166–68, 177; History of, General (course), 2, 3; human, incurably, 193; interpretation of, 227n.8; kinds of, three, 68; mathematical, 184; medieval, and conformity, 41–43; its methods, 196; its mixtures of methods, four, 65; modeling of, on science, 163–64; number of, 181; opposed, 99; original-

ity of, 174; and peace, 121; its pistic aspect, 180; plural, 115, 124, 201; and poetry, 144, 145, 149; and problems, social, 98–103; its reduction to practice, 100; practical, ends of, 201; principles of, 139, prototypical, four, 64; its retelling, 178; and rights, human, 113–14; schools of, 81; and science, advance of, 148; scope of, narrowing, 138; single, 202; and society, 98; subject matter of, 164, 199; successful and unsuccessful, 172; systems of, 171, 182; teaching of, 120; and truth, no final, 64; as truth, love of, 197, 227n.7; types of, 64, 125; understanding of, 171–72; universality of, xiv; vocabulary of, 133; and wisdom, love of, 120. *See also* Columbia University, Department of Philosophy; University of Chicago, Department of Philosophy
Physicists' cooperation, 97
Physics, 169; inexact, in Plato, 78; and logic, ethics, 82; mathematical, pre-Galilean, 20; systems of, 46
Pickwickian sense, 90
Place, 76–77
Plato, xii, 1, 2, 11, 19, 31, 52, 79, 94, 103–5, 112–14, 130, 133, 137, 143, 146, 148, 150, 151, 179, 183, 198; analogies in, 45, and Aristotle, 26–27, 195; and causes, 27; and criticism, 141; debts to others, 66; his Demiurge, 144; dialectic of, 45, 165, 195; and dialectic, accounts of, 50, 55; his dialecticians, 56; his dialogues, 45, 56, 229n.3; Divided Line of, 84; and evil, choosing of, 100; and forms, 54; and freedom, 108; hierarchies of, 55 56; history, no key to subsequent, 139; on imitation, poem as, 141, 145; interpretations of, 170; and Isocrates, 150–51; McKeon's interpretation of, 55–56; and matrix, 33; and method, 27, 47, 50; misunderstanding of, 196; motions, theory of, 78; opinions regarding, 56; his opponents, 150; as originator, 56; on poems, 140; as poet, 149; on poetic madness, 125; poets, banishes, 141; his quirks, possible, 170; on rhetoric, 194–95; on space, 76; on speakers, their

Plato, (*continued*)
opinions, 56; and Syracuse, 184; and
terms, use of, 27; and textbook,
whether writing, 55; and Tolstoy, 140;
and utopia, 122; writings of: *Critias,*
66; *Gorgias,* 15; *Ion,* 26; *Laws,* 7, 66,
180; *Meno,* 117; *Phaedrus,* 55, 66, 92,
150; *Philebus,* 55; *Republic,* xii, 6, 26,
56, 122, 141, 177, 202; *Sophist,* 25, 55;
Statesman, 55; *Symposium,* 149, 153;
Timaeus, 6, 25, 26, 56, 66, 76, 150,
196
Pleasure: and duty, 188–91; kinds of,
141; objectification of, 147
Pluralism, 210n.33; aim of, 180; and
"Chicago School," 21–22; concordant,
95; dilemma of, 181; kinds of, two,
23–24, 162–63; as label, 23; the last
best hope, 203–4; loss of, possible,
181; machinery of, 24; its monist foundation, 94–95, 201–2
Poet(s), 125, 157; as maker of plots, 148;
and scientists, 140
Poetics, 139–50; classical, 21; as critical
type, 142
Poetry: differentiation of, as thing, judgment, or effects, 140; familiarity with,
183; and imitation, 143, and philosophy, 141, 147
Politicians, 185, 194
Politics: international, 8; papers on, 94;
and power, 122; its principle, 94; and
right opinion, 117
Polylemma, 174, 178
Popularizations, 33
Positivists, 146, 202; and metaphysics, 71
Power, 97, 124, 189; and authority, force,
violence, 109; disappearing, 109;
grades of, 43; as ground for sovereignty, 109; misdirection of, 110; and
politics, 100; and rights, 114; as principle of state, 109
Precision, 66, 196; of matrices, 65
Principle(s), 197; actional, 68; Aristotle's
55; of arts and sciences, 182; and
causes, and elements, 209n.28; commitment to, 65; common, 47; and concepts, 28; of contradiction, 191; and
definitions, 183; derived from Greeks,
39; englobing, 92; formulation of, 99;

four kinds of, 87; grasping of, 54; of
indifference, 126, 144; justified by
metaphysics, 169; logical, 42; logistic,
56; metaphysical derivation of, 182;
self-reflexive, 165; and semantics, 87;
of sensation, reason as, 73; summating,
58, 63, 128; tracing through, 41; and
wisdom, 82
Problem(s): common, 86–87, 115, 131;
contemporary, 27; of ethics, 104; of individuals, governments, peoples, 10,
11; and communication, origin in, 101;
particular, 200; persistent and emergent, 104–5; philosophic, 52, 159
–60, 178; reduction of, to few kinds
not possible, 155; solutions to,
179, 200
Problematic, 54; method, 87. *See also
under* Method(s)
Profile, adherence to, 90
Proofs, two kinds of, 200–201
Proposition(s), 55; added to all others,
73; containing "pleasure," 191; and distances between, 187; individual, 83;
and inference to thinker, 74; interpretations of, xiv; metaphysical, 185; on
moral action, 190; and multiplicity of
contexts, 198–99; as *p* and *q,* 188–91;
partial and total, 177; philosophic, 84;
as primary, 63; and self-reference, 73;
semantic and syntactic relations of,
136; sentences, judgments, 83; sets of,
57; stating that and what all propositions are, 74; as substrate for truth, 60;
on totality of propositions, 73; treatment of, as contraries, 191; truth-values
of, 193–94
Prototypes, for philosophizing, 137. See
also *Urphilosophen; Ursysteme*
Psychoanalysis, not invoked, 277n.7
Publication, reasons for, 17

Query, 176–77
Question(s): Aristotle's four, 86; asking
of, 68; categorical, 82; circumstantial,
83; classroom, 11; of fact and cause,
159; and inquiry, 86; philosophic, 173;
on matrices, 63–67; their relation, to
being, 81–83; with speech, 153; splitting of, 107

Quine, Willard V., 64, 137
Quintilian, 150, 159

Ramus, Peter, 2, 52, 180
Ratner, Joseph, 3–4
Reader: and textual analogies, 184; and writings of McKeon, 16
Reality: not homogeneous, 66; objective, 71; problems of, 81–82; ways known and communicated, 71
Reason(s): and justice, 99; psychological and social, 169–70; self-arrogating, 163; three functions of, 98
Rectangles, dilapidated, 172
Refutations, 131–32; apparent, 95; confirmatory, 177; and divergent approaches to, 138; exploratory, 176–77; a rhetorical issue, 198
Relations, four, between ethics and politics, 104; logic of, 54, 75; transitive and intransitive, 81
Reminscences, termination of, 12
Renaissance: and Middle Ages, 42, 154; as "relapse," 3; and rhetoric, 154; writers of, 196
Resolution: of conflicts, 33; of oppositions, 64
Responsibility: and freedom, 127; moral and political, 112; to self and others, 114; ways to consider, 111
Rhetoric, 34, 51; its apparent advance, 165; as architectonic art, 151, 155–62; aspects of, 96; classical, 22; commonplaces of, 152, 199; counterpart of dialectic, 152–53, 158; deliberative and demonstrative, 159; enthymemes of, 152; essays on, 33; of exposition, 203; extension of, 43, 194; functions of, 155, 159; future of, 159, 163; and future of metaphysics, 165; good, and dialectic, 150; as innovative, 126; kinds of, Latin, 158; McKeon's late works on, 156; and metaphysics, 164; need for, 96–97; political, forensic, epidictic, 152–53; practical, 194; productive, 158; reformed, 155; scope of, 127; and semantics, 156; and speech, continuous, 153; its subordination, 157; and tenses, 225n.49; tradition of, 145–46; transformed, and commonplaces, 205;

universalized, 160; as used for peace, 162; vision of, new, 158
Rhetorician-historians, 4
Rights, 113–15
Rome, historians of, 208n.21
Rousseau, Jean-Jacques, 94, 109, 122
Ruler and ruled, 114
Russell, Bertrand, xi, 9, 31, 79, 95, 103, 147, 183; as historian, 202; imprisonment of, 184; and McKeon, contrasted, 24
Ryle, Gilbert, 62; and McKeon, contrasted, 25

Sacksteder, William, 11
Santayana, George, 27, 36, 103, 126, 137; and logistic approach to art, 47
Sartre, Jean-Paul, 95, 171; his *Being and Nothingness*, 15
Scale, parts of diatonic, 175
Schemata, 23; kinds of, three, 46; self-application of, 90–93; tripartite, 81. *See also* Array(s), Matrix(ces), Square(s)
Schillinger, Joseph, 126
"Scholarly," as critical type, 126
Science(s): achievements of, 179; of the actual, 74; and arts, 69, 133, 194 charts of, 72; and communication, 101; conceptions of, 48; and counting of witnesses, 118; foundations of, 43; impossible without soul, 74; and Metaphysics (course), 4; methods in, 50; model for philosophy, 163–64; natural, and productive, 125; political, and rhetoric, 153; rational, and empirical, 72; relations to philosophy, 183; of soul, nonexistent, 74; special, in linguistic approach, 81; and technology, 98; theoretical, practical, productive, 34, 82; whether undemocratic, 116–17. *See also under* McKeon, Richard: His career
Scotus, John Duns, 2, 43, 64, 112, 183; essay on, 16, 165; on being, 74–75; on trustworthiness of senses, 211n.37
Selection(s), as semantics heading, 69, 79, 88, 186, 191–92
Self: bloodless, 184; consistency of, 168, responsibility to, 114; solidity of, 185
Semantics: ordinary and philosophic, 67–70, 90; problem of, 90; square of, 86

Sense(s), 42; common, and rhetoric, 165
Seville, Isadore of, 3
Signs, 80–81
Sigwart, Christoph, xiv
"Simples," 132
Simplicity, modes of, 69
Skepticism, 96, 128, 163
Society(ies): arts in, 127–28; perfect,
   102; philosophical, xii; undifferen-
   tiated, 101
Socrates, 56, 100; his love of speeches,
   92; on method, 27
Sophist(s), 104, 105, 114, 137, 186; and
   man as measure, 145; and operational-
   ism, 69; and separation of approach, 96
Sophistic: difficulties with, 229n.7; and
   operationalism, added, 91, 107. *See also*
   Method(s)
Soul: in Aristotle, 55; in Ockham and Aristotle, 72–73; science of, whether possible, 72; as potentially all things, 74
Southern Illinois University, 68
Space, 77
Spencer, Herbert, 3; and definition of life,
   124
Spengler, Oswald, 195; and dialectic,
   129–30
Spinoza, Benedict, 3, 19, 33, 94, 108,
   168, 185; interpretation of, 36–41;
   and knowledge of God, 36; method of,
   37–40; on motion and rest, 72; and
   system, 37–41; writings of: *Correction
   of the Understanding,* 37, 40; *Ethics,* 37,
   38, 40; *Political Tractate,* 37; *Short Treatise,* 37; *Theological-Political Tractate,* 37
Square(s), 46, 58, 68; checkerboard and
   chessboard, 65; headings of, 51–52; of
   inquiry, 69, 86, KcKeon's use of, 4; semantic, 69, 86. *See also* Array(s),
   Matrix(ces), Oblongs
Statements: alternative, 46; on art, 140;
   contrast of, 193; expertness of, 198;
   metaphysical, 175. *See also* Proposi-
   tion(s)
Sternfeld, Robert, 11
Strauss, Richard, 163; and two-keyed
   ending, 165
Structure(s): common, of thought, 120;
   McKeon's own, 70; and rhetoric, 96

Students: against establishment, 115; and
   labels, misapplied, 48; as opsimaths, 8.
   See also under McKeon, Richard
Subject matter(s): generic, 182; philosophic, 183
Summaries of systems, 106
Summations: kinds of, 62; of summations, 60
Syllogism(s), 19, 63, 138; Aristotle on,
   220n.14; chain, 48
Symbols: of same kind, 66; structuring
   knowledge, 71; unambiguous systems
   of, 196
Symmetry, dynamic, 212n.44
Syntheses: and discriminations, 46; Hegelian, 192
System(s), 88; aims of, 49–50; clarifica-
   tions of, 178; closed, 180–81; and
   comparison, semantic, 86, 193; complete, 168; construction of, 182; contemporary, 180; elements of, 66; equality of value of, 193; existing and
   possible, 202, 215; and facts, 28; features of, 50; free choice of, 179; when
   formulated, 181–82; interchangeability
   of, 192; later and earlier, 30; least parts
   of, 57; and lines, fixed, 173; making
   and understanding of, 182; monolithic,
   201; objections and refutations in, 198;
   opposing, 197; original, 166; ordered,
   111; philosophic, 86, 171; pure, 187;
   semantic comparison of, 67; succession
   of, 172; whether translatable, 29, 181;
   truth of, ultimate, 28, 197; uniqueness
   of, 197; upholding of one, 111; well-
   made, 181; as wholes, 57, 67

Tasks, four, in achieving harmony, 123
"Technical," as type of criticism, 142
Tensions, 115; between cultures, 97; international, 112; relaxation of, 111
Term(s): analogical and literal, 140, 178;
   common use of, 140; constituent, 55;
   in equilibrium, 188; in essays, 95;
   groups of, 27, 214n.5; imposing of,
   196; interpretation of, 96; leading pairs
   of, 140; neutral, 171, 194; patterns of,
   170; principal, 96; retained, 67; sets of,
   57; and statement, argument, system,

155; as subject of logic, 175; as templates, 27; traditional, as commonplaces, 27; translation of, 42; in system, 197. *See also* Analogy(ies)

Text(s): analysis of, 184; corruption of, 6; ethico-political, 184; as facts, 29; interpretation of, 139; and possibility of destruction, 202

That Which Is, priority of, 81, 83

Theory(ies): of artists, 126; poetic, four types of, 207n.20; McKeon's own, 1; and practice, 98; and practice, production, 82, 144; ways, four, to present, 75

Theses: as principles, 160; repudiation of, possible, 166; and questions, substantive, 175; twelve, 166–75

Thing(s): whether amorphous, 201; and ideas and signs, 81; and property, 81; and thoughts and language, 34, 60, 92, 144; words, and actions, 155, 165

Thinker(s): disagreement of, 187; French, 3; of good will, 99; led by logic, 180; logistic, 53; problematic, 53; types of, connections between, 51

Thinking: forced, 205n.5; group, 220n.10; philosophic, 155

Thompson, Manley H., 11

Thought, modes of, 69, 86

Tolstoy, Leo, 36, 140

Topic(s): range of, 85; selection of, 133–34; specificity of, 185–86. *See also* Commonplace(s)

"Traffic jams," 25, 62

Transcendental, or idealistic, 164

Transcendentals, medieval, 31, 82

Translation(s), 6, 31, 84

Trivium, 26, 50, 126, 160

Truth(s), 11; affirmation and denial of, 73, degree of, 189; dogmatically proposed, 142; four tests for, 197; inquiry into, and rhetoric, 158; many-sided, 91; metaphysical, 75; partial, 192; plural, 128; possibilities of, 189; possible, of alternants, 191; and prejudice, 110; profiles of, 189–90; of propositions, 198–99; provisional, 193; and reflection, by category, 172; scientific, not eternal, 102; in Spinoza, 72; of state-

ments, 82; not subject to discussion, 101; supreme, 28; tables of, 189; unique, 179–80; a value, 128; as whole, 175

Twain, Mark, and cat, 199

Types, four, of philosophy, 137

Ueberweg, Friedrich, 19

UNESCO, 94, 99, 109, 110, 113, 150; McKeon's work in, 97, 219n.9

United Nations, 109, 201; "reinforced," 123

Unity, 82; and being, in Plato, 56; and diversity, 102; organic, 147; and plurality, 209n.28; and principles of completeness, 38; of sciences, 43

University of Chicago, 5, 9, 91, 99, 119, 131, 172, 205n.5, 211n.34; changes in the College, 22; changes in wartime, 11; Department of Philosophy of, xiii, 5, 9, 11

Urmethode, 147

Urphilosophen, 52, 54, 64, 81

Ursysteme, 201, 91; fixed in a changing world, 179; and flat lines, 186; four, 111

Validity, unique, not claimed, 179–80

Value(s): common, 104; community of, 127; differing, 148; ideal, 141; equality of, possible, 192; expression of, 147; in poem, four, 149

Vienna Circle, 138

Vivas, Eliseo, 11, 231n.16

Voting, 117

Warranties, 94

Wegener, Charles W., 11

Weiss, Paul, 126

Weltanschauung, 130–31

Whitehead, Alfred North, 31, 78, 95, 138, 145, 183; and theory of types, 73; his *Process and Reality*, 15, 81

Whitman, Walt, 124

Wick, Warner Arms, 11

Wisdom: and eloquence, 157, 159; language of, 1; love of, 121; and ontic questions, 82

Wittgenstein, Ludwig, 80, 95, 108, 137;
early and late profile of, 88–90; and
"extensionless point," 184; and Mc-
Keon, contrast between, 25
Woodbridge, F. J. E., 31, 36, 204
Words: ambiguous, 95; art of, 196; and
deeds, 146; senses of, 133; and sentences, 80; and texts, 199; and
thoughts and things, 176
World: government of, 43; as a machine,
78; medieval and modern, 195; peace
in, 33, 124; real and ideal, 121; and in-
determinancy, 192–93
World community, 119–20, 122, 123

World War I, 8
World War II, 10, 18, 99, 106, 111, 119,
122, 124, 179, 205n.5, 211n.34

X matrix, 128; described, 60; difficulty of
using, 186; explained in detail, 62–63;
minor of, 216n.17; and Y and Z matrices, 68

Y matrix, 128; explained, 59, 60

Z matrix, 59; described, 60; reconstructed, 84